How to Manage the IT Helpdesk

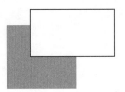

How to Manage
the IT Helpdesk

A guide for user support
and call centre managers

Second edition

Noel Bruton

BUTTERWORTH
HEINEMANN

OXFORD AMSTERDAM BOSTON LONDON NEW YORK PARIS
SAN DIEGO SAN FRANCISCO SINGAPORE SYDNEY TOKYO

Butterworth-Heinemann
An imprint of Elsevier Science
Linacre House, Jordan Hill, Oxford OX2 8DP
225 Wildwood Avenue, Woburn MA 01801-2041

First published by McGraw-Hill Book Company Europe as
Effective User Support 1995
First published as *How to Manage the IT Helpdesk* 1997
Reprinted 1998, 1999 (twice), 2000,
Second edition 2002

British Library Cataloguing in Publication Data
A catalogue record for this book is available from the British Library

ISBN 0 7506 49011

For information on all Butterworth-Heinemann publications visit
our website at www.bh.com

Composition by Genesis Typesetting, Rochester, Kent
Printed and bound in Great Britain

Contents

Contents

Case studies

Figures

Computer Weekly Professional Series

There are few professions which require as much continuous updating as that of the IS executive. Not only does the hardware and software scene change relentlessly, but also ideas about the actual management of the IS function are being continuously modified, updated and changed. Thus keeping abreast of what is going on is really a major task.

The Butterworth-Heinemann – *Computer Weekly* Professional Series has been created to assist IS executives keep up to date with the management ideas and issues of which they need to be aware.

One of the key objectives of the series is to reduce the time it takes for leading edge management ideas to move from the academic and consulting environments into the hands of the IT practitioner. Thus this series employs appropriate technology to speed up the publishing process. Where appropriate some books are supported by CD-ROM or by additional information or templates located on the Web.

This series provides IT professionals with an opportunity to build up a bookcase of easily accessible, but detailed information on the important issues that they need to be aware of to successfully perform their jobs as they move into the new millennium.

Aspiring or already established authors are invited to get in touch with me directly if they would like to be published in this series.

Dr Dan Remenyi
Series Editor
Dan.remenyi@mcil.co.uk

Series Editor
Dan Remenyi, Visiting Professor, Trinity College Dublin

Advisory Board
Frank Bannister, Trinity College Dublin
Ross Bentley, Management Editor, *Computer Weekly*
Egon Berghout, Technical University of Delft, The Netherlands
Ann Brown, City University Business School, London
Roger Clark, The Australian National University
Reet Cronk, Harding University, Arkansas, USA
Arthur Money, Henley Management College, UK
Sue Nugus, MCIL, UK
Rene Pellissier, School of Business Leadership, Johannesburg
David Taylor, CERTUS, UK
Terry White, BentleyWest, Johannesburg

Other titles in the Series
IT investment – making a business case
The effective measurement and management of IT costs and benefits
Stop IT project failures through risk management
Understanding the Internet
Prince 2: a practical handbook
Considering computer contracting?
David Taylor's Inside Track
A hacker's guide to project management
Corporate politics for IT managers: how to get streetwise
Subnet design for efficient networks
Information warfare: corporate attack and defence in a digital world
Delivering IT and e-business value
Reinventing the IT department
The project manager's toolkit

Introduction to the first edition

Why is this book needed?

Ever since computers have been used in business, there has always been user support. It goes under various names – helpdesk, technical support, information centre, etc. – and these names may also indicate very different types of services. What they all have in common is that they were created to provide technical solutions to non-technical people. This book examines that principle and how it is put into effect in its various guises.

A new industry

User support has begun to splinter away from IT to become a sub-industry in itself. This is unsurprising. Support has long been thought of as slightly outside the IT industry proper; witness the difficulty of moving from a support to a development job, or the tendency of so many companies to keep technical skills on the helpdesk at a relatively low level. These are examples of how alienated support can be as a function.

But as well as this external influence to separate support from other IT functions, there is also the pressure from inside support itself to create its own specialists and heroes. The growing similarity and standardization of computer systems and the speed with which knowledge becomes redundant have meant that a supporter's technical specialization is less of a barrier to changing jobs than it once was: technical knowledge can be gained and discarded as needed, on a continuing basis.

Technical skills are no longer enough

Much more important than technical ability for the modern support specialist are skills pertinent purely to support – like the ability to express complex technical concepts in layman's terms, probably over the telephone; or a methodical approach to problem-solving; or the ability to create a personal network of information sources. Employers have recognized these skills as being more important than the purely technical ones and have begun to hire on this basis. This means supporters can move from support job to support job across industries and technologies, and are beginning to enjoy the job mobility and variety once reserved for systems analysts.

IT's loss is support's gain

There is pressure from the supply side too. In the late 1980s and early 1990s, the IT bubble burst. IBM lost billions, Wang restructured, DEC's Ken Olsen took a back seat, PC dealers disappeared in droves, takeovers and mergers became the order of the day. Hardware sales margins diminished rapidly, putting severe pressure on IT industry suppliers to supplement product sales with services. The facilities management and outsourcing industries blossomed – support came into its own. Now user companies have to decide whether to support their own users or get an outsider in to do it for them.

We have seen huge growth in the number of vertical applications packages aimed at helping technical support departments to computerize their rather specialist administration and management methods. Call-logging, inventory and change management packages abound. In the UK and America, certain journalists are beginning to specialize in support.

To reiterate: support has become an industry in itself, with its own innate needs and specializations. This book aims to take stock of that movement and point the way forward for those wishing to be the new professionals in this burgeoning field.

More support needed

The need for support is set to increase dramatically. The amount of computing power purchasable per unit of currency has increased at a breakneck pace as DEC, Intel, Motorola, IBM and others have given us ever more capable processors. The software companies have by and large kept up with this by filling the processor with ever more software. The result of increased competition has been to drive down prices so that the machines become available to ever smaller budgets and thus an ever-widening market. The additional processing power has enabled the software companies to make the machines ever easier to use, so that more and more potential users and purchasers of the technology feel confident with it.

For support departments, this has meant ever more users of ever more powerful machines. The increased so-called 'ease-of-use' brought by graphical user interfaces like Microsoft Windows has not and will not decrease the corporate support burden; such 'improvements' will only change the nature of support. We 'supporters' were never there to help users use the machine, and increased ease of use will thus have little impact. Support was always there to help when things went wrong, or something had to be changed – and where once we were changing or assisting with a terminal running a single, character-based application or a PC with a quarter of a megabyte and a spreadsheet, now we assist when a client–server groupware system collapses taking umpteen megabytes of device drivers and related applications with it. Support is needed more than ever before; ease of use and increased availability have, in IT terms, paradoxically driven the user further away from understanding the technology, not closer to it.

This book has been written to help those companies who have realized this impact on support and need a structured approach to dealing with it.

Objectives of the book

I will define support in its various guises. I will clarify some of the different roles played by various types of support departments, their derivatives, sub-departments, and resource providers.

The emerging identity of support in its own right will be recognized, paying particular attention to the skills that make up support specialists as opposed to support technicians – in short, this will be a description of how to be a professional in this new profession.

I will also examine the 'customer service' side of support. This is a concept that by and large has not been relevant in IT until the emergence of professional user support. Building customer service into user relations is one of the traits that separate excellent support organizations from their mediocre counterparts.

The bulk of this work is taken up with the 'how tos' of user support. My intention is to examine the topic such that the reader will be exposed to enough knowledge to design a user support service, implement it, manage it and change it in a controlled fashion. Certain sections will discuss people as the key resource, in terms of defining the type of people needed; recruiting, integrating and keeping them; and the various inducements they must be given in order to keep their motivation and productivity high. I will also look at support's raw material – knowledge – as nothing more than a commodity which, like any other, must be defined, acquired, stored, used, delivered and disposed of.

Throughout the book, various points and examples of success and failure are illustrated by anecdotes and case histories. These have been drawn from real life, from situations I have encountered in my work as a support technician, manager, consultant and trainer. In all cases, the names of the individuals and organizations involved have been changed.

Who should read this?

When designing this book, I considered titles like 'Better Support Management' and 'How to Design and Run a Support Service'. I discarded them because they limited the readership. There are too many people involved in support for me to make this an esoteric work. The support movement is too young for me to pass up this opportunity of documenting the state of the art for use throughout the industry.

So, at the risk of being accused of trying to be all things to all people, I have aimed this work at anybody who is involved in support and needs an insight into its workings. That so much effort is invested in showing the reader ways of designing a support service will attract the new manager or company starting from scratch. But even for established organizations, going back to basics is not impossible and is indeed even desirable – so many support services have come into being by accident or have grown organically that a re-examination of their foundations will probably reveal flaws that this book can show them how to fix.

And I do not wish to address the management ranks in isolation; many support departments contain ambitious, educated and experienced staff on whom their manager depends. They can use this book to guide and support the manager into creating a better service for the users who need it and the people who have to work in it. After all, where will the next generation of competent, knowledgeable and respected support managers come from?

This book is there for the new support department; for the company or IT manager wishing to move from an ad hoc to a more structured user support service; for the new manager moving into old shoes; for the support organization in need of a little 're-engineering'; for the support staff member planning a career move; for the board director wondering what it is they get up to down there.

Structure of the book

Support people are busy; it is hard for them to find uninterrupted time to devote to an extended book reading, so I have had to take this into account. By all means read the book from cover to cover; I would be flattered if you did. Otherwise, dip into the part you need at a particular time. The book is divided into parts, each covering a major topic, like 'service management' and 'resources management'. Within the parts come the chapters, covering sub-topics in depth, such as forms of support, prioritizing clients, and so on. The Contents will give you a rough guide to where a topic is covered most strongly; but as so many aspects of support management are interdependent, certain topics crop up in lots of places. Use the Index for detailed study of a topic.

Acknowledgements

I must express my gratitude to several people who helped this idea become a reality. They are listed here in no particular order. To everybody who was ever part of 'The Information Centre' or its management at P&P in Rossendale, England; I learned so much from them. To Jo Palmer for her contribution to the chapter on organizing the support library. To Mark Clegg for his views on private technical librabries and technical support futures, and jointly with his colleague Mark Blinkhorn for showing me the finest helpdesk management system I ever saw. To Earl Downes and Rob Bruce at Coca-Cola and Aidan Rowsome at Quarterdeck for their help with international support. To Trish Fineran for mentoring me in the early stages of my independent career. To Henry Calero, negotiator extraordinaire, for convincing me of what was possible. To several seminar leaders at Careertrack for the means and methods of personal motivation – your seminars are worth much more than you charge. To my son Alex, who despite his few years tried hard to understand Daddy's 'work'. Most of all to my wife Karen, for her love, encouragement, patience, intelligence, proofreading skills, and unswervable ability to spot and decry bull.

All trademarks referred to in this book are courteously acknowledged.

And finally . . .

This book is intended as a practical guide. The content is largely gleaned from my own experience of many years in IT, the bulk of them in a support capacity, followed by setting up Bruton Consultancy to help companies improve user support. I would welcome your comments on this work and any ideas you think I should address in future editions. Please feel free to contact me either through the publisher or at Bruton Consultancy (email: noel@noelbruton.com), PO Box 27, Cardigan, Wales SA43 2YL, United Kingdom.

Noel Bruton

Preface to the second edition

The helpdesk industry has changed a great deal since I wrote the first edition of this book, back in the mid-1990s. In those days, outsourcing was still a distant threat for most helpdesks, and one could still draw a clear line between the helpdesk and the call centre. Not so easy now. And then there is the Internet – I didn't even mention it in the first edition as it hadn't really taken off – but the cultural changes the Internet has wrought have spilled over into our jobs such that it is replacing some of us with the burgeoning technologies of e-support.

Since I started my consultancy practice, ten years ago now, I have seen a steady increase in professionalism in our industry. Not before time, it must be said. At last, corporations seem to be taking the helpdesk seriously. Several have adopted cost-justification techniques, born of the realization of the importance of user support. Where once we were just a bunch of technically knowledgeable people on call in case of a computer failure, now in some cases at least, firms acknowledge that the helpdesk is not just an end in itself, but a means to the greater end of ensuring employee productivity. With so many workers dependent on computers, if the computers stop, the organization stops. Continuity is essential, and as an aid to that, the helpdesk has attracted more management focus and thus more adept and complete processes.

But it's not all rosy. The cultural divide between first and second line still exists. We simply must get rid of that – it belongs to an anachronistic view of IT, where the more you know about machines, the more you are respected and paid. It's divisive, meaningless and out of place.

Outsourcing has grown in professionalism and presence. It has its place, but in my experience it is expensive and does not guarantee improved service and support productivity.

There is still too much store laid by knowledge databases – as if we could effectively replace the function of the helpdesk by the output of a computer. It can be done, if one misunderstands or massively reduces the function of the helpdesk. Knowledge databases have their place – but they are not (yet) a viable alternative to human skill.

Helpdesk tools proliferate. It is beginning to look like the car market, where trivialities such as whether it has alloy wheels makes the difference between one product and another. Feature proliferation has become a chief deciding factor in helpdesk process automation. It has never been the best way to choose a management tool and it never will.

I'm older, and I like to think, a little wiser. Some of the views I held in the first edition are a shade out of date now. They need reviewing. The growth of the use of call centre tools has raised a number of issues, about which I feel some comment is warranted. We've had globalization, which is changing the rules for all areas of business, the helpdesk included. I have become a little more strident, and I want to give greater expression to my passion for this unique endeavour that is user support.

If there is one major idea that I have come to espouse more enthusiastically in the past few years, it is this. *Managers don't have time to be techies*. In far too many helpdesks, even now, there are so-called 'managers' who still spend some of their time solving technical problems. They do it because they believe their team is understaffed – they do it because they don't know any better – they do it because they believe they don't have the authority or power to take control of the desk – they do it because they've been promoted too early because that was the only way the company could afford to pay them the extra to stop them from leaving. I'll be talking more about Tom De Marco and Tim Lister later on, but one thing their work showed is that well-motivated staff are up to ten times more productive than poorly motivated ones – and all that time the 'manager' spends being a techie is time he could have spent making sure his staff were motivated, content and productive. See the arithmetic. If you have five staff, and you spend half your day helping them out, so you've got five-and-a-half staff. But if you spent your whole day being a good manager and increasing your team's motivation, then according to Tom and Tim, you'd have the equivalent of 50 staff. Pack it in. If you only spend half a day being a technician, you won't get enough practice to be as good a technician as your people in any case. Spend your time improving your management and motivation skills.

Incidentally, I've arrived at some new ways of looking at motivation recently. So if motivation is your issue, don't miss that chapter.

All these issues and more, plus gentle(ish) prodding from my publisher, have driven me to present you with this second edition. I take this opportunity to thank all those out there, who have made the effort to offer me suggestions, particularly to the truly wonderful Internet helpdesk discussion group (if you're a helpdesk professional and you're not a member, I urge you to rectify that situation today – see my website for joining instructions).

In particular, I would like to make specific mention of some individuals who have particularly contributed to my knowledge over the past few years, in addition to the recognition of others elsewhere in the book. They are, in no particular order: Philip Verghis, pioneer of the Internet's finest website for helpdesk managers, an accomplished and erudite human being and just a great bloke. Tom Heisey and Dennis Lapcewich, competent professionals who know how not to take the pressure too seriously; Dennis's own 'Prolink' website is a must-see for helpdesk managers and supervisors. Andrew Pearce, who for a while at least, ploughed a similar furrow to mine in his home Land of the Long White Cloud and contributed to my confidence. My own brother Peter, support leader cum laude. Mark Turner and latterly James West, editors of the UK's *Customer Service News*, who monthly give me two pages of that publication so I can rant about my current helpdesk management passion. Tom Leworthy, who helped me find a much-needed, very different *a priori* context in which to place all this stuff. And all the consultancy clients who in the past ten years have engaged me, trusted me and let me turn my ideas into their reality.

The problems of political correctness in writing

As do so many contemporary writers, I have struggled with political correctness in this book. It is problematical these days exclusively to use 'he'. Some people are offended and may even accuse the book of sexism. However, for the writer, the alternatives are even less palatable. To use 'she' exclusively would be just as politically incorrect, let alone statistically false – although more and more women are in positions of responsibility in helpdesks, they still do not constitute a clear majority. The other possibility is the faddish 's/he' – which itself is ugly, and gives difficulties with the accusative and possessive – S/her? S/hers? S/his? S/him?

The book's priority is to convey a set of ideas. To meet that priority, communication is paramount. To use constructed words would impede the flow of the writing and thus sully the messages. For the sake of communication and flow, I have thus used either 'he' or 'she' when the gender of the actor is irrelevant, the choice between the two largely being an act of whim. If that gender-specificity gives the reader a problem, I would politely ask the reader to remember the perspective that the book is not about sexism or political correctness – it is about helpdesks.

Noel Bruton
Cardigan, January 2002

Part One

What is 'support'?

Defining computer user support

What exactly do we mean by 'user support'? Let us start with a simple definition, based on a common understanding of the role of user support:

> *User support is the process by which technical knowledge is used by specialists to solve computing problems experienced by lay users.*

BEWARE – that is only half the story! Given that simplistic definition, information technology (IT) support is no different from, for example, a motoring organization or any good library. It is just bringing computers into it that complicates matters, as they are perhaps the most technically complex thing we have yet introduced into our everyday lives. And the main reason why they are so complex is because computers, unlike cars or most other electronic appliances, are multifunctional – the user can essentially produce a new and unique problem depending entirely on how he or she uses the machine.

So is support just a reactive bank of specialized knowledge? Essentially, yes; but of course there is rather more to it than that. The quality of the knowledge has to be considered, as do the triggers which start its delivery, let alone the channels along which we pipe our knowledge to our users.

Furthermore, we must consider why we should even bother at all to retain that knowledge in order to deliver it. For instance, why shouldn't we just give the knowledge to the users and let them get on with it? Surely that alone would reduce the support workload and leave us technical specialists free to get on with the meatier jobs of change management, product evaluation, and solutions research. We can see why we need technical specialists; but why do we need them solely to provide support?

The answer to that is the same as can be applied to so many business problems, namely cost. When we later look at support cost justification, we will see that there comes a point at which the cost of increasing user knowledge outweighs the benefit of having such high levels of IT ability at the users' fingertips. High technical competence is simply not needed often enough to make spreading it so widely a cost-effective option for many companies. So they elect to retain a few technical specialists who can be consulted as needed.

Immediately we have begun to see that there is not just a set of technical or service reasons why there is a support department; there are invariably strict business reasons why that department should exist. The reasons look very much like the ones which would call any other department, especially a non-revenue department, into existence.

1.1 Support is a business matter

Alas, it is the failing of too many inexperienced support managers that they seem to think their purpose is purely technological; in fact their purpose is, in the end, purely financial. And if support does not recognize how its esoteric function can be made to contribute to the company's business goals, its usefulness and thus its future come into question. This does not necessarily mean that support has to make a profit directly – but it does mean that it has to contribute to the means by which the company as a whole achieves its business goals. And that means that it must measure itself not in support or technical terms, but in business terms.

For a fuller picture of why support exists, we must look at this business case more deeply. How exactly does the company achieve its business goals, and how can support contribute to that process? The best place to look is at the end result and move back through the effects and causes of the profit-producing machine.

Your company makes a profit by providing a product or service for which customers are willing, for whatever reason, to pay more for than it costs the supplying company to manufacture or obtain. Therefore, what your company's end customer receives has benefited from the value which has been added to it while the product has been in your company's hands. Those people who added that value will invariably number among the users of your IT support services.

1.2 User productivity is the key

So it follows that if these users could be made more productive, then theoretically at least, they could be enabled to add more value, thus contributing further profit to the company's bottom line. One of the most popular ways to increase white-collar productivity in recent times has been to computerize the desktop. IT support services assist that end; therefore, the way support contributes to company profit is to enable the users to increase their productivity through IT.

Support delivers this increased productivity in two main ways: (i) by solving technical problems on the user's computer, so that the user can resume working; and (ii) by increasing, directly or indirectly, the user's competence with the technology. It follows, then, that an important way of measuring the success or otherwise of a support service is in terms of user productivity as enhanced by any interaction with the support department.

1.3 Is support just for problem-solving?

The way most users will encounter support is by contacting it for help when the computer fails to do what they expect it to. The reason for the problem is immaterial at this point; it may be due to a hardware or software failure, a user need unanticipated by the existing technology, or ignorance on the user's part of how to use the systems to achieve his or her business aims. Whatever the cause, it is the 'computer system' (a concept that should include the user's ability to use the technology) which is deemed to have caused the failure. Problems with the computer? Call support!

So support is naturally seen most often as a problem-solving function. But this is only a true picture in support departments which restrict themselves to a purely reactive function; and where that is true for the commonest support function, the 'helpdesk', there are many other types of support which provide a range of reactive and proactive services. As mentioned earlier, support may have a research function, identifying new technology needs, and testing various solutions; it may be testing new software in advance of it being installed, so as to anticipate problems before they occur on a user's desk; support may be involved in applications development, again for reasons of problem prevention; support may be heavily involved in user training, to try to eliminate user ignorance as a major problem cause. All in all, it is too narrow a picture to see support just as a problem-solving service.

1.4 Specialists supporting lay users?

A common image of a technical support department is of a chaotic place, full of half-disassembled electronic equipment, with technical manuals open and strewn over desks typically occupied by a highly specialized guru with a penchant for technical detail, a slender sense of humour, and a distinct lack of sartorial elegance. The ignorant user breaks the rarefied atmosphere with a mere business problem at risk of invoking humiliation at the hands of these masters of the black art of 'computing'.

Fortunately, this image is now jaded and belongs to the late 1970s before personal computers brought technological literacy to millions. True, the departments may still look like a mad scientist's laboratory, but disrespect for the users is fast disappearing. This is because users are sophisticated now; the fact is that a user who lives with a spreadsheet package four hours a day will know more about it than the support department can ever hope to. The user is less likely to ring for assistance with the technology and more likely to need an explanation of its unexpected behaviour or guidance towards making a change in his or her use of technology. The image of experts leading the ignorant still exists, but it is a branch, rather than the root of technical support.

In the late 1980s, this raw technical specialization began to gain a new maturity. As professional support tools began to arrive, helpdesks saw these as a way of imposing a shrink-wrapped production process onto what had hitherto been little more than a loose agglomeration of IT skills held by a group of technicians under a technical leader. In the 1990s, this became even more focused. Many corporations now have a defined management structure, headed by an 'information services manager', reporting to the chief information officer or IT director. By the end of the decade, the successful helpdesk had two key and inseparable skills – that of technical competence had been augmented by professional service management and service delivery. Nowadays, as a model for IT support, the disorganized group of purely reactive technicians is relatively rare. The organizational imperative now plays an equally central role, and no more so than in the providers of outsourced IT support.

1.5 A new definition needed

We have seen that support cannot be held to be a purely technical function; it has roots in business needs which go as deeply as those to be found in any other department serving the general workforce; that support is a matter of workforce productivity, not just of maintaining the technology. We see that support has a proactive role as well as a reactive one, and can guide the company to new uses of technology. And we have dispelled the outdated myth that support departments are always staffed by isolationist gurus. All of which necessitates a more complete definition of 'user support':

> *User support is a specialist function which retains, on behalf of the company's user population, technical knowledge about IT and the way the company uses it, in order to deliver that knowledge in a focused form to solve specific technical and business problems on both a reactive and proactive basis, such that user productivity is maintained and enhanced, thereby further enabling the user to contribute to the company's business goals.*

1.6 Defining the business goals

The business goals are a stumbling block; it is here that so many support departments come unstuck, and not necessarily by their own fault. Too often the problem starts higher up the chain, where the business goals should be defined. Business goals are often unclear; either the company, its business, or in these acquisitive days its management is changing too quickly, so the goals move too fast. Another reason might be poor communication channels, rendered that way by accident or deliberately in some misguided attempt to control the workforce as opposed to involving them.

It may be that the business does not actually have any goals beyond sheer survival, in which case the business probably matters rather less than the careers of its participants anyway. A further problem comes from the differing definitions bandied about as to what a 'goal' actually is. Differences in understanding of the terms 'goal', 'objective' and 'strategy' are common among managers and directors.

In every helpdesk management training course I conduct, I ask the attendees to put their hands up if their corporation has an ex-helpdesk staff on the board of directors. Over the years I've been doing this, the audience response has slowly moved from cynical giggles to a tiny minority raising faltering arms. Progress, of a fashion, I suppose. One can expect that in most companies, the board of directors is made up of staff from sales and accountancy, and perhaps production in the larger manufacturing companies. My contention is this: with no helpdesk people in positions of seniority, from where do the mentors come? Can we be sure that senior management actually understands the issues of delivering user support, the pressures, the needs, the details and the imperatives? And if they do not, can we be sure that the messages we get on the business needs for IT support will be accurate and usable? Even now, in 2002, many companies lack real strategic thinking as regards user support, choosing to leave it to the technicians, who are often too busy putting out fires to think strategically. My additional worry is that while boards are still populated by salespeople and accountants, their ignorance of IT will continue to constrain their ability to offer real managerial guidance to IT support people, while keeping anybody who understands the computers down in the computer room. This is precisely because the company cannot survive without employing somebody who understands the technology upon which the company depends. It means bleak career prospects for aspiring IT support people. And it means that IT support is going to continue to have trouble turning business goals into IT service deliverables for some time yet.

In all these environments, support has to carry on. The failings of the strategists on high can only be a temporary excuse for failing to define support services, because even if the managers cannot agree on the business purposes, the staff who turn in the work will have an idea of what computer support they need. Then the support manager makes an educated guess as to the services needed and implements them through a process of trial and error. (More on designing services in later chapters.)

For the sake of their careers as well as the business, support managers must get out of the computer room and take the screwdrivers out of their breast pockets. If senior management cannot explain business needs to IT, we will have to get out there and define those needs ourselves. We have to stop thinking, talking and looking like technicians and use our unique exposure to both business and technology. The helpdesk knows more about how the business uses computers than anybody else. It is in the unique position of seeing how the users actually use the computers, all day, every day. It can see both sides of the coin. If anybody can see the business goals from a computing point of view, the helpdesk can. Put the Javascript manual down, my friend. The management needs you to tell them how to link their computers with their business.

Never let a financial report go by without looking in it for service opportunities. If the chairman's statement says the company is placing new emphasis on European sales next year, go and see the European sales director and ask him what that means for the services he will need from you. Calculate the rate of business growth and map it onto your budget plans for support staff in the coming year. Stay abreast of the new acquisitions and disposals. Do not wait to be told about business developments. Get involved. And be careful of your vocabulary – every time you mention a specific technology, they will be wondering whether to permanently send you back downstairs to the computer room where you belong. Whatever they are doing to the business in the boardroom will have some impact on your support services. Don't ever let them surprise you. Proactivity starts with you. So does your career. If you want to stay a technician all your life, don't worry, their ignorance of computing will ensure that happens, because they cannot afford to lose your competence in the technology on which they so depend. But that may well keep you and business computing in the reactive mode that is so endemic in twenty-first century commerce.

2   Support as an IT function

User support is most commonly set up as a part of the computing function. This would seem logical on the face of it. After all, it is dealing with technical knowledge, which is only necessary because the computer is there. But by the same token, payroll should always be part of finance, because it deals with money; but payroll also turns up in the personnel department, because it deals with the overall concept of 'staff'. In the end, the decision to place the IT support department in the IT department is based on a set of technological priorities; if the company sees 'support' as a technical function, and if it behaves as such, then logically, that is where it should sit. If, however, support begins to conduct itself as a customer service centre, or a user productivity department, or a business services enabler, then the reporting structure becomes less clear. Some more enlightened and visionary support managers have been backed into a corner over this issue, but it is one that is gaining ground as the customer-service-oriented ethos progresses.

However, for now let us examine support in its more traditional role, that of an IT function.

2.1 Living with the IT department

In any organization where computing or IT is centralized, there will always be a number of IT functions, of which support is only one. Especially in a mainframe or minicomputer environment, there will be an 'operations' function, which will be given the task of ensuring that the computer system keeps running and has the physical and logical resources it needs, like online and offline data and consumables. Operations may also look after job scheduling, batch input and output decollation.

The principal relationship of support to other IT departments is usually one of query-taker to query-resolver. In its simplest form, support provides a helpdesk, simply a telephone-answering service, which can vary in sophistication from merely taking messages (using a call-logging tool) – through deciding who best to solve the user's problem – up to providing the bulk of the solutions themselves.

A helpdesk set up to allocate problems to resolvers may use one or all of the IT functions as routes to a solution to a problem encountered by a user. In some cases, the solution may have to be delivered back to the user through the helpdesk. This relationship is not without its problems, of course, as priorities differ between departments.

2.2 Living with the developers

The IT department will usually also have a 'development' function. The developers provide new software applications and may maintain the old ones. Their relationship with the user population is that of consultant to client, where IT is expected to provide a long-term solution to a major problem, and it is up to the developers to produce and implement that solution.

Clearly, support has a special relationship with development. The quality of the software solutions the developers provide has a direct impact on the support workload; basically, the flakier the systems, or the harder they are to use, the harder the support staff have to work to pick up the pieces. This is discussed in greater depth in later chapters, especially when we cover workload management.

2.3 Specialized network support

Where a more extensive communications network is in place, this will often be managed by a specialist 'networks' team, which may or may not be part of the support function, but will almost certainly be part of the overall computing function. As the essence of communications is management of distance, the networks team are often notoriously well travelled; this and the deeply technical nature of their function lends to the job a certain attractiveness as a possible career move for lower-ranking support people.

2.4 User training

Users need to be trained to use the systems on their desks. Where the software is written in-house, a specialist 'user training' department or the developers themselves may be charged with training the users. There is a direct impact on support of the effectiveness of user training – especially in those situations where it becomes easier to telephone support than it would be to search one's own memory for the solution to a problem. The more skilled the users are, the less mundane, if not the smaller the support workload.

Where the software involves standard, shrink-wrapped PC packages, training – where it is done at all – is normally available from dozens of third-party companies. My experience is that this software is nowadays so well documented and widespread that staff software training is often considered superfluous, and this becomes truer the higher through the corporate ranks you go, as if managers needed less technical training. In any case, the computer literacy or otherwise of the users has an inevitable impact on the support workload.

2.5 Deciding IT strategy

The office which decides the 'IT strategy' is where the decisions are made about what products and technologies will be used to meet the company's data-processing needs. This too has an impact on support; choices must be made which take the eventual support workload into account. It is done in terms of hardware reliability – it must be done also in terms of software and system usability.

The most obvious product of the strategy function is the list of supported products and the policy for dealing with queries on products not on that list. For this reason, support is often closely involved in this process, as they may be the ones evaluating products for general use.

2.6 Keeping the users at bay

In many organizations, one of the reasons for having a separate support department under the IT management umbrella is to provide a deliberate barrier between the computing function and the users, in the form of a customer service such as an IT helpdesk.

This can bring a number of benefits; as De Marco and Lister discuss in their excellent *Peopleware* (1987), allowing developers to be constantly interrupted breaks the flow which is necessary for creative software development, so channelling queries through a dedicated helpdesk can save money and increase quality in the development department.

It is clear that providing assistance in the use of an existing application (support) requires a very different set of skills than creating an IT solution to a new business problem (development); thus, separating these functions so that respective specialists can concentrate on them can bring the best of both worlds and prevent one from diluting the efficacy of the other. There is also a cost benefit; helpdesk staff, by and large, cost less than analyst programmers: there is no point in paying a programmer to do a job a telephonist or technician would do for much less.

2.7 Support understands the users

A communications problem arises, however. The helpdesk/ support staff become closer to the hour-by-hour, real-life use of IT than any other computing department, certainly much more so than development, who are happy restricting user access to them. It is inevitable that the users will know more about how the software behaves in real life than does support, who will in turn know the practical weaknesses, workarounds, and flaws of the computer systems even better than the developers who designed it. With this barrier between usage and development, can the programmers ever really be sure that the software they produce is exactly what is needed and as well behaved in day-to-day use and in unskilled hands as is desirable or as they intended?

This is the paradox of support within IT; by its very position, excluded from the technological process, support becomes more aware of the pressures on that process than are the very people who should respond to those pressures.

2.8 Robbing Peter to pay Paul

But as well as the communications barrier, there are some more dangerous threats posed by the separation of support from development. The main one is the almost accidental tendency to reduce the naturally high costs of development by slackening quality, thus potentially increasing the number of future problems when the reduced-quality systems go into live use.

13

Support picks up the problems, and as often as not shields the development department from the consequences of its cost-cutting measures by inventing workarounds for the usage problems and by training the users to beat the systems flaws. It appears to be cheaper this way – technicians are cheaper than analyst programmers – but it is of course a false economy, for two main reasons.

First, by a qualitative increase in the length of a finite project, the flaws would probably have been eradicated; instead the company now has to meet the daily cost of supporting a flawed system, limited only by the life of the system itself. It is the old false economy of attempting to convert a variable cost into a fixed cost; it does not work, something has to give – in this case it is user confidence in the computer system (for which a cost can be calculated) and the quality of *all* support because of the unnecessarily increased workload.

Second, there is the very real cost of reduced user productivity; while the computer system troubles or hinders the user, they are not contributing as much to profits as they might, and this is a loss which can be expressed in cash terms. Where the hindrance is caused by poor-quality software, this goes deeper than merely impacting support; it strikes at the very core of why IT exists at all. If user productivity is not enhanced, the value of the IT investment is not realized. Any action which jeopardizes that productivity must surely act in opposition to the fundamental business aims of IT.

2.9 Coming full circle?

Once upon a time, corporate computing was a cluster of huge blue (in the US) or orange (in the UK) boxes in a refrigerator, the size of a badminton court, at head office. This beast was managed by the data processing department, headed by a DP manager and top-heavy with techno-centric developers. For the users, 'computing' meant filling in forms to whatever syntax the developers deigned to offer and in whatever shade of green you could get on your 3270, C03 or VT100 terminal.

Then along came the 'microcomputer' and suddenly the users started down- and uploading mainframe information to and from Visicalc. Distributed computing was born. Who does not remember how the DP department largely despised these 'toy' computers? The technical arrogance that prevailed in those days often manifested itself as a blatant absence of customer service thinking. Before the micro, it was not a matter of what the user wanted, but of what the computer was capable.

Then, in the middle of the 1980s, we had Windows. And hardware got cheaper. The market for dumb terminals diminished rapidly. Then network servers started to have appreciable power. Minicomputers started to have the power of mainframes. Unix was a serious proposition. Hardware prices started to fall. Distributed computing led to computer downsizing, while point-and-click interfaces meant that more people could actually use the things. Microsoft, Digital Research, Lotus and WordPerfect concentrated on horizontal applications. More and more computing moved out of the temple of DP and onto the user's desktop.

This meant a new type of user support was needed. The helpdesk was born, to look after user productivity. It began to professionalize and continued to do so right up to the turn of the century. Things could only get better, especially in the area of service delivery. Or so we thought – because one dark day, somebody uttered the words 'thin client'.

Client–server computing is the zenith of distributed computing. It puts the power, the application and the data on the server. The thinner the client, the more centralized the computing function and the more the personal computer on the user's desk (the 'client') becomes a highly graphical, well-connected, mouse-endowed dumb terminal. This is great for lots of reasons. Data integrity is more controlled. Computer use can be more tightly standardized and policed. Hardware costs can come down at the client end. In other words, the benefits of thin-client computing are largely organizational and technical.

What worries me is the impact all this recentralization will have on the service ethos. Just as the helpdesk had begun to move away from the techno-centricity of old; just as it had established the new politics that make the helpdesk more than just an unfortunate and often begrudged adjunct to the IT department; just as it had become more business-aware and started to see the world from the users' point of view rather than that of the developers – the recentralization of computing threatens to drag us back to the bad old days. I foresee, and I hope I'm wrong, a return to those monolithic DP departments of the early 1980s, with their view of the world from the computer outwards, rather than the business inwards. The helpdesk was nearly there. Let's hope these new technologies do not stymie customer service in its infancy.

2.10 The 'first-line'–'second-line' divide

Historically, computing has always been about technical prowess. In our industry the more you know about computers, the more you are paid and the less of your time you have to spend on the telephone dealing with the end user. The higher you rise in the IT services department, the less stress you have to put up with and you can afford a bigger house, car and vacation, and the less stress you get at home too. Small wonder then, that given this technocratic, hierarchical situation, people want to move up through the technical ranks.

One of the most damaging consequences of this can be seen in any support department where the staff are long-serving. The longer they are there, the more they are paid, the more esoteric their skills. It is all too easy to end up with a technically top-heavy, overpaid IT department. And once the ambitious have reached the pinnacle of technical recognition, they have nowhere else to go and they cannot afford to leave. Staff motivation can become impossible, thus productivity drops and we just end up shelling out more and more money for a declining service.

This structure also gives some licence to one of the most exasperating and all too common truths of working in an IT department. If you work in the helpdesk, you are somehow worthy of less respect than if you work in other parts of IT. The helpdesk is looked down upon. Developers and system engineers routinely feel that they have progressed 'beyond' having to talk to customers. The ability to deal with the frustrated or frightened end user is often not recognized – and in making this mistake, the IT department also makes the institutional *faux pas* of forgetting why it exists. Users are everything. Those who can deal with users have an almost priceless skill.

This divide between the service and technical ends of IT is an anachronism. It belies current truths. Take systems development, for example – is that so special these days? Who really cuts code any more, now that development has been all but reduced to compiling pre-written routines supplied by software vendors? Is it really so extraordinary to be a network expert when you can get network-manufacturer certification from a correspondence course? Information technology no longer looks the way it did in the 1980s, but we still hang on to the old power structures.

Even the commercial truths dispel these outdated attitudes. In September 2000, I designed a helpdesk survey for UK IT-market researchers Xephon. The results showed that the average first line (i.e. helpdesk) technician takes 32 enquiries a day and resolves about 17 of them. The average dedicated second-liner resolves less than half that. The average salary cost of a first-line resolution is US$4.11. The average of a second-line resolution is over US$22.

One of the questions I am asked so often in my consultancy engagements is 'Where should I put my best technicians? On the first line or the second line?' Given the financial reality, the answer is quite obviously on the first line. More technical expertise talking to customers would be cheaper in salary terms, but the benefit on a corporate scale would be even greater, as users would be restored to productivity that much more quickly.

Impeding this, however, is this old-fashioned political divide. Most of our second-line technicians would attempt to avoid going back on the helpdesk – after all, they see their careers as having taken them away from all that. I have to say that in my view, this means that we have employed, and continue to employ, the wrong sort of people. If we want to recognize the business realities of helpdesking these days, if we want to make user support more cost effective, then the sort of people we are looking for love dealing with customers and are technically superb – not barely skilled technical prima donnas who by their recalcitrance and inflexibility dictate our department structure to us.

The fact is that although the developers and network engineers have their own value, unlike the helpdesk, they do not influence user productivity on an hour-by-hour basis. They are invaluable if the network goes down, but in between they are not moving the corporation's productivity forward – but the helpdesk is.

The realization that many IT departments still have to come to terms with is that IT is not just about technology any more. It is about service and service level. It is about making people, as well as machines, more productive. And those who can do that are worth far more than is pure technical competence.

Not only that, but there is also the question of money. If a first-liner takes 32 enquiries a day with a first-time-fix rate of 25 per cent and increases that through his technical skill to 50 per cent, he will be solving eight more enquiries a day. So you will need one less second line head. Which means you could double the salary of the first-liner and still justify his costs. In other words if, as I contend we have the wrong people, we can afford to pay more or less whatever it would take to get the right ones – those who would gladly work on the first line or the second line with a high level of technical competence – because they are financially worth twice what we are currently paying our first-line staff.

In effect, the productivity figures in the Xephon survey show that our techno-centric hierarchy in user support is expensive to the point that we are financially subsidizing low second-line productivity and attitudinal divides. It's time we turned the whole thing upside down. The helpdesk should not be reviled – it should be revered.

2.11 Support's higher goal

Within computing as a whole, the role of support goes much further than simply solving technical problems as they crop up. The aim of the support department should be nothing less than to act as the catalyst by which IT meets its fundamental purpose: that of making workers more productive.

It costs a lot of money to develop a program. Developers are more highly paid than helpdesk technicians. It can be tempting to save money in development. This can mean decreased usability and reliability. But it's OK – because if the users have problems after the program goes live, they can always call the helpdesk, which is often cheaper in budgetary terms than the development section. But that 'cheaper' is a fallacy. If the program is of poor quality, the helpdesk will be called more often. This is one cost. But the real cost is in the productivity the user loses while he is waiting for a helpdesk resolution. If the program had been more completely developed and the user better trained, that productivity would not have been lost. When the user is not working, this shows up at the end of the year on the profit and loss accounts as an absence of money the company could have made.

Somebody has got to make this clear to the corporation. In my view, that somebody is user support. Our job is not just to fix problems. It is to maintain user productivity through IT, and to restore to optimum that productivity, as quickly as possible, when it has been impeded by a failure in either IT or its use.[1]

---

[1] Incidentally, this sentence constitutes my favourite mission statement for a helpdesk or user support group.

And if that means that the helpdesk must defend the company against cynical cost cutting in development, or if it means they must fill the gap left by impatient heads of department who set lay users to work on computers without adequate training, then so be it – so long as they give us the budget to fill those gaps with just-in-time user support services.

3

Forms of support

IT support is to be found in a number of forms, from the simple helpdesk to the full-blown user support centre, and this chapter describes these varieties. These different forms exist in response to different perceived or actual needs and the resources available. The company or IT culture also plays a part in forming the support service, for example in deciding whether the helpdesk should be technical or whether technology should be left to the experts.

The following are only forms in which support is to be found, and they may or may not be what the support service is called in your company. Forms and titles often get confused; in many companies, the whole support organization is called the 'helpdesk', even though it might encompass technical support and development functions, and may even look after the procurement and installation of PCs. Elsewhere, a technical support function may be called 'networks and communications'. What is at question here is not what the department is called, but the form it takes. Because once the form is understood, it becomes easier to identify and solve the problems the department is experiencing, or to decide what other form support at your company should take.

It is extremely rare that any one of these forms would operate in isolation; most companies provide user support through a permutation of several of these forms. In Chapter 4 we will look more closely at some typical support services.

3.1 Helpdesk

There are two types of helpdesk – 'internal' and 'external'. The internal helpdesk supports computer users in the same organization. The external helpdesk supports the customers of that organization. So if I work for a computer or software manufacturer and I have a problem with my computer, I will call the internal helpdesk. But if I buy a computer from that manufacturer and I have a problem with it, I will call the 'external' helpdesk.

3.1.1 Typical structure and environment

The helpdesk answers the telephone. It usually has a widely known telephone number, open to all IT users at least during office hours. The number may be publicized or passed around by word of mouth. It may match shift or flexible working patterns in use elsewhere in the company. It may use other means of communication, like fax, electronic mail, or paper memorandum, but it is essentially a receive-only service, designed for reactive servicing of user demand.

A range of skill levels may be represented; at one end of the scale, the technical skill level is quite low, and deliberately so (see Case Study 3.1), making it necessary to 'escalate' all queries to a separate 'resolver'. The low-skill helpdesk exists to take queries and minimize interruptions to the development, technical support, or other resolver groups. At the other end of the scale, the helpdesk attempts to solve as many user problems as it can.

3.1.2 Advantages and disadvantages

The helpdesk usually has a good relationship with the users, built on rapport between individuals. Helpdesks are commonly staffed by individuals who have shown an interest in computing while working with a user department, or while working in a non-technical function within IT (the ubiquitous image of the helpdesk staffed by ex-punch staff, for whom a job was found when their mechanical data-entry method finally became obsolete). This usually means they have a keen understanding of how the company works and thus of the real problems faced by the users.

The helpdesk offers a single point of contact, something users consider desirable. However, the function may be repeated across many parts of a large organization; specialist helpdesks for the network, word processing, PCs, mainframe applications, and so on, plus the helpdesks created by non-IT parts of a large corporation. In this case the 'single point of contact' idea is much weakened and the users can be just as confused (see Case Study 3.2). The benefit implicit in the single contact point is that users do not have to worry about diagnosing the problem in order to decide who to call; they merely have to describe the symptoms and leave both diagnosis and solution to the helpdesk, confident that they will do all the chasing necessary to get a prompt solution.

Having one helpdesk logging all the questions it is asked into a database can produce revealing information about the company, the ability of its staff and the usability of its computer system. This can be used as raw material for improved computer software, or user induction and training programmes.

3.1.3 Common problems

Working on a helpdesk can be exhausting for the individuals concerned and *morale* can suffer. The work keeps coming in, there seems to be no end to it, and it is difficult to see the ultimate goals. It can be depressing; after all, people usually only call when they have a problem or even a crisis, tempers and patience may be frayed, and the helpdesk can get the blame for the computer system's weaknesses. One way of dealing with this is the *Smallcreep's Day* approach,[1] encouraging the helpdesk staff to take time away from the desk to improve their understanding of the company's business and to give some meaning to the work. Another idea is to populate the helpdesk by job rotation, using staff only from expert or resolver departments. However, this is difficult to negotiate and manage, and loyalties to the job cannot be guaranteed.

Image can be a problem too. If the helpdesk is seen as lacking in knowledge, then for some users, calling it only causes a delay; they consider it more effective to speak directly to the expert rather than be shunted through the system. To combat this, the

---

[1] *Smallcreep's Day*, by Peter Currell Brown (published in the United Kingdom by Panther, 1968) is a fantasy novel about Pinquean Smallcreep (works number 1644/254) whose job is to place a certain type of slot into a certain type of pulley. He has been doing this for 16 years when he begins to wonder what happens further down the line. Rebelliously, he sets off into the factory to discover what, if anything, his work means to the end product.

helpdesk manager has the uphill task of demonstrating not just the user benefits of calling the helpdesk (giving your problem to somebody else, ensuring the right resolver is brought in, etc.), but the benefits to the company as a whole (better information about software usability, measure of how much support is needed for planning staffing, etc.).

Another problem is the relationship between the helpdesk and the *resolver groups*. If the helpdesk is non-technical, it must pass on all queries it cannot answer immediately to other, more technical groups. This causes a number of problems. First, the resolvers may fall under another manager, and this can introduce politics into what should be a straightforward service relationship. This often means that the helpdesk manager may have little or no authority over the speed and quality of a problem resolution, even though he or she is likely to be accountable for them. Second, there is the necessary delay caused by having to move the query from one team to another. Third, there is the risk of garbled communications, as the user explains the problem to the helpdesk, the helpdesk then passes on its understanding of the problem to the resolver, the resolver then calls the user to clarify the problem, all of which can be exasperating. Fourth, there is the very real probability that the resolver group will see user queries as only one of their priorities, and probably not the most important; this is often the case where problems are resolved by development departments, whose primary goal is to produce the next application, not to maintain the existing ones. The result of all this is a confusion of ownership. Who owns the problem – the helpdesk, which is *responsible* for all resolutions – or the resolver groups, who *deliver* them? The users know whom they are going to call – but who do they call when the service falls below their expectations and needs?

For the helpdesk, their necessarily simple *communications* create problems. Because they are often receive-only, they have little or no control over how the users see them. The user may be harbouring unrealistic expectations of the service, or an unhealthy attitude towards helpdesk personnel. Neither the users nor the company as a whole may fully appreciate the value the helpdesk delivers, underestimating the service as a result – with the impact that can have on the helpdesk's requests for additional resources.

Many helpdesks have a problem finding and keeping the right *staff*. To be effective as a helpdesk operative, one needs some technical competence or computer literacy, considerable patience and the ability to handle certain situations with diplomacy and assertiveness. However, the nature of the job often means that there are few opportunities for career progression and salaries are relatively low. Alongside this, the pressure of the job can cause staff to burn out. Finding these skills, mixed with a necessary lack of ambition, is tricky.

The innate problems of helpdesks have caused some organizations to merge them into other support organizations to build a more complete support service; some go as far as to create a user support centre. This can open up career opportunities for helpdesk staff, enable problem ownership and place the management of problems under one manager with focused priorities. The helpdesk staff then benefit from the overall improved image as part of the larger service picture.

Case Study 3.1: Midland Aeroparts UK

The helpdesk at Midland Aeroparts UK (MAUK) was a beleaguered place, with calls coming in from users in all sectors of the company. The nature of MAUK's work – military aircraft component design and manufacture – meant that the users were often highly trained engineers with a high standard of computer literacy. They tended to use the helpdesk only after they had exhausted their own considerable technical knowledge. This made for a wide variety of highly technical queries, invariably out of the helpdesk's range of knowledge, all needing to be passed on to a more technical resolver group.

This transfer created a range of problems and costs. Every incoming query was taken first by the helpdesk, then by a technician – so everything had to be dealt with at least twice and delays were inserted into the system. Another organization might have opted for the cheaper, quicker method of training up the helpdesk to answer more of the queries. But that method would not suit MAUK for three key reasons. First, the sheer range of queries would require enormous preparation and retraining of helpdesk staff, who, because of their background, may well have struggled with some of the concepts. Second, some of the queries were on software which held militarily sensitive data, so to be able to carry out the diagnostic process some helpdesk staff would have to undergo an elaborate and time-consuming government vetting process. Third, cost was not a problem; MAUK produced high-value goods which attracted a premium price, so they could afford to maintain the type of support service which seemed most appropriate to their business.

3.2 Technical support

3.2.1 Typical structure and environment

The essence of this support service is that it is technical. Its main function is to solve technical problems, for which it takes a very high proportion of the total responsibility; that is to say, it tries to fix problems from within its own resources. If it uses external support from equipment suppliers, etc., it is more as a source of information and guidance than as a provider of solutions. The department is staffed and often run by technicians. If a helpdesk exists, technical support will often be one of its resolver groups.

As a resolver of user problems, technical support is most often found in environments which rely heavily on packaged, rather than bespoke IT products. Technical support appears most in companies using a lot of personal computers, or those with private local or wide area networks (many network support departments are typical of the 'technical support' form of support service). This tends to be a backroom operation, with a deliberate focus on supporting the technology rather than the use to which it is put.

3.2.2 Advantages and disadvantages

The main advantage of an internal technical organization is the *cost saving* to the business. With technical support behind them, IT users need to understand only enough about the technology in order to use it, whereas without such a resource, they would have to support themselves. As well as costing money in training, this would take time out of their working day and reduce the time they spend producing the company's profits. Almost without exception, it is cheaper to build or buy in a small, specialist team to service user problems on demand, than attempt to spread that ability through the whole company.

Having such a service to hand gives the corporation a certain *autonomy*, which can be translated into a competitive edge if used properly. A technical support department with a focus on enabling user productivity can provide the company with a lead over users in other companies who are probably experiencing similar if not identical IT problems. However, this process of translation may require that technical support has to be aware of its importance from a corporate marketing point of view, and has to act on that awareness – this is not that likely in most support organizations, who usually have more immediate priorities to worry about. In the end, technical support just does its job, and any commercial benefits as a result may well be incidental.

Having extensive IT skills in-house strengthens the company's *negotiating position* with IT suppliers. Technical support can be used as internal advisers, ensuring that the users' business needs can be accurately converted into a technical specification and that a supplier's proposal meets that specification.

The main disadvantage of owning a technical support department depends on how far removed from the company's core business are the technicians' IT specializations. The company is having to invest time and effort acquiring and managing skills which may not be key to its business goals. The corporation has to be expert in an area which does not make money.

3.2.3 Common problems

Simply because they are so technical, many technical support groups find it difficult to maintain a good *rapport* with all users. Language and priorities differ. Often, the user feels compelled to understand something of the technology in order to be able to explain a problem – i.e. users employ technical jargon rather than technicians speaking in business terms – and this is particularly acute where there is no helpdesk or other inter-mediary between the users and the technicians. This erodes some of the IT investment; technical support is supposed to minimize the need for users to learn about computing, not add to it. This problem partly stems from the tendency of some technical departments to recruit solely technicians, i.e. on the basis of IT ability rather than business understanding.

One way round the problem is to recruit from within the ranks of the users, usually from among the user representatives (see below). This can provide an adequate mix of business awareness and technical competence, with the knowledge gaps, if any, being on the technical side, where they can be plugged during the normal course of the technical work. It is much harder to train the other way round, e.g. by recruiting technicians and training them to understand life as a user; it is difficult to find a way of gaining that knowledge short of spending considerable time working among the users, and most technical support departments cannot afford to lose staff to long secondments, let alone ask the users to give up their time to educate this technician.

The computer industry moves very quickly. *New technology* and concepts are always on the horizon, and even IT insiders have trouble keeping abreast of new developments, let alone the problems these bring to user companies. Technical support must view new technology from two angles: first, on behalf of the users, what, if any, benefit the technology will bring to their company; second, so as to prepare for the new demand, what user support problems it will create. One way to conduct these studies simultaneously is product evaluation. A technician will experiment with the new technology or product in a structured way to determine benefits and problems.

Because it can never know where the next problem can occur, support has to be able to react. The problem some support departments have is that this *reactivity* comes to dominate everything they do and how they do it. This can result in giving the users an inaccurate impression of how quickly support will respond to or solve their problem – because in reality not everything can or should be dealt with immediately. When reactivity gets out of hand, as it often does, the result can be that if an incoming job by its nature cannot be reacted to, there is a risk of it being forgotten. It takes strong and focused management to bring reactivity under control. Like giving up smoking, the only way to stop reacting is to stop reacting. Reactivity is discussed in greater depth in later chapters.

3.3 Research and development

3.3.1 Typical structure and environment

Typically, R&D is where user support goes for a solution when its own technical or knowledge resources are exhausted. For example, this is the support service provided by the manufacturer to the user support team, particularly when a suspected system bug or design flaw is found. R&D thus has a role to play in user support, but it is an indirect one, supporting not the users, not even the product, but the individual technical problems with the product.

3.3.2 Advantages and disadvantages

The main advantage is that the existence of R&D closes the loop. It means there is always somewhere for the problem to go. The main disadvantage is that there may be no answer to a technical problem which reaches this level of escalation. As stated earlier, this type of support is often used for suspected design flaws – and if the problem turns out to be a design flaw, then the answer to the user's query is either 'can't be done' or 'will be fixed in next version'. Neither of these is satisfactory, in that neither of them fixes the immediate problem.

3.3.3 Common problems

As a user support function, the R&D department has much in common with technical support, in that it is predominantly technical and that it is a backroom operation. With these attributes come the consequent problems of user *rapport*. R&D is almost completely divorced from the user. Therefore, there may be a mediator (usually the helpdesk) between R&D and the user. Of course, the risk then is one of communication – the problem the user describes can be reinterpreted by the helpdesk before being further described to R&D, and confusion results.

There is also the matter of differing *priorities*. The main job of any R&D function is to produce the designs and systems which will become future products. A problem with an exisiting product must therefore take a lower priority. (There is a commercial imperative to this; R&D's new designs are producing future profits, where providing support only erodes profit already made.) So what started out as a user's immediate problem becomes merely one of a number of tasks for the R&D department. One way round this is to make support a commercial imperative also, by making support queries generate income for the R&D company. This will probably mean charging for support and defining service levels – and of course it only applies where there is a real commercial relationship between user and support, which is less likely if they both work for the same company.

3.4 Information centre

3.4.1 Typical structure and environment

The concept of the 'information centre' (IC) was defined by IBM in the early 1980s in response to the rise of distributed computing. Throughout large corporations, data is produced and owned by individual departments, who may have access to their own computers and not necessarily use the corporate mainframe. Indeed, given the sheer size of the mainframe, there can be many data libraries which are potential sources of management information. The job of the IC was to keep track of all these data areas and be aware of their content and then to act as a central and single source of new management information, produced by reworking these distributed data. The logic went that the answer to any given management question was probably in the corporation's computers somewhere. It was the IC's job to know where to look for it, if necessary negotiate with the owner for the use of the data and often to add value to the data by reworking it into the form needed by the requestor.

A number of software tools appeared to help the IC in this endeavour. One of these tools, the executive information system (EIS), probably contributed to the decline, in the early 1990s, of the IC. Once set up, the EIS automates the job of electronically sourcing, extracting, and publishing data in new and often graphical, easily usable, forms.

As I write the second edition, in 2001, the information centre is now virtually defunct. I have not known of a department so called for several years (although that does not mean they exist). In the UK, the self-proclaimed professional body for the format, the 'Information Centre Manager's Forum' has changed its name and its form completely, so the idea of the IC has to all intents and purposes lost its focus. This is a pity – the forum was a splendid and strategically oriented body while it lasted, and in these days of reactivity and obsession with the bottom line, in my view we need more of that kind of thinking.

The software of data-warehousing has largely taken over from the labour-intensive IC. Corporations adopting the idea know where and what their data are and improved searches and reporting have made the data available in automated ways. By and large, it is safe to say the manual information centre had little to offer that nowadays the computers could not do for us.

3.4.2 Advantages and disadvantages

The IC has a distinct user bias. Rather than being intended as a service for resolving system failures, its job is to put the 'information' in 'information technology'. This function can produce real, new benefits by making the whole of the corporation's electronically held data add up to more than the sum of its parts. The IC's main disadvantage is the narrowness of its scope. Because it deals in information, the product of the technology, it can lack technical knowledge overall, making it a very incomplete support provider.

3.4.3 Common problems

The true function of the IC is not often understood. It is user support in the truest sense, but its specialization often gets lost in the other types of user support it frequently gets roped into providing. The IC concept was born at about the same time as PCs began to become widespread. Partly because of the user orientation of the PCs, partly because some companies did not know how to support them, and partly because many data-processing departments did not take PCs seriously enough even to want to support them, PC support became the job of the IC. For many ICs, this new support requirement swamped their original purpose and transformed them utterly.

3.5 User support centre

3.5.1 Typical structure and environment

The user support centre (USC) is an attempt to solve all the problems associated with having several groups providing user support, by putting all responsibility for user support in one place. It manages the helpdesk as well as the resolvers, and also has a technical support function. On sites doing their own applications programming, it will also retain a programming staff whose function is systems maintenance as well as solving problems which need investigation by an R&D function. It will typically also be responsible for the specification and installation of desktop computing equipment and connection to the corporate network, which it may also manage. The USC will also take responsibility for the management of relationships with external support providers, such as computer maintenance companies and network data carriers.

3.5.2 Advantages and disadvantages

On the face of it, the USC is everybody's dream come true. To the users, it is a single point of contact, a single point of resolution, no matter what the query. To the developers it is the solutions machine which relieves them of the burden of having to support what they have already written as well as composing new software. To the company, it is all of a vital function under one budget and cost centre. To USC staff, it opens up career paths. Within the USC, the benefits for the management of support workload are considerable: no need to negotiate with other department managers for the use of their resources, which they may not be able to provide; improved communications (potentially) for moving problems between resolvers; improved speed of response (again, potentially); broader skills mix; greater skill and headcount redundancy, so better able to withstand sudden staff absences.

The main disadvantage from the user's point of view is that the USC has a monopoly on user support in the company; if it cannot or will not solve your problem, nobody else can. This means the USC has to be seen to be flexible. Another disadvantage is that it is expensive, but this can be offset by the easier identification of the costs of user support and the greater control gained over them.

3.5.3 Common problems

The USC's very size and comprehensiveness can be its weakness. The variety of services it offers makes for a sizeable management overhead. The right manager may be difficult to find. The job requires considerable breadth of experience and aptitude and in many corporations, even now, user support has not yet reached a level of maturity to deliver many managers of this calibre: the company going for this kind of support structure may do better looking at ex-IC rather than ex-technical support managers. There is also a risk that the USC may become bureaucratic, forced down this path by the need to document changes in ownership as a query passes through various hands, or by documenting response and fix times to comply with service level agreements.

Another risk is that the service will be oversubscribed: its sheer competence will attract work, putting more of a strain on resources than it can cope with. So user expectations need to be tightly managed, probably more so than with any other form of support; but this has to be married with a certain flexibility of service so that users do not miss out.

Case Study 3.2: when helpdesks proliferate

It was the day when both her secretaries were away that the comptroller's laptop happened to misbehave once too often. She knew about the helpdesk, but didn't know the number, so she looked it up in the corporate telephone directory. There was a page-and-a-half of telephone numbers of one or another helpdesk. Forty-eight of them, in every location from Minneapolis to Montreal, keen and communicative company departments offering help and knowledge of all kinds. She found what appeared to be the right one at her third attempt – a good ratio, three out of 48 – but she began to wonder whether the cost and time-saved benefits were being eroded by user confusion just as she had suffered.

It took nine months to decide on a solution and another 18 to implement it, using expert help as they went. The company libraries at head office, the operations and network helpdesks from the computing section and the corporate R&D helpdesk were all amalgamated under the one manager, a rather innovative individual from customer relations. The workplace support centre was formed. Theoretically, they could take any call, on anything, from anywhere, and any time zone. It took a lot of negotiating with resolver groups and the introduction of some unpopular job rotation. Some of the users were sceptical, others pragmatic, retaining their own in-house experts for the specialized queries. But the dream of 'one-stop knowledge' was made real.

3.6 Technical library

3.6.1 Typical structure and environment

The technical library manages technical documentation. As a support form, it differs from all the others in that it is the only passive support provision. All the others deal with the users' needs directly, where this one only provides the users with the means to help themselves. In practice, it tends to exist as part of another computing function such as software development, i.e. because the documentation is there, others might as well use it also. Such a library is not normally needed for user support, especially if good training, user documentation, or online help are available.

3.6.2 Advantages and disadvantages

A technical library is probably the cheapest way of supporting the users: headcount investment is minimal and the documentation would normally have to be provided for computing purposes anyway. However, as a form of user support, it is extremely limited and unlikely to be appropriate for most companies. By its nature it separates computers from the users and demonstrates a policy of leaving the users to their own devices.

3.6.3 Common problems

Any technical or development function will need a library of some description. Often these are informal, with each technician or programmer keeping the documentation they need for their work (in other words, in much the same way as users keep documentation); there may be some commonly available documentation as well, perhaps kept by the department manager. It is very difficult to ensure that informal libraries are kept up to date. There may also be duplication or omissions, and no one person could be said to be responsible for the integrity of the library. User support organizations without a proper librarian are much more common than those with one. The type of documentation in a technical library may also decrease the library's usefulness to the users, as it will also usually be written by and for technicians.

3.7 User group representative

3.7.1 Typical structure and environment

In any group or department of computer users, there will usually be somebody who is more computer literate than the others, and acts as a first line of computer support to them. The job may be official but more often it is not. Either way, this person will usually be known to the support department and will have built up a rapport with them. Where the job is official, part of the representative's job will be to filter out and probably solve a large number of the problems, particularly those that have more to do with the users' specialization than they have with the computer system. Another job may be to act as the local co-ordinator for equipment installations. Sometimes this is done by the local manager, but more often now it is being recognized as necessary and the job delegated to one who shows a specific aptitude.

A study conducted by the Gartner Group showed that the significance of this function is recognized by 78 per cent of support departments interviewed, and that for PC users at least, providing this 'hidden support' constitutes the overwhelming majority of the corporate cost of PC ownership.

3.7.2 Advantages and disadvantages

The users benefit from having local support. Because their specialist is 'one of us' rather than a member of the computer department, accessibility is high and communications relatively free-flowing. However, the user representative is usually not a computer technician by career, but has come into the position by aptitude. His or her knowledge may well be incomplete, and more akin to that of the hobbyist than the professional. The support department usually has little control over the quality of support provided through this channel. However, support can be fairly sure that when a query comes from a department which has a local representative, that it will already have been through the obvious possible solutions and is likely to be well qualified for being dealt with by computer specialists.

Often, it is at the user representative that the worlds of business and computing are bridged. The user representative under-stands the impact of each on the other and can smooth the flow of communication between them.

User representatives are usually a good source of computer support staff. They have already shown interest and ability and they know the user environment. For the time being, however, their primary job is not user support – they have other priorities which can quickly remove them from the support chain, and put the burden of their support work back on to the support department. And given that it is not uncommon for user representatives to spend up to a quarter of their time supporting their peers, any withdrawal of their assistance can be a big headcount problem for the support manager.

3.7.3 Common problems

Because they are not officially computer technicians, it is much more difficult for the user representatives to justify spending time keeping their knowledge up to date – after all, they may have no reference whatsoever to peer support in their job descriptions. The user is actually at risk of being given flawed information through this channel.

Having the representative there can place yet another hurdle between the user and the computer system. In some companies, the standing rule is that all IT queries go to the user representative first (making them a kind of local helpdesk), thence to be passed on to the IT helpdesk. This can introduce problems with individual queries and cause the user to have to explain the query three times – to the user representative, helpdesk and resolver – and this can be exasperating. Clear lines of ownership, responsibility and query flow must be drawn up between the user, the representative and the support team to avoid confusion.

3.8 Workstation management

3.8.1 Typical structure and environment

Workstation management looks after the users' desktop computing equipment. Typical tasks may include assisting the user to draw up a specification for the required equipment and then moving that through the procurement process. When the hardware or software arrives, support may install it, connect it to the company network and, if it is for a first-time user, may give a brief introduction to use of the equipment.

This network connection element is important. Users may be able to buy and start up their own PCs, but connection to the network will usually need a technical specialist. This also means that workstation management is needed if any desktop machine needs to be relocated. There is also the question of system security, for which the computing function will most likely be ultimately responsible, hence the need for them to be involved in connection of any devices to the company network.

3.8.2 Advantages and disadvantages

One advantage of workstation management is that standardization is made easier, and this brings with it numerous opportunities such as better-prepared support, high availability of assistance from one's peers, even cheaper equipment as it can be bought in bulk. This is offset by the negative side of uniformity of equipment: the user with a genuinely non-standard application may be left with a reduced support service.

The main disadvantage to this aspect of user support is that the user absolutely depends on it wherever connection to a network or remote peripherals is required; and this means that the user's need for that and support's ability to comply within the right timescales have to match. If not, this can be a source of frustration and possibly lost productivity for the user.

3.8.3 Common problems

Problems with workstation management include fitting in with the users, agreeing on delivery times and establishing that the user will be physically available for installations, acquaintance with new equipment, and so on. It is also desirable to dovetail the moves and installations with other necessary functions like the provision of power and physical space, both of which may well be handled by separate departments. Network planning is also necessary so that equipment is not delivered to a place where no network connection can be achieved.

3.9 System maintenance

3.9.1 Typical structure and environment

Traditionally, hardware maintenance has been the role of the hardware manufacturer or a third-party repair company. This situation is changing for PCs at least – as the cost of hardware comes down, some support departments have found it cheaper and more convenient to buy extra machines to the same standard as the installed base, to be used as spares in the event of a hardware failure. PCs are becoming increasingly modular and spare parts widely available.

3.9.2 Advantages and disadvantages

The advantage of system maintenance as done in the traditional way, with engineers visiting to effect a repair, is that users do not need to worry about the failure or the diagnosis; all that can be left to a specialist, while they just get on with whatever other work they can. But therein lies the disadvantage; users have to wait for an engineer to call before fault diagnosis or repair can even begin. When the engineer arrives, he or she may well decide that an immediate repair is impossible, the equipment must be removed to a specialist workshop, or discover the correct spares are not to hand, making a further delay and second visit necessary. Small wonder that so many user companies are seriously considering holding spares on-site. System maintenance is a case of support for the machine, not the user.

Another disadvantage of system maintenance is that it is limited in the type of problems it can tackle and the completeness of the solution it can render. For instance, if the hard disk on a network server fails, an engineer is usually called to replace the hard disk. However, the contents of the disk, its operating system, network configuration and user data will all subsequently have to be rebuilt, and the machine reconnected to the network in order to restore user service. Clearly, the maintenance engineer can seldom be expected to conduct the whole repair, as so much of it is in the domain of the user company. Some maintenance companies have recognized this failing and are rebuilding their engineering force to be able to rebuild the computer *system*, rather than just repair the hardware. There is a cost to any user company which does not have engineers this competent; in several user companies an internal network technician has to attend a sizeable proportion of engineer callouts in order to check or rebuild the software or network link.

3.9.3 Common problems

The *image* of hardware repair now is that it is less demanding from a skills point of view than systems support. With computers diagnosing their own faults and the repairer relegated to a position of merely changing the subassembly identified by the computer, hardware repair is now held by some to have more in common with the job of a fitter than a computer expert. The image is probably some way from the complete truth, but where it holds, it will damage the credibility of the industry.

As it becomes ever more *competitive*, the repair industry is now becoming more confusing for the user. Decisions about engaging a third-party repair company are often based on price rather than a detailed assessment of its ability to provide the required level of support.

As regards supporting individual users, hardware engineers have the same problems as anybody visiting the user's desk – getting schedules to coincide so that the user can be there with the engineer to describe the problem, provide access to the office, etc.

Communications can also be a source of difficulty. How is the helpdesk to know whether the engineer visited at the time promised, fixed the problem as described, kept to the service level agreement, and so on? All these things have to be taken into account. The job of managing any external service provider has to rest somewhere, and it is not always clear whose responsibility it is.

Case Study 3.3: managing external support

Rita was the user support manager for BCT, a very high-profile retail company. Specifically, her job was to look after the 250 or so users in corporate central office. These were all very influential people, ranging from senior managers, through divisional directors, to the board of the holding company. From a career point of view, her job was very high risk.

The consequences of computer failure at this level could be catastrophic. These computers, which on other desks in the company might be word processors or low-level databases, here were making rapid decisons about investments in millions, communicating the chairman's thoughts to the shareholding institutions, and making sure the company's thousands of employees and suppliers got paid. They had a four-hour turnaround on any hardware failure, with high-priced teams of engineers floating around the head office campus, and penalties to be paid if service dropped below certain levels. It was vital not just to provide good hardware support – but to know that it was being provided.

The first step was to increase the speed with which hardware failures were reported. Initially, the helpdesk technician would report by fax, but this was replaced by a modem connection to the repairer's local office with a terminal showing hardware failures as logged at BCT's helpdesk. This meant that somebody had to keep an eye on the terminal – so eventually that became a PC, which automatically scanned BCT's call-logs for hardware failures and moved them straight into the repairer's job allocation system.

At the user end, the engineer carried a pack of visit cards. At every desk visit, one of these cards would be left, showing the job number, time of arrival and departure, and result of the visit. After the engineer was supposed to have visited, the BCT helpdesk called the user and requested the information on the card. Any failure to meet the service level agreement was immediately identified and went onto the agenda of the monthly service review meetings.

Rita was justly proud of the system she had devised; but she was prouder still of the spirit of co-operation it signified between her department and the repair organization. She also knew that none of their direct competitors had anything like it – a fact she made sure was well known by the influential decision-makers she had to support.

3.10 User training

3.10.1 Typical structure and environment

There are several ways of ensuring the user has the knowledge needed to use the system. Some companies attach a training function to the computer department. This can be in the form of a programmer or perhaps professional trainers training the users in a newly developed system; or a support technician spending a short while with the users of a newly delivered machine so that they can get started on it (sometimes called 'user acquaintance'). It is quite common for a user's line manager to take ultimate responsibility for their ability to use the computer, as part of the overall responsibility of ensuring an employee is able to do the job they were hired for.

3.10.2 Advantages and disadvantages

The advantages of user training are clear. For the support staff it means more competent users, delivering fewer queries, and with improved computer literacy, so that when they do come across a problem, they are better able either to solve it themselves or to describe it more accurately to the support organization. Also, they will be better equipped to understand the solution as explained to them. It is an unfortunate truth that some less computer-aware users will ask for technical assistance and not understand the advice given, yet fail to mention that they do not understand – so the problem and the frustration go on. Training is the only way such knowledge gaps can be eradicated; but one must take care that users such as these are actually open to training.

Training tends to be associated with a single event or stage; ongoing training in the same topic, simply ensuring the user has grasped and can use everything covered in the training course, is much less common. However, this is where user support has to pick up the workload. People are seldom able to take in everything in a training course and will usually need some guidance in system usage, but they often get this from their peers as well as the helpdesk. But the snag with traditional training is that once it's over, it's over.

3.10.3 Common problems

Leaving the user's level of computer skills up to a line manager is like leaving their competence in foreign languages up to a confirmed monoglot. It is a rare manager, in the UK at least, who is fully computer literate, and 'delegating' the computer to one's secretary or the young, recent recruit who learned about them at school is still embarrassingly common. Clearly, it is unsafe to place the onus of ensuring a respectable level of technical skills (or any office skills for that matter) on middle management. Responsibility for ensuring users are educated should be taken by the organization with most to benefit from having a more knowledgeable user base – naturally this means the support organization. The training section (or in some companies the personnel office) should not be seen as being responsible for technical knowledge, but merely as one of several means of delivering that knowledge.

3.11 Call centre

3.11.1 Typical structure and environment

The call centre is the archetypal front line of the support machine. It takes the incoming telephone calls. The traditional call centre is more of an extrapolation of a sales technique towards the helpdesk, rather than the other way round. Helpdesks have always taken telephone calls – but call centre techniques offer a focus on and special expertise in the art of managing incoming calls. This is why larger helpdesks, taking large call volumes, often separate the front and back lines, so that these can build their own particular procedural benefits.

If I call an airline to book a flight, I can imagine the scene at the other end of the line. A veritable factory floor of cubicles, each containing an isolated agent wearing a telephone headset and logging calls into a computer, which is itself linked to the telephone system. The computer may have identified the caller by recognizing the telephone number he is calling from ('Caller Line Identification') and looked that number up in a database, which then feeds the agent with known information about that customer and other enquiries he may have already placed. The agent's job is to answer the call, respond to the enquiry and note both enquiry and response in the computer before moving to the next call.

The response may take one of two forms. The first is to resolve the enquiry, and this is the usual purpose of a call centre in a sales or sales support context. For this, the agent may have access to a knowledge base, providing the requisite information. The second is the 'catch and dispatch' helpdesk, whose job is to note the nature of the enquiry and pass it to a second-line resolving agency, e.g. a hardware engineer, desktop support technician or indeed a warehouse to fulfil a sales order.

3.11.2 Advantages and disadvantages

Not all helpdesks need call centres and not all call centres are helpdesks. Call centres are great at taking calls. They are response factories, and as such they deal in mass-production. In a small helpdesk, they can be overkill. As a support mechanism, they are only part of a larger whole. Their response-only culture tends to preclude diagnosis, meaning they often cannot resolve the problem but they may be pretty good at passing the enquiry to somebody who can.

The technologies to aid call centres are broad and sophisticated. Their specialization in one limited aspect of the customer support relationship means that they can perfect the art. Productivity tends to be high – for just getting calls in, the call centre is king. They fit best where the anticipated number of calls is high and the expected response is either from predefined knowledge or an obvious course of escalation.

The reason call centres are ubiquitous in a sales environment is because of the predefined nature of the information they must deliver. Do you have a flight to New York tomorrow? Yes. Have you seats available in Business Class? Yes. How much is it? So many dollars. What time does it leave? 10:45. How long is the flight? Three hours. Can I get lunch on the plane? Roast chicken or vegetable ratatouille. What time next day is the return flight? And so on and so on. This is rather different to 'My printer won't print', which may be as much to do with the caller's comprehension of and ability to explain the problem as it has to do with the complex diagnosis of what may be, for this enquiry, a unique and previously unseen set of circumstances. Once we move from delivering predefined information against anticipated enquiries, to diagnosing our way through both technical and behavioural circumstances, we move also from an environment a call centre could handle to one more suited to a helpdesk.

3.11.3 Common problems

In a survey in March 2000, market researcher Mintel reported that 61 per cent of the UK population would prefer to avoid having to deal with call centre technologies. The robotic 'press one for this, two for that' offering of the Interactive Voice Response unit ('IVR' or 'VRU') has people hanging on in frayed patience waiting to hear what button to press to speak to a human being. In one helpdesk I know, using call centre techniques, there are tape machines playing reports of the known problems so if yours is one of those, you can have confidence that the helpdesk is already dealing with the problem and doesn't want to hear about it any more, thanks all the same. The caller can press a button to skip the tape announcement. Most of the users have programmed this selection into the speed dial for the helpdesk, so they always skip the announcements in the hope of getting more quickly to an agent. As a result, whenever the network goes down, the helpdesk agents get swamped with hundreds of calls, precisely the situation the tape machine was meant to avoid.

The call centre is often sold as being of a benefit to the caller – in reality, many callers see these technologies as being designed to benefit the call centre. Call centres are unpopular. However, the phenomenon does seem to be gaining acceptability (if not popularity) as it wends its way into people's lives. A survey conducted by Xephon PLC of Newbury, England (on which I was a consultant), showed a distinct correlation between those helpdesks scoring least in customer satisfaction and those being fronted by call centre telephone technologies such as Interactive Voice Response (IVR). By the time we conducted the survey again in 2000, the correlation had disappeared.

One the call centre's inherent problems is staff retention. In my experience, this is partly due to the uncommonly low salaries. At the time of writing, I know of call centres here in the UK paying their staff around £14,000 per annum, while the average wage is something over £22,000. In the context of a helpdesk service, whose job is to get users working again when the computer fails them, this is startling in its narrow-mindedness and false economy. The compulsion among some companies to pay what they can get away with is in my view directly damaging corporate productivity. It makes far more sense for companies to ignore the market rate and pay instead what the job is worth. It makes for higher quality and better motivated staff who have a reason for staying. This should lead to a more integrated IT department and increased continuity of service. Skill levels can be increased, so the first time fix rate goes up and overall support costs drop. But that of course only works where the call centre moves towards the helpdesk model, where it attempts to fix as well as take the call. Where it is just catch and dispatch, salaries can stay low and the call centre risks being replaced by e-support, which I cover below.

The catch and dispatch call centre also may lose staff because the job offers few prospects for improvement (except perhaps a salary rise by becoming a team leader or supervisor) and a job that is the same all day, every day, for the foreseeable future. People are not machines – for the most part (there are exceptions) they have aspirations, a variety of skills and interests and an innate source of self-motivation which is worth seeking out. Find those things, feed those things and you never know, They Might Be Giants. Give staff a job with too little money, no intrinsic incentive and routine exposure to clients the company has let down, and sooner or later the best will leave and you will be left with dregs. The call centre probably needs more attention to staff motivation than most other forms of user support. For the call centre to succeed on a staff front, it needs an impassioned manager with vision, leadership and a sense of innovation. When you lead your call centre, how far do your staff follow you? To the ends of the earth, or only as far as five o'clock?

3.12 E-support and the Internet

3.12.1 Typical structure and environment

It is the age of the Internet, and with it has come e-mail, e-commerce, e-trading, e-business, e-transaction, e-support (and e-what-next? one may wonder). In the IT industry, 'e' has become the coolest letter of the alphabet. In support terms, the 'e' refers to providing user support electronically rather than the old-fashioned way of having people talking to one another through that outmoded medium, the telephone.

E-support consists of four main components:

- Support provision by e-mail rather than voice.
- User self-help by provision of online manuals and downloadable solutions.
- Remote control of distant computers.
- Automated problem diagnosis and resolution.

We can see from that list that e-support is not new – the technologies have been there for years. The only thing that is new about it is that we now have a convenient category within which to include these electronic provisions, and in the Internet, a convenient and ubiquitous way to deliver them.

E-support then is another marketing construct (like 'CRM' below). It is more accurate to call the rise of e-support a marketing rather than a technological consideration.

But before dismissing it so cynically, one ought to see why it has arisen. The main reason is the cultural change that the Internet has brought about. We have become accustomed to the immediate availability from our desktops of all kinds of information, such that we now expect and demand that a supplier should make any public-domain information electronically. I bought a CD player recently – discount, no manual. No problem. I just presumed that I would be able to download the manual. Five years ago, I would have had to contact the manufacturer, find a part number, send off a cheque, hope the manual was not out of print or discarded to make room for new models. The Internet has changed our expectations about the availability of product support.

The other reason for e-support is the high – in some cases unaffordable – cost of traditional support models. In my local computer store, I can buy an anti-virus package for £30. Take away the store's margin, the transport, printing and disk pressing and development costs, the manufacturer's profit, tax and the shareholder dividend and there is not a lot left to field a support team to deal with the technical enquiries. But that manufacturer simply has to offer some kind of support, or he will lose sales of even such an inexpensive product as this.

It is for this reason that e-support is still predominantly an external support provision, but it is becoming more common in internal desks too. Helpdesk costs are falling, but the financiers still find the cost of such a labour-intensive service intimidating. E-support is tempting, because as a way of providing support, machines are cheaper than people.

3.12.2 Advantages and disadvantages

And there's the first advantage. E-support is cheaper to provide. If the users help themselves, fewer support people are, or should be, needed. When the computers can diagnose their own problems and automatically locate solutions and repairs across the Internet or intranet, repairs and system updates can be quicker and systems more standardized.

But while e-support is a no-brainer for the provision of external support, the apparently reduced costs of e-support for an internal helpdesk are an illusion. The salary and accommodation costs of the internal helpdesk are only part of the picture. The real and much larger cost of internal user support is in the productivity lost by the user while his computer is unavailable – and that lost productivity, as I endeavour to prove in the chapter on cost justification, although often unnoticed by the finance director, is terrifyingly expensive and comes right off the profit and loss bottom line.

In my experience, there are few helpdesks that could not benefit from the provision of some form of computer remote control. It often pays for itself very quickly, by avoiding expensive deskside visits by second-line technicians and the inherent delay in escalation. It can prove to be essential in those organizations where users are located in offices distant from corporate HQ and in populations too small to warrant onsite technical staff.

Support by e-mail can help when support has to be provided across time zones. A problem may occur in the remote office while the HQ staff are in bed, but an overnight e-mail will guarantee a solution is waiting when the remote office staff report for work tomorrow. This is an advantage in that remote offices can be supported – a disadvantage in its lack of service immediacy.

3.12.3 Common problems

All this online help – this copious problem solving website – these succinct and precise e-mails – this all-embracing knowledge database – who's going to write them? In external support, a cost–benefit analysis may show that effort invested in writing self-help systems will pay off in terms of support staff not needing to be hired. But the truth about external support is that the profitability of the customer is not the problem of the vendor. It may well not be the vendor's concern that the customer (rather than the vendor) has to expend the time and effort extracting a technical solution at the cost of his own lost productivity. For the vendor, providing electronic rather than human support reduces his costs, thus boosting his own profitability – so the value of the investment is clear.

For the internal helpdesk, however, the value is less clear. As such, the helpdesk may simply not have the staff, the time or the skills to create the website. For e-mail support, precise communication in the written word is a crucial skill. The helpdesk therefore must have staff who write well.

E-mail support has the other problem of being a one-way medium. There is no discourse, so there is often a lengthy and involved exchange of typed messages, when a brief conversation would have been much quicker.

The main problem with online manuals is that the user's problem must have been experienced hitherto, so that the experience could then be documented for the future benefit of other users. If the problem is a new one – or it stems from some unique mix of this particular problem and this particular user – the website may not be able to solve it. Although websites and knowledge databases may be able to diagnose the computer's problems, they are often unable to diagnose the user's problem, especially if that problem is more associated with the user's comprehension or IT competence than with any mechanical failure.

3.13 Customer relationship management

3.13.1 Typical structure and environment

'Customer relationship management' (CRM) is not really a form of support as such, but an industry term for a method of working and range of technologies. CRM is a way of governing all the ways in which the organization interacts with its external customers. These interactions thus include those made by the helpdesk, which will by definition be an external helpdesk (see 3.1 above).

A company that adopts a CRM methodology is one that has identified all the points at which customer contact has involved, and then implemented umbrella procedures that all those points must follow. The procedures will usually be enshrined in a universal database system in which all customer interactions will be logged. The system will have a helpdesk component – but usually, it also will comprise all sales contacts made with the customer, as well as ordering patterns, call-off stock levels, credit ratings, market sector, history of that customer's involvement with marketing promotions and all the other paraphernalia of proactive marketing. As such, CRM is really a marketing concept of which both the pre- and post-sales support functions are merely components.

3.13.2 Advantages and disadvantages

A CRM strategy can be a boon to an organization, where the management wants and needs as full as possible a picture of the behaviour of its customer base and the company's contacts with it. There are no particular advantages from a solely support point of view. However, the use made of the helpdesk by the customer may be of particular interest to the sales department. Where the helpdesk is free of charge, the sales department has a negotiating tool because the availability of the helpdesk constitutes an additional value in the product sale. Added value is of use in keeping selling prices high, and differentiating the organization from the offerings of its competitors. Where the helpdesk is chargeable, the cost of the helpdesk then becomes another item for negotiation. CRM is a sales and marketing tool, and the helpdesk's role thus becomes part of the sales and marketing propositions.

3.13.3 Common problems

One of the most common problems in CRM is database integrity. All interactions with the customer, no matter in which department they are made, go into the same database. So the data are owned by everybody, and thus by nobody in particular. And where there is no ownership, errors and omissions may occur. The essence of CRM is its universality, the benefit of which is that any department can use the whole picture. But if, for example, the sales department makes no use of the entries logged by the helpdesk, then the CRM system is in effect behaving as though it were a suite of separate systems used by separate departments.

If that turns out to be the case, then the justification of a fully fledged CRM system is questionable. A system that tries to be all things cannot be guaranteed to be especially good at any one thing in particular. If the whole system is not used as a whole, then perhaps the helpdesk would have been better off with its own system, specifically designed solely for user support, rather than being part of a greater whole.

From the helpdesk's point of view, it is perhaps better to look at the problems of being an external helpdesk, rather than those of existence merely as a part of a CRM strategy. And invariably, those problems are usually to do with the relationship between support and sales.

I have been a technician in, designed and run a few external helpdesks. They have their own special issues. The helpdesk can become a pawn in the sales negotiation with the customer. A customer complaint at the support service level puts the sales department under pressure, and the helpdesk may be indicted (i.e. blamed) for lost customers or otherwise unnecessary discounts having to be given. The helpdesk itself is under pressure – it may often be seen as a drain on the company's profitability, so its costs may be resented – as a result it may be difficult to increase helpdesk investment, which may depress service levels and the whole thing goes full circle. And all too painfully often, the value the helpdesk adds cannot be measured, so there is no algorithm for justifying a proper level of investment. To this end, I have offered just such an algorithm in the chapter on cost justification.

3.14 Triage support

3.14.1 Typical structure and environment

'Triage' is a service function commonly used by hospital emergency departments to sort patients into priorities for treatment and to deliver service on the basis of expediency rather than need. It is a term I have come to use for a new adjunct to the helpdesk.

The traditional route for helpdesk enquiries looks like this:

Function	Activity
User	Reports problem to helpdesk
Helpdesk (first line)	Attempts to solve by telephone – otherwise logs problem and assigns (escalates) to resolver
Resolver (second line)	Claims assignment and solves problem

Where a 'triage' function is deployed, the route changes:

Function	Activity
User	Reports problem to helpdesk
Helpdesk (first line)	Attempts to solve by telephone. Otherwise, assesses whether a telephone fix would be possible given time, in which case passes caller immediately to triage desk for 'hot' resolution. If telephone fix impossible, logs and escalates problem to resolver for 'cold' resolution
Triage desk	Takes calls passed from helpdesk and spends time fixing by telephone. May escalate to second line if telephone fix impossible
Resolver (second line)	Claims assignment and solves problem

The reason for the terminology of 'hot' and 'cold' resolution reflects the fact that the helpdesk passes the caller direct to the triage desk while the caller is still on the line, in other words while the enquiry is still 'hot'. Success at the triage desk means that the caller sees, in effect, a first-time fix. The idea of a 'cold' resolution reflects the fact that the logged, escalated enquiry must spend at least some time in the helpdesk system until the second-line resolver can get around to fixing it.

3.14.2 Advantages and disadvantages

The 'triage' desk is especially useful for what has, in recent years, become the most common helpdesk enquiry, namely 'How do I . . .?' A few years ago, the two most usual helpdesk enquiries were 'I've lost my password' and 'My printer won't print'. Those days have passed, as software has become increasingly feature-rich. The triage desk deals with this new demand, effectively by offering just-in-time training over the telephone. It is therefore also the best place to put applications usage support, the remote control service in the e-support helpdesk or call avoidance in the field maintenance support desk.

With a triage desk in place, the helpdesk need no longer worry about spending too much time on the telephone supporting one user and thus presenting the busy tone to other callers. If the problem could be fixed over the telephone, it can be passed to the triage desk, leaving the first line helpdesk free to take new incoming calls.

Triage can be extremely cost effective. I recommended one for a field maintenance company. The number of problems it solved over the telephone meant that for every full-time equivalent (FTE) employed on the triage desk, six fewer were needed in the field. The users may appreciate it too – for them it means more first-time fixes and a more rapid return to productivity.

3.14.3 Common problems

The main problem with the triage desk is finding the staff to put on it. The necessary skills and motivations are considerable. A high level of technical competence is a prerequisite, as is contentment with spending much of the working day on the telephone.

Another is the identification of the types of problems that could be solved by the triage desk – but all that needs is a regular trawling of the call-log to see what sort of enquiries are being escalated to the second line and which of those escalations could have been solved by triage.

Typical support structures

4.1 Who supports what?

There are several elements to a computer system, all of which require support. Support for each of these elements may come from a different source. Figure 4.1 shows the usual sources of support for a typical computer environment. Note that the helpdesk or equivalent provides only a part of the support needed by the whole system. Note also that support tends to become more vague as the problem area tends towards the user's specialization; for example, the use of computer aided design (CAD) software requires specialized engineering skills, and those skills cannot be expected of the computer support team. Similarly, a finance specialist writing macros in a spreadsheet may also find that he or she is alone, as may any programmer. At this level, users often fall back on their own resources, training they have had, or contact with other users with similar problems.

One conclusion we can draw from Fig. 4.1 is that one method of delivering support is rarely enough. The same can be seen from the individual weaknesses of the different forms of support described in Chapter 3. The rest of this chapter describes the support set-ups of a variety of company types. It shows which forms of support are deployed for the particular circumstances of the company and where each of these succeeds and fails. Of particular interest are the various permutations of support forms in order to meet different types of user support needs.

Problem area	Support provided by
Advanced usage (e.g. programming, macro editing)	Peers, product author, user representative (if a programmer), user training
Usage of application	User representative, user training, possibly helpdesk
Application installation and interfacing to system and peripherals	Helpdesk or equivalent (e.g. technical support)
Environment (system interface, e.g. Windows, Shell)	Helpdesk or equivalent
Operating system	Helpdesk or equivalent
Firmware (BIOS)	Manufacturer (via helpdesk)
Hardware	Maintenance company (possibly via helpdesk)
Implementation (e.g. network connection)	Helpdesk or equivalent

Figure 4.1
Who supports what?

4.2 Support scenario 1: computer sales

The company is a computer reseller with its head office and several branches in the UK and branches in two other European countries. As well as having to support its computer clients, it also has several hundred users of its own internal computing systems. Broadly speaking, the company sells a different type of computer system to the one it uses in-house.

Support to external users is slick and professional. Its customer support services are split into two separate organizations. The first is a *'system maintenance'* operation. Mobile engineers ring into an *'administrative helpdesk'* (where customers will have reported their equipment failures) to pick up repair jobs, then visit the client to make the repair. The engineers also have a further *'technical helpdesk'* which they can contact for assistance with the repair. The helpdesk has an extremely high spot rate, so it rarely needs to pass on queries; it keeps this spot rate high by maintaining a good *'technical library'*. The technical helpdesk also recontacts most clients prior to an engineer's visit, first to see if the problem can be repaired without such a visit, and second to decide what additional spare parts may be needed to be despatched to meet the engineer.

The second customer support service function is the *'systems helpdesk'*. This is dedicated to solving problems on software and communications (including networking). This has two tiers: first, general query-and-answer helpdesks, one in each of the operating countries, for pre-sales and simple post-sales support calls; and second, a chargeable premium support helpdesk for customers requiring a fully fledged problem-solving service (e.g. when their own support organizations are overstretched or have a problem outside their specialization). All the helpdesks have a strong emphasis on user relationships, choosing to build up a rapport with the user. The helpdesks take queries from customers who are also technically competent (usually calling from a client's internal helpdesk service), answer those they can immediately and pass on what they cannot answer to a separate, central, *'technical support'* function, which solves the problem and contacts the customer. Technical support also provides software solutions to the system maintenance helpdesk. Also, clients and the company's sales teams can use the technical library, which as well as retaining a professionally managed catalogue of technical volumes also offers online technical documents.

Support to internal users is slender. The central computing department has a *'development'* function which answers the occasional user query but does not operate a formal helpdesk. User training is virtually non-existent – users are expected to learn from their office colleagues and no responsibility for the standard of user ability is taken. A single, overstretched *'technical support'* operative moves from user to user, solving problems reactively.

4.2.1 Success or failure?

The contrast in this scenario between the professionalism of customer support and the sparsity of internal support is not uncommon in the computer industry. Customer support grows out of commercial imperative under the watchful eye of senior management. Internal support can risk a little complacency, for it can always turn to its better-equipped and better-financed colleagues down the corridor. However, the lack of internal user training and poor internal support reduces the effectiveness of the workforce and worsens the learning curve for new recruits. It also occasionally causes customer support to be diverted from its true purpose in order to help out with internal support.

That the customer support side is successful is not in doubt. With such a broad range of services, plus a technical library to catch those support queries which don't fit the other services, their coverage is as broad as could be expected. They have separated loss-making from profit-making customer support work and use one to feed, finance and necessitate the other.

The separation of helpdesk and technical support causes problems in some implementations; however, here it is a distinct advantage. Great store is set by the helpdesks' ability to answer queries on the spot. This pleases the clients, who of course want the fastest possible answer, as well as minimizing the number of staff needed in technical support. In order to make sure technical support does not get out of touch with customers, job rotation takes place between helpdesk and resolver functions. The main weakness of this focus on a high spot rate is the tendency of some helpdesk technicians to mark a query as closed, when in fact the client may have wanted more. To control this tendency, the helpdesk manager needs to keep a careful watch on answer quality.

Where the systems helpdesk fails is in its inherent inability to manage user expectations for its free-of-charge, general support services. In order to attract custom, the company's salesforce naturally tends to overstate the capability of this service, and this increases demand to a level at which the quality of support becomes unsustainable. (This is common in the computer industry – sales staff are often more optimistic than pragmatic about the capability of their offerings.) The lesson here is that if support is free, it will be oversubscribed, whether it is needed or not. The chargeable, premium support is in a much better position to control expectations through service level agreements.

On the maintenance side, the separation of the administrative from the technical helpdesks causes considerable duplication of work. This confuses some customers who see no reason for two contacts on the same topic before the engineer comes, when one would have done. From the company's point of view, there is a trade-off between reducing technical people to logging fault calls from users and having a separate, less-skilled but expensive service just to answer the telephone. Another computer maintenance company has solved this dilemna by issuing its clients with batches of fax header sheets, preprinted with their account details, for reporting faults. No administrative helpdesk is needed, the faults come straight into the technical helpdesk, who can then decide whether to call the client for further information before passing the report on to an administrator to allocate the job to an engineer.

4.3 Support scenario 2: retail chain

This company has medium-sized retail outlets in many British cities and several European ones. It sells a mixture of mid-priced goods, aimed at a considered-purchase market. It trades on its reputation for customer service, and encourages this 'quality of service' culture to run right through the organization. The company makes extensive use of electronic point-of-sale (EPOS) computer systems, which monitor every sale, make stock-reordering decisions, and report turnover and product-line popularity very rapidly back to head office. An increasing number of the outlets depend to such an extent on the EPOS system that without it, parts of the store can cease to function, showing up as an immediate impact on turnover. For this reason, the company has invested heavily in EPOS support, separate from the systems support it needs for users of its internal management systems.

EPOS support is divided into a 'helpdesk' and *technical support*. The helpdesk has to be open before the stores and close after they do, every day except Christmas Day for up to 14 hours. Uploads of sales figures and downloads of pricing information take place every night under the auspices of a general network control function; any failures of these routines are reported automatically to the EPOS helpdesk, so they can begin to solve the problem and attempt to redo the up/download before the store opens. Good communications links allow the helpdesk to take complete remote control of the instore systems. If a hardware fault is diagnosed, the external *system maintenance* provider is alerted by direct links with their fault report system and the store is switched over to a backup system.

During the day, store-based users may contact the EPOS helpdesk with general queries. These tend to be on a limited range of topics as not much use is made of computers in the stores other than the EPOS systems. The helpdesk assumes a low level of user expertise to shift rotas and staff turnover; in the store, no one person is responsible for the EPOS computers, so callers will differ. To deal with this, the helpdesk has recruited most of its staff from stores or warehouses, to ensure the helpdesk speaks its users' language with patience and understanding.

As well as solving problems which cannot be solved at the helpdesk (very few: less than 5 per cent), the job of the technical support function is to act as *workstation management*. They will test all new products destined for store-based systems, whether obtained from internal *development* or from outside the company, before arranging and conducting the rollout of these new additions, both in the UK and Europe. Some helpdesk technicians naturally see the technical support

department as their next career move, to increase their knowledge as well as their salary.

4.3.1 Success or failure?

The EPOS system is vital to the business; but as a computer, it
cannot truthfully be said to be 'used' by any one person, rather
by the store as an entity in itself. EPOS support has thus taken
the decision to concentrate the support effort on the computer
system rather than on the user, a decision that makes perfect
sense in this scenario, where it might go completely against the
grain in another. This separation is understood and welcomed
by the users, who would rather leave the computers completely
to the specialists so that they are free to get on with selling the
stores' merchandise. In this respect, the EPOS helpdesk is clearly
a great commercial and support management success.

However, the limited purpose of the computer systems makes
for an unchanging and uninspiring workload – which along
with shift and weekend working creates an unusually stressful
job. The problems of this helpdesk lie not in the management of
its systems and methods, but in the management and motivation of its people. The situation is exacerbated by the perceived
higher value and more glamorous job of the technical support
staff. Where these pressures cause motivation to slip, productivity falls, which in extreme circumstances could cause stores sales
points not to open on time and turnover to suffer. It never comes
to this: when crises erupt, the professionalism of the staff takes
over and the problem is solved – but the frustration has to come
out somewhere, and it can be in productivity elsewhere and
resentment of support management.

Once this potential was spotted, the support management at this
site acted decisively to improve internal communications and
job variety. In addition, they increased emphasis on and
recognition of the success and productivity of individual
members of the support staff in areas other than the helpdesk.
The result was a turnround in morale and productivity.

4.4 Support scenario 3: manufacturer

The company designs and builds transport systems and vehicles
for a limited, specialist, international market. The product is
commissioned rather than purchased, and is produced on a
project rather than a production line basis. The company is
therefore highly skilled at the management and support of

large-scale, high-value, long-term projects. It is safe to say that this skill has become rooted in the corporate culture and crops up in the computing function. In one form or another, the company has been in existence for several decades. This has lent a traditionalist, conservative approach to many of its methods, as continued success in a changing world is seen as giving some value to this conservatism. On top of this, it is a career company – whole working lives are conducted within it. Couple all this with a vibrant political environment, and the result is a ship that takes careful and considered steering.

At the heart of corporate computing is a very active *'development'* function. Here the culture of project management comes into its own. In addition to overall administrative software which rarely changes except for the usual revisions, whole systems have to be written for each new manufacturing project. These have to be supported during the course of the project and possibly discarded afterwards. Both *'user training'* and *'technical support'* are provided by the development department, usually by the individual programmer responsible for the application.

The entire support function is fronted by a central *'helpdesk'*. This publicizes a telephone number and all users are encouraged to place all queries through it. The central helpdesk has only a modicum of technical knowledge and expects to pass on all queries up to one of many programmers and project teams, depending on the product displaying the problem. In practice, a user experiencing several problems with a given system will discover the name of the appropriate programmer and contact him or her direct. The usual reason given for circumventing the helpdesk is that it is unable to answer the query anyway, so there is little benefit to the user in calling the helpdesk.

The assumption is that most queries will be about mainframe-based systems. However, PCs have been spreading rapidly through the company. A decision was taken to hand over both the PC helpdesk and PC workstation management to a local PC supplier. The prescribed route now for a PC support query is to the central helpdesk first, who then invariably pass it to the outsourced PC helpdesk, who in turn may contact their own company's helpdesk.

The job of the central helpdesk is then to ensure that the user gets a fix in a reasonable amount of time, which means contacting the PC helpdesk and the programmers on a regular basis for status reports on the problems which have been passed on to them.

57

4.4.1 Success or failure?

The helpdesk was created to protect the developers from excessive interruptions by the users. However, the helpdesk has limited knowledge and passes the majority of its queries on to the developers. The number of interruptions has thus decreased much less than could have been the case. In addition, for some users, the helpdesk is nothing more than a hurdle to be cleared before finally speaking to the support service; in other words it is seen as an increase in bureaucracy rather than as an increase in support. As such, the helpdesk is not making the best possible use of its people investment.

The helpdesk staff do not actually come from a computing background, but are ex-data entry clerks. The development department is opposed to any increase in their knowledge, fearing that a little knowledge is a dangerous thing; the helpdesk may actually do more harm than good by overestimating the usefulness of its limited knowledge. A more cynical observer may conclude that some developers are clinging to power for its own sake than for the sake of improved service.

In its present support structure, this company is deliberately underusing its helpdesk staff. It has been unable to subsume the demands of the new technology of PCs and has created an unnecessary chain of escalations in a half-hearted attempt to cope. In effect, no one group is responsible for user support, and the resulting hotchpotch delivers an outdated and substandard level of user support. Exacerbating this is the fact that the helpdesk, although held responsible for the speed of support service the users receive, can in practice do little to influence the speed at which the resolver departments work. The overriding principle appears to be the protection of the status quo rather than delivering increased productivity to the user population.

The fact that the helpdesk does not service user needs as required is clearly demonstrated by the users' attempts to avoid using it. The result of this, as well as undermining the main purpose of the helpdesk, is that the company misses an opportunity to use the helpdesk to measure the support overhead more precisely. Questions like how well the users are trained, how well the software performs, how respected is the system usability, what size the helpdesk needs to be, and many more could be answered from the call-log of a properly used helpdesk, and used to make decisions about the effectiveness or otherwise of the IT investment. In conclusion, this is a helpdesk that purports to be a user support function, but in fact is not.

Support functions

5.1 Lines of support

The provision of user support is often divided into 'lines' or 'levels'. The 'first line' is the helpdesk, taking the incoming calls, solving what can be solved quickly. It escalates more involved enquiries, or those needing a higher level of technical competence to the 'second line'. The particularly tricky or technically specialized issues go to the 'third line'.

My problem with that model is where does it stop? Easy problems to first line – difficult ones to second – really difficult to third – and, one supposes, the really, really difficult to fourth and the really, really, really difficult to fifth? This is not a service delivery model – it is a simple pandering to technocracy. It keeps the helpdesk technically ignorant and puts the power in the hands of the technically certified. It is an anachronism and presupposes technical competence to be more important than service delivery.

A more strategic approach would be to ask 'what has to happen, why and where?' In essence, the job of user support, at any so-called 'level', is to restore the user to productivity. In my view the definition of the lines of support should rest not on who has the skills, but where those skills should be. The requisite skills for user support should ideally be in the user support department.

I propose an alternative model, based around the deciding factor of whether a change to the system is needed to resolve the user's problem. In that model, the first line continues to take the call and resolves by telephone if it can (this may include a 'triage' desk – see 3.14). Where longer diagnosis or a deskside visit is required, the enquiry is escalated to the second line. But the mission of both the first and second line is to resolve all enquiries *where the system options already exist*. This would imply that a 'third line' is superfluous – either the problem can be fixed within the existing system structure or it cannot. And if it cannot, the only other possible course of action is to change the system.

In this model then, the third line should only be invoked when a change to the system is needed, and of course at that point, the change management procedures come into play. The model also means that responsibilities are clearer. In the traditional method, it is all too easy for one line to escalate to the next line just because they find the problem too difficult. But that's how delays creep in and backlogs increase, because the technocratic structure allows people to avoid taking responsibility for and ownership of the user's problem.

5.2 Ten key steps for successful support

Success in user support can be achieved step by step. One could say there are ten of these steps, each an area of support management focus in itself, as shown in Fig. 5.1. These steps are listed roughly chronologically; they are in the order you would consider them if you were starting a user support service from scratch. This is a different order to the way they are covered in the book. The reason for the discrepancy is that these steps are only intended as a simplified guide to a complex process. In practice you would not really do things in such a staccato fashion – several of the steps would be going on in parallel. The

Figure 5.1
Ten key steps for
successful support

Ten key steps to successful support

1. Know your resources
2. Know your customers
3. Launch your services
4. Manage the support workflow
5. Ensure good problem closure techniques
6. Instant workload status reporting
7. Be proactive – take control
8. Regular contact with customers
9. Conduct surveys
10. Redo all the above every 4 to 6 months

---

order they are covered in the book makes more sense for the purposes of study and reference.

1   Examine your resources to find out what you're capable of delivering and what you're not, and implement ways of improving your skills, equipment and contacts.
    Resources management – see Part Five; staff management – see Part Six.

2   Identify your customers, both users and non-users of your services, and list them in order of priority. Be pragmatic – their priority may come from their importance to the company and its business, or it may come from the political power they wield.
    Client management – see Part Two; workload management – see Part Four.

3   By way of a service statement, launch a set of services that meets the majority of customers' needs. Encourage any customer who finds the services inappropriate to consider the service statement as merely a basis for negotiating a special service level agreement with them.
    Client management – see Part Two; service management – see Part Three.

4   Establish effective workflow management in the support department. This should cover call management, query prioritization, job allocation, problem escalation and staff motivation. Note that this is done after launching the services, for two main reasons: (i) it is a higher priority to service the customers and (ii) you will not be exactly sure how to manage the workload until you know what it looks like.
    Workload management – see Part Four; staff management – see Part Six.

5   It is not enough to solve the user's technical problem. Establish query closure methods, to encompass ensuring customer satisfaction as well as analysing recently completed jobs to see what lessons can be extracted from how they were handled.
    Client management – see Part Two; resources management – see Part Five.

6   Set up your reporting routines to provide instant snapshots of the current workload status as well as routine historical information. This will enable you to make decisions about how to deploy your resources.
    Resources management – see Part Five; workload management – see Part Four.

7 Look for and implement ways of dealing with the workload proactively instead of just reactively. Don't let the workload control your department – you should control the work.
Workload management – see Part Four.

8 Communicate with your customers, through newsletters, workshops, knowledge provision, and, most importantly, personal contact – get out there and mix.
Client management – see Part Two.

9 Establish ways of surveying your customers for their views on how the service is being delivered. Use this information to make improvements to your support service and always report your findings and your subsequent actions to your customers.
Client management – see Part Two; service management – see Part Three.

10 Don't rest on your laurels no matter how good you are. Go back to step 1 every four to six months and review your whole set-up.
Resources management – see Part Five; service management – see Part Three.

Part Two

Client management

What is a 'customer'?

The most obvious answer to the question of who might be the customers of a user support department is 'the users'. And as usual, this is only a fraction of the picture. Rather than look at detail, for a moment let us look at what makes a customer a customer.

6.1 A matter of terminology?

The *Oxford English Dictionary* calls a customer 'one who buys, especially from one seller' – a useful definition for a support department, if we interpret 'buys' loosely. *Webster's Dictionary* goes further, giving as its main definition 'a person wishing to purchase from a store or a firm'. It is that element of 'wishing' that brings some uncertainty, and helps us towards a better definition of who support should concern themselves with. It is not just those who use our services – I prefer to call them 'clients' – but those who have not yet decided whether to use our services.

In support, when we are not calling them 'users', we often use the word 'customers' to define those whom we exist to serve. Indeed the use of the word in this context seems to have industry-wide acceptance – for example, the UK's Helpdesk User Group's monthly magazine is called *Customers*. But what is a customer, and what is the difference between a customer and a client? In support, we interchange the words 'user' and 'customer' almost freely; I have done it myself throughout this book. There is no doubt that we must number users among our customers, but there are many more we must also not forget.

'Customer' is a general term, used to encompass any individual or institution that can influence or is influenced by the support services. They may be users of our services – in which case they become clients every time they do so. But even when they are not in the act of using us, i.e. not clients at the moment, they must still be treated with the respect deserved by customers.

I have my own favourite definition of a customer and it is this:

> **Your customer is anybody . . .**
> **who consumes anything he perceives**
> **you to have produced . . .**
> **whether or not his perception is correct . . .**
> **whether or not you intended to produce it . . .**
> **whether or not you knew you had produced it.**

The reason I use this definition is to remind me of the truth of customer satisfaction. I can improve my services continuously, keep increasing my service levels, keep solving the problems, and so on. But those are only the things that I know I have produced. If my customers measure me on that alone, then that's terrific. But they don't. They may measure me on anything at all that in their imagination or opinion is an output from the helpdesk. So what if my response times far exceed the industry average? If the customer couldn't care less about response times I've achieved nothing. Conversely, even if my response times are comparatively superb, if my customers don't think they are good enough, then they are not good enough. Keep this definition in mind when you read about expectations in the next chapter.

6.2 Do not forget non-customers

Why should we also be considering those who are not so obviously our customers? That question is relevant to any industry, not just user support. It is precisely because they do not use our services that we should be concerned, especially if we cannot be sure why they do not use us. It may be that our services do not appear to them to match their needs – in which case, is there an opportunity for us to provide them with a service they need, or is it simply that they do not understand our services so all that is needed is clearer explanation? On the other hand, there is a risk that the reason they do not use us is more negative than that – that they do not trust us, or have heard too many horror stories about our service level. If that is the case, we need to know about it. They may be harmless and ignorant of us, or they may be negative and badly informed. The latter type is a problem, especially if they are encouraging their opinions to spread – but both types are an opportunity.

We treat our clients with respect because they can influence our budgets, income, staffing level, resources, and so on, by the very fact of using us. Even if we do not charge for our services, as most support departments do not, if we fail to attract custom we lose our point; and when that happens, those who finance us are likely to become less disposed towards doing so.

6.3 Clients and customers

So those who use our support services are our 'clients'; those who do not (yet) are our 'customers'. Both need the attention of support management – non-clients in particular, either to ensure that they get the best possible IT support in their and the company's interests, or to ensure that they are not spreading an unjustly negative picture of the quality of support. The client/customer window in Fig. 6.1 illustrates how passive and active clients and customers can influence support.

The passive client uses support on a regular basis, and apparently presents few challenges. She is broadly satisfied with the service, at least to the extent of not having to think about it too much. If

	Client	
Passive	Use of support service part of office routine. May be conservative, unwilling to accept radical change. Otherwise, predictable	Highly demanding, knows what he wants. Use of helpdesk may be challenging but sporadic. Expectations may be unrealistic	Active
	Is ignorant of, or does not understand, support service offerings	Aware of own needs for IT support – may have considered using your service, but also may be sourcing elsewhere. Could be a useful ally if converted	
	Customer	

Figure 6.1
Client/customer window

pressed, her view of support will at least not be negative and probably positive (especially if she is surprised or flattered to be asked for her opinion). It is gratifying to have this kind of client, they seem to justify IT support on their own. However, there is a latent threat here: this passivity may run a little too deep. This user may be doing what she is doing with the computer largely because that is what she has always done. She may not take kindly to any change in service, for she sees all change as radical, and will be unwilling to examine potential benefits. She may well be underusing the technology, which denies the company a potential benefit, and boring the living daylights out of the technical staff, which can be a headache for the support manager.

The active client will probably contact support rather less often than his passive colleague. However, his service demands, when they come, may be more challenging – even to the extent of being outside what the support service is actually there to offer. Often, these are the clients who take up most of the support manager's time, because they play an active role in the progress of their query through the support mill. The key to handling this client is to play close attention to his expectations of the service and to the priority of his query compared with support's other outstanding work.

The passive customer is a floating voter, who has ignored you by default rather than choice. She may be 'in the market' for your services, but does not realize it yet. Begin your approach by first defining the root of this ignorance – is it you she does not know about, or is it her own needs which she does not understand? Or both?

The active customer will probably already have made a decision about IT support services; for or against, provided out of his own resources or outsourced, company services or third party. For him, using IT support is a considered purchase, and do not forget that he may consider he does not need it at all. It is not just what he feels about your services that you have to root out, but why he feels the way he does. There is a risk of extremism from this end of the market – see Case Study 6.1.

Case Study 6.1: militant non-clients

Anybody who ever considers or observes the support service, for whatever reason, has a potential influence on its success, whether they eventually become clients or not. There is evidence for this all over business – witness the currently popular practice of militant consumers boycotting goods and companies to bring about changes in business practices at those companies. These consumers, unlikely ever to become clients, are nevertheless directly affecting the success of those companies. Whether it is refusing to eat tuna because you've heard tuna fishing methods hurt dolphins, or refusing to use the support department because you've heard the technicians are rude and dismissive, the effect can still close the shop.

Take a look around your own potential userbase: are there any departments who refuse to use your support services? Why is this? Irrelevance or something more sinister? What is your support manager's attitude to it? If the support manager is merely grateful for the relief of not having to support those departments, is there not a risk that he or she will allow existing clients to go the same way? After all, there is every possibility that these maverick users may talk to other groups and turn them into mavericks too. If too many users go their own way to get IT support, that introduces risks of service duplication and non-standardization that brings problems when they depart your services. It is probably in the company's interest that support pay particular interest to straying user departments – they might be mavericks.

6.4 Basic types of customer

Users are only the most obvious of our customers. They are the first layer. They use our 'core services', namely those services that exist to fulfil our primary mission – for most of us, keeping the users' machines going and keeping their ability to use the machines relatively high. So core services usually include things like running a helpdesk, solving technical problems, user training, and so on.

There are three more layers of customers to worry about (see Fig. 6.2). The second layer contains clients of our non-core services. Non-core services are those that exist because of the existence of the core – like reporting to managers, maintaining the company technical library, or IT companies where the support is looking after the company's customers, this may mean keeping the salesforce supplied with ammunition. Remember non-core services have a clientele also.

Customer type	Consumes
Core service client	User support services
on core service client	Ancillary conse uent services
ecision maker	Commercial imperatives, culture
Influencer	Image

Figure 6.2
Basic customer types

The third layer of customers consists of those who use neither type of service, but can still affect our existence. These are the comptroller who yeas or nays our budget, the vice president with the power to reorganize support out of existence, the external supplier who feeds us with technical information. We shall call these the 'decision-makers'. The fourth layer of customers consists of almost invisible people. These are the clients and non-clients who trade opinions and impressions about our service, and create between them the almost intangible culture of acceptance or stigma which surrounds us. This is the most dangerous layer: it is so difficult to identify, yet we must do all we can to influence how and what it thinks and more importantly, what it says and to whom it says it. We shall call the members of this layer the 'influencers', and the effect they have on us, although indirect, can often be even more important than an outstanding query list. We will go into this in more detail later – for now, the maxim is:

> **Remember that the decision-makers feed on the influencers – how else will they know which way to decide?**

6.5 Customers – the main priority?

6.5.1 A caveat for the newly commercial support manager

It is currently fashionable for some companies to state how they put customers first. One member of the IT industry announces publicly how its priorities are customers, staff and profits, in that order. The implication is that the customer can expect great respect and be treated accordingly, and I am sure this is the case in many companies who state such policies.

By and large, however, statements such as this should be treated with considerable scepticism. It is very difficult to check their authenticity. First, the statements are usually made by a public relations function such as the salesforce or advertising department, whose primary function, to which *all* other considerations defer, is to impress potential customers and attract sales. Second, they may be associated with a specific campaign or with the current state of the company, in which case they are transitory. Third, they cannot be checked against the actual corporate objectives, which are the prerogative of the board of directors and usually discussed in closed session; most board objectives are financial, not customer-oriented. Fourth, they are clearly self-contradictory: if a company makes service a higher priority than commercial success, it will not be a company for long. Fifth, there is no way of knowing how committed the incumbent staff are to the policy, seeing as the vast majority of them have no public face. Sixth, it is often difficult for customers of a company to compare their experiences of the truth with other customers, so one can really never know whether the policy is true or not.

However, the support manager is in a particularly difficult position working inside a company which fosters such a public face, especially when the truth is closer to one of the six reasons above. With all the service bias support managers often have, it is easy to believe the 'customer service' marketing and assume that one is following the stated company goals; but unless one's immediate superior measures support success in those terms, the result can be confusion.

In fact it is *extremely rare* that customers and service are the company's prime orientations. Customers are almost never the most important factor in any business. Customers are merely one of several raw materials to be processed to make the company's final product. Nor is the final product the object or service the company sells. That too is only part of the process. For many companies, not even profit is the final product, nor turnover. For most companies, the final product is either its own continued existence or the dividends payable to the shareholders. Every other single corporate function contributes to one of those two ends. To state that customers are the corporation's prime focus is at best hyperbole, invariably confusing for the workforce, and at worst internally confusing and eventually divisive.

I further encourage your cynicism by affirming that in some companies, the ultimate business goal may in reality have nothing whatsoever to do with the business – it may be something as crass as the furtherment of the careers of the board members or a steady growth of the chief executive's personal fortune. I point this out for a purpose: to succeed in that company, the support manager needs to know what the real goals are, and strive towards them regardless. Whether he or she finds those goals acceptable, or even ethical is an entirely separate issue, because walking away means that success in that company has not been chosen.

Let me make it clear. Customers are invariably *not* your company's main priority, no matter what their marketing says. You disagree with this contention at your peril. Why? Because even if you as support manager are measured on the level of customer service, the company directors are not – and it is what the board is measured on that dictates the company culture, because the board will make decisions on that basis – and support will be influenced if not directly impacted by those decisions.

You may believe that by adopting a 'customer service' stance in a company which proclaims customer service as its end is a sure-fire recipe for success. This is naïve, and if you are very lucky, somebody may give you a little nudge in the right direction. But if you find you are left to discover by yourself, the safest policy is to assume that customer service is just another product your company sells for a profit. Keep one eye on the money: it is the main reason your company exists, and your department is only there to contribute to that, no matter how obscure that contribution may be.

Case Study 6.2: 'Our Customer – Our Priority'

Dave B. was a support manager for a manufacturer of communications switching equipment. They had a wide market, and because of the specialization, as well as looking after internal users, Dave and his team had to take the occasional call from external clients.

As a true professional, and as a middle manager wanting to rise through the company, Dave took his job seriously. He adopted the prevailing company culture and took it upon himself to believe in the company slogan: 'Our Customer – Our Priority'.

One Friday afternoon, in the weekly report session with his manager, Dave was having a hard time explaining why his team's performance was lower than usual. His boss was

---

worried: service levels were important – they were seen as a measure of the quality his department delivered, but more importantly, the sales department used them as a differentiator, to show how much better they were than the competition. Dave described how his department had been busy looking after a particularly troublesome customer, and did not want that customer to see him as not committed to service quality. Dave was shocked to hear the boss say, 'Oh that account? Forget it – they're not a target this year.'

For days after, Dave pondered that. Clearly priorities were operating here; but what the advertising told him and what his boss had said seemed to conflict. Customers were clearly less important than targeted business. Armed with that conclusion, he rejigged his department to offer new and improved services to the new business team and their customers. The following Friday, he had a question for his boss: why had he not been told of the real policy before?

What do they want?

7.1 All customers need managing . . .

In Chapter 6, we identified four basic customer types. As each of these is a customer, each can affect our success, even our very existence, by our relationship with them. The fact that they have this influence upon us, be it potential or realized, means that there is a relationship. We can choose to ignore that relationship – and take the risks which go with that ignorance – or we can choose to manage it.

Because they are customers, they are consuming something we produce. They may not be consuming what we want them to, or they may have a distorted impression of our output, but it is still our output. Customers will always form an impression of the product they receive. If we do nothing to influence that impression, it will be formed by default – and it may or may not be accurate, indeed it may or may not be rational. This is why we must always strive to manage our relationships with our customers, so that the impression they have is a favourable one. And this is equally important at all the four layers of custom described in Chapter 6. It is particularly important at the intangible fourth layer, for they have no real service to consume, they trade in opinion and anecdote.

7.2 . . . Not just the computer users

Clearly the 'computer users' will continue to be the prime example of our customer and client base. But now we know of the additional dimension, we must identify what these other customers and clients actually consume. Our customers and clients may be our customers and clients for several reasons, and not just because they use the computers (and *ipso facto* our technical knowledge).

The very existence of support inside any company means there must be a variety of services. Yes, variety. Even if your support offering is a 'simple' hotline, it still puts out a variety of services. It does not just take calls, or just solve problems, it does many other things. They may be subtle, and they may not be publicized, but they are still there. The support department does not exist in a vacuum, it is part of the corporate entity as a whole, and that fact alone generates several customers with service needs.

To get these other customers, and their needs from the support department in perspective, brainstorm everybody who is even remotely impacted by the existence of 'support'. Do not be afraid to cast your net wide. Make a list of who you come up with. Next to their entry in the list, note the 'services' they get from you, along with anything else they get as a result of support's existence. *Tip*: Get all the support staff involved in this exercise. They may be able to identify some customers you may have overlooked. But an exercise such as this also gives them chance to take ownership of their client base, i.e. to see it as theirs, and not just the manager's, or the IT department's.

An example of such a list is given in Fig. 7.1. It describes what the customers get from the support department in a typical company, where a hotline takes users' queries, answers those it can immediately, and passes the trickier ones to other technicians in the same department for resolution. Sometimes the technicians have to travel to remote sites; on other occasions, the fix can be implemented by the users' local IT representative.

Remember the list in Fig. 7.1 is just a sketch. It will look different for your company, and in any case will probably be much longer. You probably also just did the exercise off the top of your head. You could do a lot more with accurate information, so that is why to do this exercise for real, you would probably interview several users, the chief of IT, the accounts supervisor, and so on. Not only have you identified who your customers are, but by the same exercise, you have noted what they want from you.

Let us take a closer look at that list and see what we can learn from it. The first thing it shows is that lots of other people need you and your professionalism so that they can get on with their jobs. You

Customer impacted by user support	What they get
Users	■ Availability of helpdesk ■ Prompt service ■ Estimated fix time ■ Guaranteed response time ■ Correct answers ■ Monthly newsletter ■ PC installations ■ 'Get you started' sessions
User IT representative	■ Good information flow
Support staff	■ Pride in working for a successful team ■ Pride in perceived quality of their work ■ Good leadership ■ Feeling 'involved'
Support manager	■ High profile to help career ■ No surprises ■ Pride in a motivated and diligent
IT general manager	■ Regular and accurate reports ■ Notification of emergencies ■ Contribution to IT department image ■ High profile to help career
IT development department	■ Accurate and timely bug report ■ Protection from users' questions
IT operations department	■ Protection from users' questions ■ Well-written system job control routines
Corporate facilities department	■ Advance notification of power points needed
Training department	■ Timely notification of user knowledge gaps
Accounts department	■ Everything within budget ■ Accurate expenditure reports
Cash office	■ Expenses claims in on time
Personnel department	■ Job appraisals handed in on time
External service providers (e.g. maintenance company)	■ Good problem diagnosis ■ Accurate user location information
External helpdesks	
Sales office	■ Notification of support use by clients ■ Outstanding customer problems ■ Monthly newsletter ■ Support makes sales department look good ■ 'Commercial awareness'

Figure 7.1
Sketch of who gets what from the support department

will have to keep that fact in mind when designing services, as we will do in Part Three, and sorting out your resources, as we will do in Part Five.

7.3 A varied market

The variety of both customers and services is startling. Some of the customers are a logical progression of supporting users, such as one's own manager needing reports for business purposes, or corporate facilities needing to know where support is going to need electrical sockets for the computers and printers they are installing.

In this perspective, even the support staff become their own customers – and rightly too. They need to get some satisfaction from the department they work in, otherwise they may come to regret working in it and eventually want to leave. So support has to deliver personal satisfaction on several planes. This is one example of the intangibility of some of the end products support must deliver – another is the high profile some people will look for to carry them into the next stage of their careers.

The more tangible products, like good problem diagnosis, reports, newsletters, and so on will be relatively easy to deliver. They are often thrown up as part of what the support department does anyway. They also can be produced largely from the skills one would expect to find by default in a user support organization. But some of these intangibles, like 'commercial awareness', may be impossible to satisfy.

7.4 Focus on the expectation

Where the intangibility of the service means that it is too difficult to manage, then worry less about the service itself than about the *expectation* of the service. For instance, in Fig. 7.1, development want support to deliver some protection from the users. How to deliver that protection? Protection is hardly the sort of service that can be written into a service agreement, yet development will consider the support department to have failed them if that protection is not forthcoming. The key is to look at protection from development's point of view. On the face of it, it may look as though there's a big sign on the development office door: 'No Users!' Look at it more closely, it may be that development does not mind talking to users, but only at development's choice and only about new developments. If pushed, development staff will talk to a user to solve a problem, but only after the helpdesk has tried to fix it. Aha! Even when the service seems intangible, there is always an expectation down there somewhere waiting to be rooted out.

Another example of this is the manager's expectation of 'no surprises'. What it actually means is that the support manager does not want to hear of a user problem via anything other than the official channels. What she is trying to avoid has nothing to do with the severity of the problem; it is the embarrassment of hearing about it direct from the user or from the user's manager – because that means the support service has failed to respond adequately, so support, and by association the support manager, are not doing the job right.

7.5 How are we being measured?

Where phrases like 'respond adequately' spring up, alarm bells should ring. If the service is deemed inadequate, then there must therefore be a point at which the service would have been adequate. There is a measure in force here, and the support manager needs to find out what that measure is. 'Adequate' means different things to different people, depending on the service, and depending on the expectation. If users believe the support team to be understaffed and underfunded, they may well set their expectations lower. The service delivery which is considered 'adequate' by somebody who holds this belief may well be held to be 'deeply unsatisfactory' to a user who thinks that the support department is a bunch of wild-spending incompetents.

7.6 Key concepts

'Expectation' and 'measurement' are key concepts in any user support environment. They are inextricably intertwined. You and your support service are measured against somebody's expectation to see if that expectation is met. Yet the expectation is that both parties use the same measure. The problems only really occur either when the measure is left to float, so that it is interpreted differently by service provider and service client, or when clients are left to set their own expectations.

An expectation must have three attributes. It must be rational – within the client's real needs and within the company's objectives. It must be reviewable – subject to negotiation and flexible in the face of a change of circumstances or environment. And it must be realistic – meaning that it must be possible to meet that expectation within available or obtainable support resources.

> **Expectations must be Rational, Reviewable, Realistic.**

- *Rational.* Who knows the client's *real* needs? In the end, it probably is not the client, who, being human, will sometimes get a need confused with a desire. Nor is it likely to be support alone, who after all are worried about being able to register success with this client in the face of other pressing demands on limited resources and budget. However, with the right information about how the user uses the technology, support is likely to be able to estimate the needs with some degree of accuracy. For example, users do the bulk of their data entry on a Thursday, but Friday is pretty quiet – mind you Monday is difficult because that is when all the queries come in regarding last Thursday's data entry. The support manager gleans from this that it is best to take the data backups on Thursday night and test them on Friday, because they sure better be there if anything goes wrong next Monday. The 'sure better be there' bit is the expectation. Of course the ideal way of ensuring rationality is by each of the parties, users and support, coming to understand the needs and limitations faced by the other.
- *Reviewable.* In business, change is the only real constant. Your customer's circumstances will change, and they may just be too busy dealing with that change to get round to telling you how it affects their service relationship with you. But one thing is sure: that when their needs change, support has to change to meet it – and a change in support can only come from within support itself. So you have to watch their market almost as closely as they do, because only you, the support manager, know what you have to do to your department/function/service to meet their inevitably changing needs.
- *Realistic.* Only support knows what resources are available or obtainable internally or externally. Users will need to be briefed on this or else their expectations may wander unrealistically high.

In all three cases, the attributes of expectation involve both the support department and the users in setting the expectations. But it is clear that most of the running should be done by support. If there is a key to success in support, the management of customer expectations is it. Conditioned to being a reactive force, the support department need never move from its office, except to jump when a user calls. Meanwhile, users may be gaily setting personal expectations of the service which may not be rational, are based on past circumstances and thus overdue for review, and are in virtual ignorance of what is possible.

7.7 Great or lesser expectations?

Try a simple experiment next time you go into a store or shop you have never visited before. Before you get to the store, based on what you have heard of it, form an impression in your mind of what it will look like, how the merchandise will be laid out, how available the staff will be, how easy it will be to park the car nearby, and so on. Get to the door of the store and check back on those expectations. Have they been met? And what has instantly happened to your impression of that store and your inclination to buy something there? We all make these prejudgements, subconsciously, all the time. It is a very human trait to try to compare the misunderstood with existing experience, in order to make it easier to cope with the constant bombardment of new experiences. So we filter things out by saying to ourselves that this experience is not new, I have seen it before and it looks like such-and-such.

For users faced with the support department, this means that by the time they come to use your service, they have already come to expect something from it. It is a purely natural thing to do. And in the absence of anything else to guide that process, they will set those expecations entirely from within their own (possibly irrelevant and almost certainly non-specialist) experience. Which does not portend well for how realistic that expectation will be, let alone how rational.

Without playing an active part in users setting their expectations, and that invariably means proactively seeking them out, the best the supporter can hope for is that the users will set their sights low. But that will eventually have a negative effect in the support department, because an expectation that is too easy to meet will not inspire the staff to do it with quality.

7.8 Your measure or theirs?

Every time you provide any client with anything, ask yourself the following three questions:

1 Who is measuring my service and how I provide it?
2 Against what criteria are they measuring me?
3 Do they measure me the same way I measure me?

Some users refuse to have their expectations adjusted or manipulated, possibly because of the control it places over service delivery. They would rather be in a position to bend the rules when it suits them. The solution to this comes from the very irrationality of such a refusal. User support customers will set their expectations in the absence of having anything else by which to measure you. Business is (in theory) a rational process – but expectations set by any means other than measurement or negotiation will be intrinsically emotional. There is a basic tension here between the rational and the emotional which the support service provider can use to bring the wayward user into a more manageable service relationship. A service relationship based on purely emotional expectations would be a very insecure one. People do not feel safe measuring a business issue by an emotional yardstick (unless they are politicians, but that is another issue). They need a better yardstick and will look to the support department, overtly or covertly, to provide it. And conveniently, it is the support department's job, as well as being in its best interests, to provide that yardstick.

Case Study 7.1: the practice of expectation-setting

If support does not dictate what it wants to be measured by, then the users will measure support against their own, irrational, possibly irrelevant conclusions. That is why you probably did not read the inside of this book first. You wanted to know what to expect, so you paid heed to the marketing first. The marketing which preceded the book, the blurb on the cover, all this serves not just to encourage you to buy the book ('use the service') but also to help you set your expectations of the content of the book and the experience of using it; and to set those expectations in my terms as well as yours. The publisher and I did a lot of research about you to find out what you would need. We spoke to dozens of people in your position and came up with a list of expectations we anticipated you would have. Then we described them in our terms in the marketing – our goal was not only to meet your needs but to ensure as far as possible that you would be satisfied with what we eventually provided you with. You will be measuring how much use this book is to you – that is why the publisher's marketing department has tried to give you a way to measure it.

Your marketing communications with your users should have the same dual purpose: to encourage them to use the service as well as to help them set the expectations against which they measure the usefulness and success of the service for them.

7.9 Implementing the definition of a customer

You will recall my definition in the previous chapter – 'Your customer is anybody who consumes anything he perceives you to have produced, whether or not his perception is correct, whether or not you intended to produce it and whether or not you knew you had produced it.'

This definition highlights the importance of managing the customer's expectation. Try this exercise – list all your customers and what they require from the helpdesk. Users want quick solutions, yes. But then you have to get down to the more obscure ones. Financiers want value for money. Managers want accurate reports. Board directors want a quiet life with no surprises. Your staff want job satisfaction. The second line wants well-documented escalations.

So to satisfy your customers, all you have to do is identify them all and what they require. That's hard enough – did you manage to identify everybody, yes everybody who would match the above definition of a customer? Of course you didn't. It's impossible.

And even if you could identify all your customers, what about what they require? Users want quick solutions? Oh really? So how quick is 'quick'? And is the definition of 'quick' open to change? What is quick enough for this enquiry may not be quick enough for the next. What is quick enough on a lazy summer afternoon may be exasperatingly slow on a filthy day in winter after the user had a domestic row before leaving the house this morning and then the car broke down and he was pulled for running a red light and he got a coffee stain on the tie his mother-in-law gave him when they went to Florida for Christmas that time so it's sentimental and, and, and. . .

This is how it is. No matter what the service level agreement or performance targets say. . .

You are not measured on your service level –
You are measured against customer expectations.

And yet it is impossible to uncover who the customer is, let alone what he expects today. Your only option for achieving customer satisfaction is to tell him what to expect and to keep reminding him of it, so that he becomes conditioned to measuring you on what you want him to measure you on. If you do not do this, there is no telling what you will be measured against, and you may be completely powerless to improve customer satisfaction, because left to its own devices, customer satisfaction is irrational.

This means that you *must* be able to offer a precise expectation as to when the second line will call the customer back. You must tell him in advance what services you provide and what you do not. And you must keep him up to date with those expectations, because his priorities are his own and it is not his responsibility to memorize your service level statement.

7.10 Performance versus expectation

Figure 7.2 compares high and low performance with high and low customer expectation, giving us four comparative outcomes.

Performance high, expectation high – here's the ideal. Everybody's happy and the situation is stable. The users expect a given service level and get it. There's a rapport between the service provider and consumer – the provider keeps reminding the consumer of the expectation and then delivers against that promise.

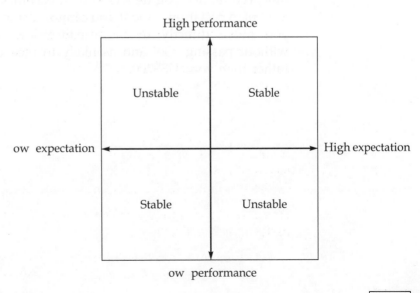

Figure 7.2
Comparing performance with expectation

Performance low, expectation low – this is stable too. I was engaged by a helpdesk in the UK's National Health Service (NHS). The NHS is notoriously underfunded as a proportion of gross domestic product when compared with other western industrialized nations. That has come to be an accepted maxim in much of the NHS. The newly appointed IT services manager had called me in to make recommendations about how to improve the helpdesk after his predecessor had underinvested in it. Technically speaking, the helpdesk was one of the least cost effective I had seen. It had all the problems: low productivity, service levels and morale. I interviewed several of its users for their opinions of the helpdesk. I was stunned to find that the users pitied rather than complained about the helpdesk – as one interviewee put it to me, 'I suppose the helpdesk could be better – but they're just like us, they're understaffed and underfunded, so you have to accept it really.' In other words, here was a helpdesk whose service was so poor it could not support the demands of the business, but as far as the users were concerned, *it did not matter.*

Performance low, expectation high – the one every helpdesk manager dreads. You just know your boss is talking to the outsourcing companies. But hey, things can't get any worse, can they? Oh yes they can . . .

Performance high, expectation low – wouldn't this be great? Doesn't matter what the users expect, you can deliver better. They are delighted, surprised at how much you have exceeded their expectations. You get away with this once maybe. The next time, the service you delivered then becomes the norm of their level of expectation – and if you cannot sustain that service level, you move directly to performance low, expectation high, without passing 'Go' and as likely to pick up your pink slip rather than your US$200.

8

Prioritizing clients

In any environment where there is more work to do than there are resources to satisfy that demand, prioritization becomes an essential way of making sure the most important things get done. Then if there is any time left, we can do some of the less important things. Nowhere is this truer than in a user support office. With services that so many people need, with a hotline that users call when just opening the manual would do, with support unable to control demand by charging for its services – while all these things continue to be true, support will always have to prioritize. Support has to prioritize (i) because there are not enough hours in the day or people on the payroll or money in the bank or enough potential reward to do everything, and (ii) because some people and some jobs are simply more important than others.

In Part Four we will discuss the concept of prioritization as it applies to the pile of jobs in the department's intray, but in this chapter we will look at prioritizing our clients. It is essential to acknowledge that some people are more important than others. Even if we look at it pragmatically; Susan in marketing is one of the nicest people in the building, you get pleasure just from answering her questions about her spreadsheet software; but when the divisional director of sales is on the other line, sorry Susan, but I'm going to have to consider the director first. When you have two urgent and important problems in the queue at the same time, it comes down to a matter of which is the most important department: payroll or purchase ledger? staff or sales office? despatch or design? recruitment or research?

8.1 The purpose of client prioritization

When we assign a priority to a job, we are considering that job's immediate urgency – specifically, does the job have a deadline associated with it? Will the company suffer damage if we do not solve this problem within a given timeframe, and if so, let us give it such-and-such a priority. This is *query prioritization*. It cannot be done until after we know what the query or problem is. (Query prioritization is studied in more depth in Part Four.) The priority is set *at the time* – but that is not the whole picture. The priority we give that query will be weighted by the importance of the user delivering the problem. This is *client prioritization*. And where it differs from query prioritization is that it can and should be set *in advance*.

One of the purposes of client prioritization is to weigh the relative importance of support clients against one another, then to apply that weighting to the intrinsic priority of incoming client problems, in order to bring into sharper focus the relative priorities of the support workload as a whole. The other is so as to gain the best return, in terms of service level appropriately delivered, from the helpdesk resource investment made.

The end result of this process will be to be able to decide whether the failure of one department's computer is more or less important than the failure of a similar computer in another department. Because once you know that, you will know where to focus your best resource first, fully confident that you are acting in the best interests of all concerned.

The question is one of delivering service levels that meet the needs of the business. The helpdesk manager knows instinctively that some user departments are more needy, in terms of enquiry urgency than are others. An inappropriately low service level given to the sales department at the wrong time could mean that the company loses an order, so there is a cost in revenue. A high service level given to a department that doesn't need one could be at the expense of another department that does.

We can see from Fig. 8.1 what happens when we deliver a 'blanket' service level that does not reflect the organization's true needs. In this case, the helpdesk is delivering too high a service level to human resources and facilities *at the expense of* the service level to those departments who really need more. The helpdesk has opted to give the same level of service to everybody, and as a result is wasting the company's money delivering a high service level where such is not necessary – and

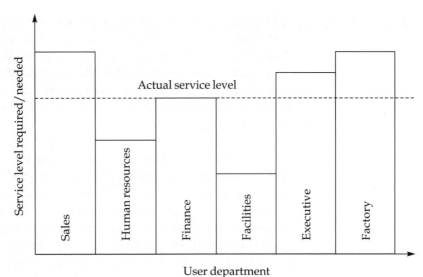

Figure 8.1
Required versus actual
service level

because the really needy departments are suffering, the company as a whole is probably not as successful as it otherwise could be.

Think very hard before you offer a 'blanket' service level. It's true that blanket service levels are tempting – it is easier to train support staff how to do it, easier for the users to understand so easier to set expectations, in fact from the helpdesk's point of view, it has all the benefits of any mass-production strategy. But it may ultimately be damaging to the financial health of the organization.

8.2 Where client priorities come from

A client will be allocated a high or low priority based on two criteria: the power the client wields, and the value of the client to the various parties who will be impacted by the level of this client's priority.

8.2.1 Power

Let us look first at power, which itself may either be real or bluffed. A healthy respect for power, regardless of whether that power be used fairly or unjustly abused, is a perfectly legitimate criterion for allocating a high priority to a client. If you were support manager at Ewing Oil and you had to assess J.R.'s priority, let's face it, there'd be no question. There are four questions to be answered:

1 Does this person or group have real power which can damage the interests of the support service or its other clients?
2 Is support threatened with the use of that power by not allocating this client a high enough priority?
3 Is the threat credible and likely to be carried out?
4 Is the likely, resulting damage a realistic price to pay for not heeding that power?

If the power does not exist or can do no real damage, then move to an assessment of the value of the client. Otherwise, we are looking at whether the support department (its bid for next year's budget, the career aspirations of the individuals within it, its ability to meet its other high-priority commitments, etc.) will suffer damage if we do not use this opportunity to prove to this powerful customer how good and worthwhile a service we run.

8.2.2 Value

Examine the value of this client from three separate angles: the value to the *business*, the value to the *company* and the value to *you* and your support function. It is often difficult to separate the 'business' from the 'company', but it is an important distinction to make. The business entails the activities carried out by the company to achieve the financial goals set by certain members of the company and its shareholders. In this sense, 'business' is a relatively short-term consideration, associated with the current sales and expenditure targets. Business is a purely financial, essentially non-political issue. Is this client of high value to the business? This is something that can be measured quickly and numerically. A major-accounts salesperson is important to the business; so are the sales ledger department and the warehouse; the personnel department, however, is not.

In most private-sector companies, contribution to the business takes the highest priority and this should be reflected in the priority support allocates to those users whose importance to the business is clear. However, in some sectors, or for certain issues, value to the company is seen as at least as important as value to the business.

Take an R&D department, for example. Here is a user whose contribution to the business is debatable – but their value to the company is clear. It is developing the future means of income for the company, even though its results have little immediate relevance. In most private-sector companies, R&D will take a lower priority than business-oriented users by default, unless of course the company's end saleable product is research itself.

The final consideration is the value of this client to you as support manager, to your department, to your goals and aspirations. The work some users could grant you may be fun or educational to do. It may stretch or motivate your suppoɪt team. Association with this user may further your career.

You may desire to actively attract work from a client who can provide your department with such stimulation or support, and so you set their priority (artificially) high so they get an increased and more attractive service level than they may commercially deserve. To a certain extent, the priority you set a client, if that priority is based on considerations other than business or professional ones, is a matter for your own conscience. However, it may be that some of your personal priorities stem from your interpretation of what is important to the business or the company. After all, you work there too.

8.3 Putting client priorities in place

8.3.1 Internal helpdesks

The organization knows instinctively which are the most important departments. If you're lucky, they may even tell you formally. This is another reason I urge you to keep an eye on the statement made by the chairman of the board or chief executive officer in the company's annual report, because there may be an indication of next year's corporate strategy, from which you may be able to glean which user departments may consequently become a higher priority. For example, if the CEO says there is going to be a big marketing push into the Russian market next year, go and see the head of division, Eastern European Sales and ask him what new or enhanced IT support services and service levels he's going to need as a result of this new pressure on him.

But the other thing here is proactivity. If you can identify in advance the relative priority of the various user departments, you can get that list of priorities signed off by the board, and then enshrine those priorities into your helpdesk management software. What you have then done is prioritized the users in those departments *even before they have had a need to call the helpdesk*. So when they do call the helpdesk, all you have to do is assess the impact of the enquiry (is their system down? how many users are affected? what time criticalities are indicated? etc.) and you have a unique priority for that enquiry that truly reflects business needs. The beauty of setting out client priorities in advance this way is that no user can then put you under illegitimate pressure to offer him an artificially high priority. This is because that user's level of priority has been set by licence from the board of directors. So if that user thinks he needs a higher priority, it's the board he has to convince, not the helpdesk manager.

8.3.2 External helpdesks

For external helpdesks too, client prioritization can be especially important. The Italian mathematician Vilfredo Pareto (1848–1923) came up with something now commonly called 'the 80/20 rule', which can be universally applied in business. Eighty per cent of the company's business, profit, etc., tends to come from 20 per cent of its customers. If that's the case, why not reflect that in your service levels? Implement a premium helpdesk for those 20 per cent, offering a higher service level, quicker response time, and so on. The sales department will love you for it, you will get the reputation of being 'business aware' (a rare accolade in IT) and you will be making your own contribution to increasing the company's repeat business from its highest-spending customers. This contribution to repeat business can be especially useful for justifying investment in the external helpdesk, as we shall see in the chapter on cost justification.

Keeping in contact

9.1 Why keep in contact?

As we established in Chapter 7, if support does not have a hand in setting its customers' expectations, then their performance will be measured against benchmarks which may be unreasonable or even irrational. So support has a duty to itself to get and stay in contact with its customers, to ensure expectations are reasonable as well as to know what services to offer. But there has got to be more than this – for if communications are left to be just as perfunctory as that, we will achieve very little, and at best no more than we are achieving now.

In principle, we have to communicate to keep things positive, to increase understanding between ourselves and our customers. There is a natural gulf between computer specialists and computer users, a legacy coming right from the early history of computing where the only people who understood computers were scientists. In the 1970s and 1980s, some of the larger computer companies contributed to this obfuscation by marketing their systems as instruments of corporate control rather than the tools of user enablement. They also advocated huge IT departments to run these machines, speaking a language which by its nature would abbreviate and confuse.

Even now, with the ubiquitous PC, computers are still the prerogative of a technoclass, and that image alone alienates many users from us. The PC has not delivered a new user independence. It can do increasingly little on its own, is utterly emasculated if it loses contact with the corporate network, and with 'client–server' computing, is becoming little more than a graphical terminal. It had to happen – computers are still instruments of control, engendering feelings of mistrust. Against this backdrop of unfortunate but unavoidable technological alienation, users can easily form unjust impressions. Coupled with the image of the supporters throwing their hands up in despair at the user who will not even read the manual, the total picture is not an encouraging one. Left to their own devices, the emotions of ignorance, prejudice, suspicion, and even fear can contribute to inaccurate pictures we build of one another.

To see the need for proactive communication with the users, let's look at the world from the user's point of view. The company hires him, gives him a job description and tells him that his performance will be measured against that job description – and that his performance will affect his salary, his chances of promotion and his level of day-to-day power and influence. They also tell him that the way to deliver that performance is through the use of his desktop computer. So the computer has been foisted upon him, he is compelled to use it, and the behaviour of that computer now has a direct impact on his personal and professional success and happiness.

So how does he feel when the computer fails to deliver? He never asked for the computer, he uses it because he has to, his life depends on it and now it has crashed yet again. What's the number of the IT department? I'm going to call them up and give them a piece of my mind! Oh, there's no number for the IT department and they don't have a complaints desk. What's the next best thing? The helpdesk! Right, now they're going to get it! Pass me that phone!

The helpdesk is the customer face of IT. Most users, quite rightly, cannot get a mental bus ticket in between the concepts of the IT department and the helpdesk. The two are one and the same. If the IT department fails, the helpdesk gets it in the neck.

This means that by default, communications coming from the users into the helpdesk are overwhelmingly negative. So the standard relationship between the users and the helpdesk is also negative. Most helpdesks defend themselves from this negativity instinctively, by hiring nice people who are good at dealing with complaints, good at calming angry, excited or frightened users. But that simply is not enough. A smile will get you so far. But this is business. And to deal with that properly, you need a business methodology. There is only one solution – the helpdesk must communicate proactively with its customers.

It cannot just wait for the customers to ring in because when they do, it will be because in their eyes, the IT department (i.e. the helpdesk) has screwed up yet again.

The implications of this for service management are enormous. In order to be successful, the helpdesk must set client expectations. In order to do that, the helpdesk must set the agenda by which the service is measured. In order to do that, the helpdesk must communicate. In order for that to be successful, the communication has to be proactive at the helpdesk's instigation. But communications coming out of the IT department must take a lower priority than the tasks of the user's day, so for the communication to be successful, it must be composed from the point of view of the user, not from that of IT. But if it is from the user's point of view, it will talk about IT in terms that IT professionals may see as trivial, but that's OK because that's how the users see IT, as just a tool, the technical details of which are relevant only to the IT department.

If we take that logical train of consequences into account, this means that the successful IT department must talk to its users in trivial terms. And this is the absolute opposite of what most IT departments do, which is to make their communications to the users as if the IT department were trying to show off how clever it is.

It is one of the central purposes of this book to entreat user support to play an even greater role in breaking the legacy of poor communication between users and information technologists. Many support professionals are self-taught and come from a user background rather than from a computing background. This is the basis of good communications in the future. Good communications not only have to be maintained for the purely practical purposes of expectation management and market research, but must ensure that IT as a whole, in your company, in your business, in your life, is delivering the increased productivity and the promises of new business opportunities we all assume are to be expected.

In the face of this massive challenge, it is a sad and pathetic fact that in some companies, this new and better business world which IT could bring about is in the hands of support leaders whose idea of communication is to sit behind a PC screen and wait for a user to ring up and complain that he cannot get a £ sign out of his printer. I am not asking you just to go and ask users if they are happy with the helpdesk; I am asking you to get out there and change the world.

> **Regular, varied, quality communication with our users is crucial:**
>
> *Tactically* – so we know what to expect from each other
> *Emotionally* – we're only human, and we'd rather be friends
> *Commercially* – so we can make the machines make us richer

9.2 Communications routes around user support

For most support departments, the most obvious way of keeping in contact is via the problem reports the users will pass to the helpdesk or equivalent. However, there are several routes to communications, each of them with a purpose, each with its own potential advantages and disadvantages. There are so many of them, and so much passing along them that a map would be useful. Figure 9.1 illustrates this.

Figure 9.1 is meant to give a general impression of the sort of communications which might be going on in a typical user support organization. It is much simplified. The inner circle is the technical function within the user support department itself, here divided into three separate areas: a *helpdesk*, which takes all incoming queries and either solves them on the spot or passes them on to the *resolvers* (sometimes called 'technical support') for solution. These two areas are backed up by a *library*, from where they get their knowledge and to which they pass all newly created knowledge for storage, and eventually retrieval to help with new queries.

The solution to the user's query will come either from the helpdesk or from the resolver. Either way it must be established whether it has actually resulted in a solution, hence the need for quality checks carried out by support administration. Note that the second circle is divided into support administration and users. In a sense these groups are on the same level – caught halfway between the purely technical and probably non-business-oriented support machine and the ultimately commercial and absolutely business-oriented outside world. The commercial pressures imposed by the outside world affect both the users and support administration/management, but are much less likely to be directly felt by the technicians solving

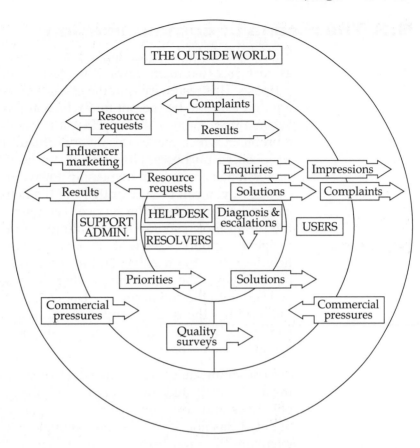

Figure 9.1
Communications routes
around user support

problems. However, they must be made real to the support department so that it knows who and what it is important to support, hence the need for support administration first to discover, then to understand these pressures, and immediately to convert them into clear priorities for the resolvers.

However, as well as being IT support customers, the users are also part of the outside world. They are representatives of the business and the company. This means they communicate with it by default, and as the outside world is the domain of the influencer and the decision-maker, this is a communications medium we should make it a priority to tap into. The success of the users is paramount, not only because of the commercial imperative, but also when they fail, the last thing the support department wants to be is the scapegoat for that failure. Hence the importance for support administration to find out what the users are being measured on and to whom they report, so it is clear where support should be concentrating its limited resources.

9.3 The means of communication

The helpdesk, although a legitimate means of communication, as such has two main flaws: it is reactive and it has a limited purpose. This reactivity is in the essence of user support, which after all exists to be the pot into which all problems are tossed. When a user contacts the helpdesk it is usually because there is a problem, which makes this a very difficult medium to exploit for positive purposes. However, it can be used to convey the professionalism and job-ownership ('leave it with me, I'll take care of it, you can be sure of that') of the helpdesk staff and the comprehensiveness of the service. The user will read this from the promise of response and resolution. To convey a complete image of support as we wish it conveyed, we cannot rely on the helpdesk. It is too reactive, and in most companies too busy to be worrying about anything other than getting the user's problem into the solving-mill. Also, we are not in control of the interaction – the user is. And if we do not have control of the communication, we are in a very weak position to address any agenda we may have.

For communication to be truly effective, it must be proactive. It must be instigated by support and designed to meet our objectives and cover our agenda, in a palatable and customer-oriented fashion. So it is not enough just to wait for the telephone to ring, because even when it does, the resulting interaction is not conducive to getting the support message across. The only truly effective support communications are those made by, not to, support.

So what communications channels exist between support, the users and the outside world? What communication is passing along these channels: are they well or badly used? How many of the following exist in your company?

- The helpdesk, taking all calls, answering those it can, passing those it cannot fix to the resolvers.

  For: A truly helpful team who take not just the physical telephone call, but also full responsibility for the problem as reported and the fix to be delivered. Consistently friendly, helpful and diligent.

  Or: A barrier put there to keep the users away from the proper computer people. Not sufficiently knowledgeable, always trying to fob the caller off, giving the impression they have limited time to take your call, get rid of you and get on to the next caller.

- Visits by support staff to users, for solving and diagnosing problems, installing and configuring new equipment.

  For: Shows support for the professionals we are. Users are always glad to see us and clearly get a buzz out of watching an expert working. Gratitude in abundance when SuperTechy flies in.

  Or: Adds to the distasteful image of support staff as just a bunch of plumbers with disks instead of wrenches. Nothing better to do than push computers round on trolleys all day wearing jeans with screwdrivers sticking out of their pockets. Technicians expect the users to stop what they are doing and let these intruders tamper with the machines, which never work the same after they have meddled.

- Usage reports compiled by support and passed to users, showing how many questions they have asked support and when.

  For: A useful account of the use such-and-such a user department makes of the support service, showing how often a techy is needed and who of the user staff could benefit from more training. Also illustrates how much the users are saving by not doing this support themselves.

  Or: In effect, these reports are no more than a bill for services rendered. They are just a dry list of statistics with no interpretation, clearly put out more for the convenience of the support department than for the convenience of the customer. They read like they are a whitewash and show support up for being out of touch with what users want.

- User forums, in effect open days, where the users can come to visit the support department to hear about new products and technologies that are going to affect them, perhaps even to experiment with and evaluate this new technology.

  For: A chance to see the new technologies outside the hype of the media and to look at how they will help or hinder this company; and with the support department's technical experts always on hand. A good place to clear up all those niggling little technical questions that have never been worth logging a call.

  Or: A nerd's day out, only ever attended by hackers and users who wish they were techies, where all they do is play with irrelevant and gimmicky toys. They talk bits and bytes among themselves with never a thought for what this product means to the company.

- The user newsletter, written by support to provide the users with useful information.

  For: A reliably regular publication, easily obtainable and containing real information of direct relevance to the users and clearly designed to help users do their jobs better, despite the computers. Shows how support are truly switched-on to user needs.

  Or: A dry-as-dust corporate memorandum which comes out once every blue moon, every time with a different writer and never to the same format. Only ever goes to department heads, so the people who could use it never see it. Written in a style clearly designed to bore rather than inform, too technical and almost always out of date. Shows again how out of touch they are down there.

- Service review meetings.

  For: Regular meetings, with an invited audience yet open to all, where mutual impedances to better support service are openly discussed and solutions which benefit all are thrashed out. Shows that we are all in the same boat and helping each other. Nothing is ever allowed to escalate into a crisis, and this co-operation means we have got everything under control.

  Or: The support department's chief defence mechanism. These meetings take place irregularly, behind closed doors, start badly and degenerate from there into accusations and blame-slinging.

9.4 Other communications methods

The problem with all communications is that to be effective, they must be consumed by the target audience. There is no point, other than perhaps one of prestige, in producing a communication that is summarily ignored. In all cases, write or speak the communication in the consumer's terms, not in your own.

The *intranet* (for external helpdesks, read 'Internet') is an electronic noticeboard, to which items of interest, notes, hints, requests for assistance, and so on can be pinned. There are several kinds, from the basic browser running on a PC and through which users can tap into pre-written information text pages, through to fully managed, purpose-built systems with the sophistication of an executive information system. Either way, if support publishes one of these, it must make sure a technician looks at the intranet site regularly and that support is as involved in it as the users are. Sophisticated helpdesk presences on the intranet can offer links to the helpdesk system so that users can monitor progress on their outstanding enquiries or indeed submit new enquiries. The intranet can also link to online help or computer-based training systems.

The *user booklet*: some support organizations identify new users in advance of their arrival and issue them with a kind of introductory guide to being a user of this computer system and surrounding services. In the booklet will typically be their username and introductory password, with instructions as to how to change the password immediately after logging in for the first time; a list of the applications to which they have access; a description of the computer system with details of how often it is backed up; the name and address of their local IT contact; how to recognize a computer problem; what hours user support is open, how to contact them, and what information will be required; who to complain to if user support does not deliver; how to get printer paper, toner, disks and other consumables; where to go for training; how to propose software improvements; a description of all user support services and service levels which the user can expect; which of the services the user is currently entitled to and how to increase that entitlement. The user booklet is a powerful communications medium precisely because it is proactive – user support takes control of the relationship with this user right from the start, setting the agenda and showing they are 'on the case'. The user booklet screams ownership – its very existence shows that user support has the user's interests at heart, that they want the user to get productive on the computer system as quickly as possible.

The *hints manual* can be useful where the product manuals are too complex and give too much cover to features this company or these users do not exploit. Where hints manuals often fail, however, is when they are handed out to a populace in addition to or in replacement for the official product manuals, when that populace has already shown that it does not read manuals and prefers to call support.

9.5 The effective newsletter

The newsletter is one of several types of documented communications which can pass between support and the users. To produce an effective user support newsletter, first decide on its purpose. If the purpose is unclear, it may have trouble attracting a readership as users will find it difficult to comprehend whom it is written for. Your purpose may be 'to promote a positive image of user support while providing the users with information they ought to know', or it may be 'to further the efforts of user training by cementing the lessons in the courses they give', or it may be 'to raise the profile of user support as the ambassador of IT in this company'. Know what your purpose is and stick to it, and above all, make sure you can see your purpose in at least 80 per cent of the articles you print. Magazines stop being read when they forget or lose their purpose, or when the market for that purpose dwindles. Remember you are a magazine publisher, so think like one.

Second, be careful about competition between the newsletter and other written media, e.g. product evaluations, a BBS, broadcast electronic mail, a 'hints and tips manual'. By all means have these other things, but let the niche of each of them be clear.

Third, be careful about the writing style and content; write to inform, not to impress or gloat. Write from the point of view of the reader, not from that of the writer (this is probably the commonest and most damaging failure of the support newsletter).

Fourth, humanize it; do not write a newsletter from manager to manager, use memos, meetings, e-mail, or lunch to do that. To humanize a newsletter, start from the premiss that the readers are all people before they are workers, that people have fears, aspirations, cynicism and a sense of humour (particularly this last category – most people are not pompous asses, even though their section heads may be). Remember that people are more interesting than things, so profile your own staff and their contribution to the support effort in the newsletter. Even better, consider letting your own staff write in the newsletter, so long as they can write the way ordinary people would want to read. This mixes the writing style a little, introducing a little variety: a newsletter written by one person in one style can be boring if the writer is not a particularly creative one. Have an editorial section – it sets the tone for the entire publication and opens and closes the experience of reading this edition of the newsletter, as well as pointing out what is the 'big issue' of the moment and that support are thinking about it. Encourage your users to submit their writing to the newsletter: one of them may have discovered a really hot workaround to that annoying and perennial problem with the sales ledger, and everybody could benefit.

Fifth, consider digestibility. Most users will get one chance and only one to read the newsletter – the moment it lands on their desk. That means they have to feel that they can afford those few precious moments to read it. Long articles dissecting the intricacies of a new word processor are out. Remember, this is a news document first and foremost. If there is a need in your organization for long, technical reports, put them out in a separate publication. The newsletter, and everything in it, should be brief, to the point and an all-round good read.

Everything in the newsletter should be oriented towards what benefit it delivers to the reader. Do not just state that the XYZ company has just launched the gee-whizziest software; say how the software will benefit the user. Do not just say that your technician Fred is the best networking man this side of the equator; say why it is important that your company has such a highly paid guru. Do not just say that you solved 1000 user problems this month, say that it is 10 per cent more than last month, and 15 per cent up on last year, with the same staff, but user satisfaction is still going up. Do not just say that you have got the ear of the IT director, explain how that helps problems to be solved more quickly because problem escalation is slicker.

Assume that the first time users pick that document up, they will be thinking that it looks interesting, but what is in it for them? Why should they spend time and effort reading and thinking about this thing? Tell them why, with the first thing they read – and do not assume they will start reading at the top of page 1.

Do you have somebody in support who is good with the written word? No? Then find somebody else, perhaps in marketing, who is. The ability of the newsletter to get read is more important than the information in it. If it does not get read, you will never know about it, and the information and effort in the newsletter will have been wasted. But if the newsletter gets read, even if it only provides half the information it could, at least those who wish to know more will be aware of that and will know where to go for more. In a user newsletter, good writing is more important than good content. If it is difficult to read, people will not bother: ask any newspaper editor. Remember, there is no comeback on users if they do not read it, because if a problem crops up, whether it was mentioned in the newsletter or not, they can still just pick up the phone. And even though users may have benefited from reading the newsletter, there is no point in delivering a potential benefit to a user then obscuring it behind a morass of turgid technical jargon.

9.6 Customer surveys

It is vital that we know what our customers think about the support service. By visiting them, mixing with them, conversing with them, we can find out a great deal. But these methods are non-scientific, they can give us nothing we can measure against a scale, to see how much effect our efforts to improve ourselves are having. In the desire for a more scientific way of measuring user opinion, we invariably turn to the customer survey.

As a way of discovering what the users think, it is at most the best of a bad bunch. It is intrinsically flawed. We realize the customers will have neither the time nor the inclination to fill out a freestyle survey; and the more freestyle the replies, the harder they are to measure, thereby defeating some of the point. On the other hand, if we ask set questions and solicit multiple-choice replies, then we are setting the agenda, inviting the criticism that we only want to hear about what is important to support and not what is important to the customer.

9.6.1 Multiple-choice questions

To see the weaknesses of multiple-choice customer surveys a bit more closely, let us take the following example. While filling in a customer survey, clients are invited to consider what happens when they ask the helpdesk a technical question and respond to the following question by circling one of the five possible replies:

I usually get the right answer to my question . . . Strongly agree, agree, indifferent, disagree, strongly disagree.

The users read this question and think about it a while. What they actually believe is that of late they have had to adjust their questions down to a level they think the helpdesk can cope with. And yes, now that they have done that, they are forced to agree with the question/statement, because they can always answer these watered-down questions: they have designed them so the helpdesk can answer them. What they actually want to say is that the helpdesk does not appear capable of answering the right questions, and as a result they feel that their department is missing out on a heap of technological progress they could be making; and more frighteningly, they suspect this is causing them to lose the competitive edge with a similar department in another company.

But that is a long and complicated answer to such a simple question, they do not feel confident in going into writing about it, and they have no real proof of their contention that the helpdesk is not doing its job; they suspect other users are probably having the same problem, so they will put it on their survey form, besides they do not have the time or the inclination to do all this replying, and nothing will change anyway, then there is nowhere to put all this on the form and they do not really want to get anybody into trouble; and it is true, the helpdesk does answer all the questions they feel they can trust it with – and with all these excuses coursing round their brains, they take the easy way out and circle 'agree'.

When the survey forms are analysed, support measures this as a success! When with the right information they would see it as indicating that they were short on knowledge, out of touch with these users and lacking the right mechanisms to discover the failing. In this case, what support charts up as a success, if they just lifted the curtain a little higher, they would see to be an abject failure in at least three areas – a serious weakness rather than the acceptable service level indicated by the survey.

There is some debate about whether multiple-choice questions should have an odd or even number of possible replies. Current thinking appears to be in favour of an even number of replies, because that forces the respondent not to sit on the fence and plump for either 'I love it' or 'I hate it'. It seems that 'Actually, I couldn't care less' is not the answer survey designers want to hear. But I'm not so sure.

If I were to put out a standard survey form to be completed by every user in the company, I would expect a return of about 15 to 25 per cent. I would expect a respectable number of positive responses, a disproportionately high number of negative ones (often from users who were using the survey form to complain about a couple of isolated incidences of bad service and almost none from those who were apathetic about the service or did not see it as a priority to send the completed form back).

The thing about service apathy is that for a service delivery like a helpdesk, the level, scale and quantity of apathy is important. If the user couldn't care less one way or another about the service, then as far as he is concerned, the question of whether the service needs to be improved is simply not important enough for him to take the time to complete our survey form. In other words, what apathy tells us is that for those who did not fill the form in, the service is adequate – meaning that *the customers are satisfied*.

To get a true measure of customer satisfaction, we therefore need to measure how many people couldn't care less. Which means that in our customer surveys, there has to be an odd not even number of possible responses to any question measuring satisfaction (and ideally five rather than four).

The reason even numbers of responses are so popular comes from the market research industry. The questions they tend to ask are along the lines of 'Would you buy this product?' or 'Will you be voting for this party?' In those cases, there is no need for a safe middle ground, because that would mean 'Maybe' – and in terms of 'Would you or wouldn't you?', 'Maybe' means 'I might' or 'I would given the right conditions', or in other words 'Yes'. If the answer is in effect going to be either Yes or No, then there is no need for a middle option. But if we want to measure apathy, a middle option is essential.

The problem with measuring apathy is that to include it, you have to get a captive audience who must reply, so you get a 100 per cent return. And you cannot do that with the printed survey form, because not enough people will complete it and send it back. Which is another reason for the random, telephone survey I propose at 9.6.3 below.

9.6.2 The type of respondent

Who replies to customer surveys? It takes a certain type. This person has to be sufficiently confident in their opinions to commit them, along with their name, to paper and probably be measured against them. They have to believe, or perhaps have not ever considered, that the company will not witch-hunt those with unfavourable opinions which contravene the company line or are interpreted as being 'negative' (see Section 9.6.4). Many people actually shrink from writing anything, perhaps fearing that their language skills are inadequate or that their opinions will be considered naïve or simplistic. Experience shows too that IT surveys tend to attract IT-aware respondents – meaning that those clients less aware of the computer, those who see the computer as nothing more than a simple tool like the telephone, and those who consider themselves too senior to use the computer will see the survey as largely irrelevant to them and will either ignore it or will make it so low a priority that they next see the form after the 'please respond by' date. The IT-aware clients will also be the ones who tend to have a positive view of what the IT department is delivering; those with a complaint will either have already made it their own way or will opine that the IT people are already so far gone they would not listen to, understand, or do anything about a complaint anyway. So the respondent will also have to believe that your survey will bring about the change he or she wants to see.

9.6.3 An alternative to the customer survey

All that said, clearly the customer survey attracts a limited and typically artificially positive response. Add to that the survey climate, which can also cause deceptively positive results. One way to combat the weaknesses of the customer survey is to conduct more of a surprise attack. One technique is the *random client poll*, which works best against the backdrop of a helpdesk with a computerized call-logging system. Once every two weeks, say Friday afternoons, generate at random five call-log numbers. These should be numbers of calls which have been placed to the helpdesk in the last two weeks, and you should have no prior knowledge of their content. Pluck those calls from the call-log, call up the clients who placed them and ask a short list of questions to find out how they were dealt with on that call only. This method has several benefits over the formal customer survey. First, it shows the clients and your own staff you care about quality. Second, it gives you a measure of quality (so we will be covering this again in Part Four). Third, it tends to catch the client slightly more off-guard than a formal survey would, so you may get less fence-sitting. Fourth, it forces you, as support manager, into the discipline of keeping in regular contact with your clients. Fifth, it exposes you to the way the clients are really treated, incident by incident rather than just hearing their impressions of how they are treated overall.

Ideally, you would use the random client poll in conjunction with, say, a six-monthly survey. Each will attract a different type of response and you want the most complete picture possible.

9.6.4 The survey climate

Before polling your users for what they think of your service, consider this: is your company the sort of place where a customer survey can be conducted safely? Is the environment conducive to objectivity, criticism and self-examination?

There was a company whose fortunes I had cause to watch for some years. Through sound investment at the right time in a booming market, they gathered a large, strong team of exceptional people, leaders in their field. Yet they managed to keep these gurus to themselves, where some companies may have found the attentions of their experts divided between work in the office and their own public careers. For a couple of years, everything clicked and business was good. Then the recession bit, almost overnight. The company responded in true western style: training, salaries, miscellaneous costs were all cut. A sound, if short-termist, business move. Then restructuring: another sound move, get ready for the upturn. But the restructuring went on and on. No time for anybody to settle in, then another reorganization. The board tried to steer their way through the chaos by saying the reorganizations were part of a master plan – but when they were not believed, they got defensive and declared anybody not with them to be against them. The experts they had recruited could not do the job they came to do. Disagreeing with the ruling party, privately or publicly, risked the accusation of negativism and cost a couple of people their places in the new hierarchy. To blazes with user surveys; in this company, which changed so radically and tailspun so quickly from brash self-confidence to paranoia, asking for any opinion produced a glut of fence-sitting and apathy. They even stopped performing employee appraisals.

The end of the story? I watched with a kind of sadistic delight as the talent and expertise bled from the company. Those who could get out, did. Those who could not, stayed. Within 18 months, the company went from sharing market leadership to an advanced state of mediocrity, where at the time of writing it still languishes, with staff who dedicate much of their effort to keeping their heads below the parapet and a board which, if it were not for the indifference of the stock market, would be furthering their careers elsewhere. They are so paranoid, they probably think this story is about them (with apologies to Carly Simon). Suffice to say the support manager was one of those who left.

Case Study 9.1: the wrong end of the stick?

Robert was a support manager, or so it said on his payslip. His company had never quite been able to decide what its user support strategy was. The IT director was more concerned with hardware costs and the almost uncontrollable nature of software development, so in the midst of all this, user support got forgotten. Except by the users – who were convinced the support could be better and were getting steadily more vociferous about their conviction.

They complained that support's helpdesk was always engaged, that the technicians often heard about the latest bug in the software after the users got to experience it on the screens, that the helpdesk always had to go back to development with everything, so what was the point?

Down in support, Robert was getting ever more despondent. He knew that his troubles came from the state of the software, but software development was not his department. The users were unfair in blaming him, they had got the wrong end of the stick. Still, they were right about one thing – the helpdesk did not seem to be able to cut it these days, at least on the mainframe software; every query had to go back to development. On the PC side, though, they were answering 90 per cent of the queries they got on the spot, but nobody wanted to know that.

Upstairs in the boardroom, the furore from the users was getting noticed. The IT director realized she had to do something or it would be her neck. She called in the mainframe manufacturers, JCN, and had them put a bid in for taking over support. Six months later, JCN had the contract and Robert was out of a job, the scapegoat for the problems which had apparently been because of support. He never saw just how JCN fixed the problem.

JCN had realized from the start that they could not make their bid based on fact, because they had no history of providing support in that company. The best they could do was trade on their image – but they knew that was enough, for although Robert had not had a history of success either, he had also had a weak image. The result was that on balance, JCN looked stronger, with only intangibles as evidence. JCN are not fools: they knew that if Robert had kept in contact with his users, the users would probably have preferred the devil they knew – but as they did not know Robert either, it would be pretty straightforward to convince them that JCN could only be better.

The first thing JCN did was get rid of Robert and put their own man in. They kept the helpdesk, the people and, by and large, the overall structure. But they gave their own man a brief of setting up a regular dialogue with development, using support statistics of software failures, to force them to improve quality. The results of this dialogue were regularly published in the new support newsletter, showing the users how support was working on their behalf. To deal with the short-term problems in the meantime, the help-desk was briefed to handle calls on mainframe software slightly differently. Whenever a mainframe software bug was reported, the helpdesk had to try to find a workaround as well as passing the problem to development – in effect, to keep the user working while somebody looked at their problem. The users perceived this as a great improvement – even though in effect it was largely a repackaging of what had gone before.

Customer service in IT support

It follows that if we have customers, we must also have customer service.

10.1 Serve your customers or the competition will

There was an office-wall poster going around a few years ago which stated quite forcefully that 'Customers Make Pay-days Possible'. That is certainly true. Add to that, the 1990s were supposed to be the decade of customer service. As companies and products get more alike due to research and marketing departments coming inevitably to the same conclusions about the markets they are trading in, something else will have to differentiate your company if it is not going to fall victim to competition. For many, that differentiator is *customer service*.

The idea is no less relevant, nor the need no less pressing for the user support organization. User support is just as much up against it as is the host company. It is a common misconception that in-house user support organizations have no competition. This is the arrogance of perceived monopoly and as the saying 'pride comes before a fall' teaches, such self-importance has often been dashed along with the aspirations of the over-arrogant.

User support has competition all around it. It does not have to come from the ogre of 'outsourcing' (bringing in a specialist company to take over support – a move usually associated with redundancies and upheaval). There are several sources from which users can get the same knowledge as they currently expect from user support. Some of these are quite subtle, others are radical. There is competition from the computer press, bending over backwards to advise users on technical matters for no more than a few tax-deductible dollars a month. There is competition from the users themselves, who may either beef up their own knowledge or appoint specialists from among their own ranks to support their computer usage. There is competition from the various bulletin boards and CD-ROM support databases now available. There is competition from computer manufacturers and retailers, many of whom offer premium support services for a fee. There are the third-party maintenance companies who have realized their market is becoming ever more limited as hardware gets cheaper to replace than repair; they are retraining their technicians to take over more aspects of support, starting with rebuilding the system on which they have just replaced a failed component and moving into full-scale network support. There are the contractors who have a certain software specialization and may convince the users they can provide a better support service than a generalist, in-house team.

This competition is going to get worse. Better, cheaper communications and remote-control software, all of which now help the user support organization to support remote sites, will make low-cost remote support more freely available and attractive; at the time of writing, at least one company in Russia is offering to write programs for the PC environment for ludicrously low rates. Simply because of the difference in living costs, a network in Frankfurt-am-Main could be supported by a party in Bucharest for a far lower hourly rate than the Frankfurt team could afford, and with virtually no language barrier; similarly, a network in Paris could be supported from Algiers, one in Sydney from Kuala Lumpur, one in Hong Kong from Shanghai – at least in theory. And what about the training companies who have realized they can back up their service by inviting software queries on premium-rate telephone lines – all the right expertise, without the overheads; the hardware manufacturers who have come full circle and are trying to attract market share by offering so much support for free?

The in-house support team simply must differentiate itself from all this, or be swept away by one or the other trend when the next recession bites. They have one shining advantage: they are there on the ground, and can exploit their presence and closeness to the user.

When the same product is available from several sources, that product becomes a commodity. Fundamentally, the only way to differentiate between suppliers of a commodity is price. Now it may be that your helpdesk does not charge for its services, and so price may apparently not be part of the equation – but it is, nevertheless. Looking at the use of your helpdesk from your users' point of view, what does it cost them to log a call with you? How long do they have to wait before getting through to a technician? How long for a response? How long for a fix? In other words, what does their use of your service cost them, if not in money, in their time and effort? And do they have other sources of the same information, which are more convenient to use?

If the helpdesk cannot provide what the users see as a convenient and appropriate level of service, they will go elsewhere for it. That makes the helpdesk less relevant, with obvious implications for the manager's career. But it also means the organization is getting its user support from many, undefined sources with no governance on the quality or accuracy of the answers so invisibly requested and supplied. It is the duty of the helpdesk to deliver a good and easy-access service for the good of the company as a whole.

Take the example of one of the helpdesk's classic competitors, the technical or desktop support department. The user wonders why he should call the helpdesk, when they will only put him through to a desktop support technician – might as well go direct. How can you compete with that?

You compete with that the same way you would compete in any commodity-based market. When the commodities are the same, but one is cheaper (the desktop support technician only costs one call and the answer is immediate) the competitor must differentiate himself by *adding value*. The usual way of adding value is to offer a service element on top of the commodity product. For the helpdesk, this means that we look at our service provision not just for what it is – e.g. technically inferior to that provided by technical support, however unofficially – but for what it means to the customer. A broader proposal is required, more in keeping with the user's needs.

Mr User (the proposal goes), that second line technician you call – does he promise to be available from 8am to 6pm? Well, the helpdesk does. Does he guarantee a service level and response time? The helpdesk does. If he cannot solve your problem, does he have a means of escalating it to somebody else? The helpdesk does. And if he did pass it to somebody else, would he undertake to chase that assignee up on your behalf? The helpdesk does. Does that technician take full ownership and responsibility for your enquiry? The helpdesk does. Mr User, given all the customer service elements we offer over and above the commodity of a technical solution, don't you think you would benefit more by coming through the helpdesk?

10.2 What is customer service?

Customer service is the art of giving the customers precisely what they want, with a professionalism and flair they would not expect. That professionalism comes from the service providers' unique understanding of their own job and the clients' real needs, rather than just their expressed desire. Customer service is essentially anecdotal – it is difficult to describe in a brochure or in a statement of services offered. It is the individual touch, the comprehension and exploitation of the fact that the problem the user reports is part of a relationship between people (the technician and the user) and not just between somebody's job and their tools (the user and the computer).

Customer service is not solely a management issue – it works much better when the service is seen to be provided by the individual technician out of personal professionalism, rather than out of an instruction provided by management. That is why phrases like 'Have a nice day' can grate so much, because it often sounds so insincere, as though it comes from the staff handbook rather than from the heart.

10.3 When customer service is wasted

The key concept to customer service is *value*, and it is double-edged. The customer has to perceive some value in the quality of the service over and above the value of the service itself – otherwise there is no point in adding the quality. And the service provider has to see the value in adding the quality, for the whole commercial point of customer service is that it differentiates the service provider from the competition, thereby ensuring con-tinued custom and, *ipso facto*, hopefully continued profits.

But how much value should be added? For the key to this, we must look at the expectations of our users. By now we should know precisely what the users want – after all, if we have been doing our job correctly, we will have been managing their expectations of our service to the extent that they will choose their expectations from an agenda largely set by ourselves and our service marketing. However, service quality does not come from simply meeting the users' expectations, for if we do that, we are only doing our job, merely meeting the expectations we set.

The trick to quality customer service is to over-achieve, to deliver more than the users expected – to surprise the users with our professionalism and dedication. But this can be overdone. The principle is that quality customer service is an expression of professionalism. It is designed to appeal to the emotions by going beyond the call of duty. But it is done not for emotional or professional reasons but essentially out of commercial motives. We are really good to our users, not just because we want to be (which we do of course) but because if we were not, there would be a medium-term risk of them going elsewhere and rendering us redundant. A certain, relatively small amount of effort is all that is needed to achieve the surprise that goes beyond the call of duty. Any more than the minimum effort to denote quality will cost the company more money than it needs to spend; it will cost the support department more of its resources than it needs to dedicate, and will therefore be wasted.

> **Good quality customer service is the art of doing just enough more than just enough.**

That is why when I hear customer service anecdotes about the shop assistant who drives tens of miles and goes through purgatory and back to deliver the item which the absent-minded customer left behind, despite the fact that the story may pluck the heartstrings, I reach for my calculator. It is worth your while to occasionally let the delivery of quality customer service get out of hand – but such over-delivery and expense should be reserved for the after-dinner stories, not for the business norm. Do not let over-delivery become a habit: if you do, you will set a customer expectation you may not be able to live up to, and that is enormously counterproductive. Keep a close, judge-mental eye on what is professional and what is wasteful.

10.4 Who benefits?

Everybody benefits from good customer service. The support department which values and practices it will have a lot of friends. The culture of professionalism and ownership necessary for quality service will generate an atmosphere of genuine concern for the users' problems, but it will be a pleasant one rather than the gloom which could be created by merely worrying about the problems. The technicians will benefit by having a psychologically rewarding working environment. The manager will benefit by having an interested, involved and motivated team. The users will benefit by having their precise needs met, and then some. The company will benefit by having a better-served user population.

10.5 How to deliver good customer service

The delivery of good customer service starts before the customer makes an attempt to use the support office. How easy was it to find out about the helpdesk and how to contact it? Is that information available through official channels or just word-of-mouth, and if the latter, what other laudatory or derogatory messages about user support accompanied it? When they made the call, was the telephone answered promptly? Or was it allowed to ring just that bit too long, then answered with an excuse or an apology? Did the person who took the call understand the question? Were they friendly and approachable, yet simultaneously assertive and confident? Did the helpdesk use the right register, i.e. did they speak to the user on his or her level, or did they let the user speak business while they responded technically? Did the helpdesk appear to have enough time for the user or was there a distinct impression of the interaction being hurried along, like the feeling you get in some hamburger restaurants? Was this query welcomed with open arms, or was it jostled roughly into a queue of other outstanding work? Did the technician leave the user with the confidence that the query was safely delivered into the hands of dedicated professionals, or was the acceptance of the query vague and its future uncertain? Does the user know what will happen next, when and at whose hand? And when the solution is delivered, does the resolver check that the user is happy with the resolution?

In short, can users clearly see ownership of the problem being willingly taken from them and exchanged for a certainty of purpose and result as regards this query? Because if not, they may suspect that the problem-logging process exists and is run for the convenience of the support staff and not, as should be the case, for the purpose of seeing their problems get the best possible attention they can in an atmosphere of competence and determination.

It is true that in essence, users and their problems are only raw materials to be processed by the support organization to make their desired end product of improved user productivity, and thus contribution of support to the overall business effort. But in real life, this must never be as dismissive as it sounds: the users and their problems should be treated with the respect due to such a precious raw material.

10.6 How to deal with complaints

If users have a complaint about the Support service, they have three options. They can do nothing, they can tell you, or they can tell everybody else. If they decide to do nothing about this complaint, this may have a beneficial effect, depending on why their complaint arose. For example, if the complaint stems from the fact that they were expecting too much of you anyway and you failed to deliver against those expectations, then doing nothing may be part of the process of adjusting their expectations down to more appropriate levels. But this is a slender hope: doing nothing about a problem they have with you is more likely to be part of a more general cessation of dialogue between your department and theirs – and any failure of communications is a bad outcome. For this reason, you must strive at all times to keep communications channels open with all users, so they always feel they can bring a complaint (or a congratulation) to you.

Another option would be for the users to tell everybody else about the bad experience they had with you. In keeping with the principle that bad news sells newspapers, horror stories enliven conversation. The cause for complaint you have given these users will spread far and wide, because everybody loves a good anecdote. Sooner rather than later, this anecdote passes into reputation, and if it is backed up by other complaints from other users, the souring effect increases exponentially. Nor is there much the support department can do about it, for all this usually goes on outside their earshot. In fact the only way to deal with reputation and rumour is to run your own counter-reputation and rumour mill. This requires a large and constant marketing effort but is always advised – for a constant, positive reputation will nip in the bud any complaints which are not really complaints but just sour attempts to start a good anecdote.

> **To err is human.**
> **To admit it is professional.**
> **To fix the damage you caused is essential.**

The third option is that the user tells you. Some users do not like to do this – they worry they may be seen as whingeing. But their complaints should be encouraged, because you can and should always do something about any complaint you receive, so strive to ensure that the users understand this. For hints on how to handle the actual incoming complainant, see Case Study 10.1. Keep a tally of complaints, who and what they were about – they can and should be used as a measure of your service (more on measurement in Part Four).

Always handle complaints, always produce a result of the complaint itself. This is essential in a service industry like user support, and also particularly difficult. We produce no tangible output, no product which can be replaced if the customer complains it is faulty. Part of our end product is the confidence users have in us and our ability – it is this which is most damaged by our failure, it is this which would cause the users to consider the competition, and we must use the complaint as an opportunity to repair this damage.

When a user calls in, it may look like an isolated incident. It may be no more than an unfortunate set of circumstances, which in an uncommon co-operation has produced this particular, one-off situation for this user. It will fix with a few quick procedural nips and tucks. Or it may be the only glimpse you will get this month of a deep-seated malaise running through the whole support department, and by the time you get the next obscure clue to its existence it will be too late, the cancer will have spread too far. You do not know. Treat every complaint with the suspicion that it just may be the last hint you will get of a rot that will eventually destroy you, then rejoice if you find it is something you can fix quickly.

10.7 Seeing things from the user's viewpoint

It is difficult to see things from the user's point of view. We are service providers, not users – we have our own, intricate, specialized problems and priorities. The world looks different out there and in here, and for all we know we may not even be speaking the same language as our users. Take every opportunity you can to see things from their point of view. This is extremely difficult to do. Like many support managers, I called my own helpdesk to see how I was handled, but they recognized my voice, my style and I cannot be sure that they did not adjust their behaviour accordingly. So I asked somebody else to do it for me, but they used their own style and could not ask the questions I wanted asked, study the outcomes I wanted studied. So you have to find another way, and one method is to stand back and look at any service operation that falls within your own experience. Next time you see a service operation screw up, pay particular, scientific and objective attention. Note particularly how you are feeling as the screw-up progresses.

Being in the position of customer will give you clues and insights as to what is going through your own customers' minds. I have recently extracted lessons from two stores in my home town. In the supermarket, a new checkout clerk tried to service us quickly, thinking that speed was most important – but she was pushing the items through the checkout too quickly, damaging cans, disregarding our struggles to fill the bags against this onslaught of groceries. She had got my expectations wrong: yes I wanted speed, but not at the cost of personal attention and certainly not at the cost of even trivial damage to my purchases. Complaining was easy – they even had a special (slightly too complicated) way of accepting them. And my complaint produced a rapid, personal result from a senior representative, who both understood my problem and offered to improve the clerk's training, thereby benefiting both me and future customers. Conclusion? I feel good – I'm convinced this was an isolated incident, and that the store cares, both about me and about their staff. And training the clerk so she will not make the same mistake again – well, that means the supermarket has enabled me to make the world a slightly better place. Will I go back? Of course I will.

A little way up the road, in a well-known electrical store, customer service is a very different concept. Trying to buy a telephone for my business produced several problems, ranging from staff trying to sell me something I did not want, through to the manager not accepting a complaint and a refusal to provide a tax invoice. The letter I had to write was passed to a complaints department with no authority to do anything about my problem. When I pressed them, they chose one item from the complaint and put the onus back on me. Technically, they may have been right. But how do I feel as a customer? That this company does not really give a damn, that they have a department designed not to accept complaints but to defend themselves from them, that they cannot see the big picture that this complaint hints at (the complaint was a composite of experiences in two stores in the chain). I came away with the conclusion that here a customer is not a customer, it is a credit card with legs. I bought a tumble drier a couple of months later. Did I go back there? The store has two direct competitors on the same shopping mall . . . Do not make the mistakes they do.

Neither of these were IT support environments, but the lessons are there to be extracted. First, be willing to accept the complaint, and on the customer's terms. Second, take ownership of the complaint, all of it, not just the bits you think you can fix. Third, make sure the complaint gets to and is acknowledged by somebody who can change something, even if nothing will change. Fourth, tell the customers what action will be taken and ensure they have your sincere gratitude. Remember that sometimes circumstances conspire against us and we all make mistakes; you will be judged more on how you repair your mistakes than you will on having made them.

Case Study 10.1: if you get a caller who has a complaint

1 Stay calm and competent, but genuinely concerned. What you have is an unhappy user, who thinks his problem is your department's fault, and at this stage it does not matter whether it was your fault or not. Your objective now is to take the complaint; you will take ownership of the complaint, even though you may not take responsibility for the cause of it.

2 Acknowledge any anger he is expressing – if he feels he has been badly treated, then he is justified in being angry about that perceived treatment. Say that you can understand why he feels the way he does.

3 Make sure you take down as much information about the complaint as possible. You may need to help the caller here – he may not be thinking clearly, so state your understanding and summarize as you go.

4 State what will happen next, especially what action you personally will take. You must sound competent and decisive at all times. You may in reality have no authority to make changes or decisions on this complainant's behalf, but you must commit yourself to doing whatever you can – for example, making sure the boss sees this

---

complaint immediately. The caller wants to deliver his problem into your hands, not walk away with it still in his; and he wants to know that something will happen, quickly.

5 Finish the interaction with sincere gratitude for the complaint – after all, you could not fix what you did not know about. Give the caller any help you can with getting round the problem in the meantime. Then go away and do what you said you would.

11

A view from above

There are those who will observe the support organization with a particularly detached eye. Their view is not of how support contributes to its direct clients individually, or service by service, but how the existence of support contributes to the company; and within that framework how that contribution matches their understanding of what a company contribution should look like.

These are the especially senior observers. It is gratifying to know that they are watching at all, for their attention will strengthen any bid for improved service or resources support may make – so long as they like what they see.

This chapter is placed here for the sole purpose of encouraging a little healthy paranoia. The view from above and outside matters a great deal and is often difficult to discern. The support manager sensitive to the view from above can come to glance, even briefly, on the 'big picture', a view it is so difficult for a middle manager to take, smothered as he or she is by the daily duties of line management – but a view which can show the future brightly enough for the astute and more dynamic service manager to see which way to steer.

11.1 Casual observers

Individually, I call these seniors the 'casual observers'. Not accustomed to direct use of support services, they nevertheless appear to take an interest in the successes and failures, waxing and waning profile and predominant image of support. These casual observers certainly fall firmly into the category of influencer; that comes from the loftiness of their position, whether they are involved with IT or not. These are the unmanaged influencers. The discovery that they exist, and that they are commenting on support's existence, may come as a surprise.

'What on earth has support got to do with her? She doesn't even switch the computer on!' was a question a support manager once asked me when I told him that the director of international sales was particularly complimentary about his department. It turned out that this director regularly and anecdotally described the support department to her international clients as proof of how efficient head office was in general – there being few other departments about which it could be said.

Your first goal on discovering a highly placed commentator such as this should be to find out who it is. Names are only the beginning. Find out also who might be the audience of the observer, for this will give some idea of the context of the observation. You need to find out why he or she is watching, or indeed whom. Is it the department which attracts the interest, or one individual in the department? Is it the support service catalogue in general or just one service? Is it the service level to the company as a whole or just to one group of users?

Is your casual observer an opinion former – in other words gathering information to serve his or her own impressions – or an opinion moulder, using that information to feed the opinions of others?

And most importantly, what is this person comparing you with? What are the terms of reference, the benchmarks of measurement of this observation?

All these things will indicate whether there are new criteria in high places for the examination of the support service. In the end, support exists because of, at best, the active and positive decision of senior management, at worst, their acquiescence in support's existence. Any handle you can get on that process can be one of the keys to the future of the service.

11.2 A board's eye view

The view of the casual observer is usually much magnified when it is the view of the board as a whole. Let us look first at the board's likely focus. First, their active attention on the support department is likely to be fleeting, as they have other distractions to contend with. Support is just as likely to come under active scrutiny as any other cost centre. However, we must also be aware that once the existence and various contributions of IT support have been noticed, they will continue to be the subject of low-level monitoring for some time after. The support management team's job here is to make the most of the active monitoring to get across the most accurate and positive impression possible, while ensuring that the tiara does not slip when the monitoring becomes more passive.

Support is not unique in attracting this attention. The board will examine the activities of any company function against probably four criteria. How would your company's board of directors rate your support department's compliance with 'company policy' – after all, they are the architects of that policy and ultimately must therefore police it. They will also be looking at the *service to the users*; not necessarily from the point of view of policeman this time, but more to ensure nothing gets in the way of the users' contribution to the company's business ends. Next, there is the question of their perception of the *performance* of the support department, but again against business goals, such as control of expenditure, headcount restriction, abuse of power, and so on. Finally, they will be looking at *individuals*, but here they are more than likely to be assessing the management team, e.g. the success and productivity of the relationship between support manager and IT manager, than that of the individual technicians.

11.3 Board-level priorities

To complete the picture, we must consider which of the board's priorities are impacted here. The first of these will probably be financial, typically *profit contribution*. User support may well not be in a position to make a direct profit, but is certainly able to influence the productivity of those users who do manufacture the company's profits. Does your support function recognize this role they have? The directors will often themselves be measured by the shareholders on the profit, and thereafter the share dividend they can generate. It is to be expected that they will examine the various corners of the company for weaknesses in that effort.

Another of the board's priorities is compliance with the 'company culture'. Company culture is nothing more than a set of emotions which happen to be fashionable in that locality. All fashion is set by the process of followers falling in behind leaders. Sometimes the culture springs up organically, for example from the personality of a despotic chief executive officer (CEO); other times it is set by rules laid down in the boardroom (I once read a memo from a managing director which effectively described what the company culture was about to become). The board are the ones who are looking for compliance to the company culture, regardless of how it was created; after all, directors make it to those dizzy heights by embodying the 'culture' and being fit to carry it forward.

It is good to see others succeeding – and success breeds success. At board level, this principle continues, probably even more so. The directors want to see that *everybody looks good* – this is one of their priorities. After all, an environment where one is surrounded by people who are seen to be just as competent and committed as oneself is inspiring and motivated, if not healthily competitive. This contributes to the overall productivity of the company.

And one reason the board will look down is to see who is coming up. It is a wise manager who keeps an eye to the future by *watching for the pretenders*. They will be the ones to carry the company and its culture forward. Who in the lower ranks is beginning to exhibit the skills and vision required of the next generation of upper managers? Could it be that talented and well-read individual who is doing such a great job keeping the computers going and the users happy?

Marketing the support department

12.1 Support service, who are you?

When somebody outside your support department looks at it, what do they see? Can they even discern it at all? Some support departments are part of IT as a whole. Some are loose, project-based operations which form into a service to solve a certain problem, then disband. Some are just a group of PC technicians who report, through their team leader, to one of IT's managers. And then some helpdesks purport to be the whole support service, when in fact they only front it. For some companies, support is what the developers do when the telephone interrupts them from their developing.

If the *identity* of the support service is unclear, that lack of clarity will pervade all the dealings the service has with the outside world. It will be unclear who provides the services, ergo who owns the problem. It will be unclear who the overall leader is – which in times of failure or shortcoming invites the perennial cry of 'Who's in charge here?' It will be unclear whether a given service is a support service or not. The deliverables of that service will be similarly vague or lacking in credibility.

Conversely, a strong identity is a sound foundation upon which to build so many more of the essential attributes of a successful user support service. With a strong identity in support, the users can see precisely who is responsible for delivering their service, and with whom they should negotiate improved services. It is obvious who is to blame or who is to be congratulated. Giving support an independent identity gives the ultimate recognition to the problem of lay users forced to use complicated computers.

Once the identity is established, benefits can be extracted within support also. Staff have something to belong to, a purpose shared with others under the same identity. From an identity can grow a group *mission*, and from that specific goals and objectives.

On the other hand, the identity, intended as it is to attract attention, can also attract less desirable forms of attention. One of these is jealousy – some may see the strength of the support identity as attracting more attention than it deserves, and conspire to tarnish that identity or even damage the support department itself. Another problem is colourfully described by the proverb 'the higher the monkey climbs, the more it shows its bottom' – as support's profile increases, then the more public will be its failings, which will be exaggerated by the high profile. This is why the support department with a well-established identity must simultaneously be taking good care of how that identity is perceived and interpreted – the process of managing your *image*.

12.2 A managed image

IT support does not turn out a product – it offers a service, usually in the form of a repackaging of a cluster of items of technical knowledge, arranged in such a way as to offer a solution to the problem as initially described by a lay user. Whether the user's problem was solved can be open to interpretation – for instance, sometimes the only solution is to offer a workaround instead of a solution. When the support services, the technicians' knowledge and the users' problems are all distilled away, we are left with intangibles, in the form of expectations and interpretation.

If we try to meet this intangible demand with a tangible product, for example a service level (e.g. '85 per cent of all queries answered on time') we will not be tackling like with like. Put yourself in the user's shoes – when the user is unhappy with something as vague as, say, 'how she was treated by the helpdesk', to reply that 96 per cent of users are happy with the helpdesk, or that all helpdesk staff go through three hours of user-happiness training a month is to miss the point. You tried to handle an intangible with a tangible. Politicians do it all the time – tell a politician that people are homeless, he will probably tell you how much his party spends on shelters – of course this reply is irrelevant because it does not address your particular question, and worse, it is all the more annoying because of its irrelevance. The only solution is to meet this demand for an intangible with an equally intangible product, namely the image rather than the actuality of the support service.

Start by deciding what you want your customers to think of you, what your message is. You have now taken the first step towards manipulating their opinion of you. Do not jump back in horror at this point – manipulation such as this is not bad, it is necessary. As we have already discovered, out there are possibly hundreds of users, 80 per cent of whom love your support services, 20 per cent of whom dislike them. There will always be this difference in opinion. You cannot please everybody because you do not have infinite resources. These 20 per cent, if their opinions are vociferous, can do a disproportionate amount of damage to your reputation and the confidence held in you by the other 80 per cent. For the good of the company, for the productivity of the users, for the morale of your staff, this cannot be allowed to happen. So you must make sure you have a defence against it, and that is to ensure that all your customers, and particularly the 80 per cent who are the potential victims of bad news put out by the other 20 per cent, have a balanced view of the services you provide. Therefore it is your bound duty to influence the opinions of your users and customers over and above the opinions they would arrive at on their own, because if you do not, somebody else will, probably without your best interests at heart.

Next, decide how that image would be most easily digested by the users. What will establish the identity and the image of the department? What is needed is a simple and ubiquitous image, easy to grasp and retain in the memory, which precisely embodies what the users need to know about the support department and the services and value it delivers. The identity must stand alone – not as a part of anything else, even though support may in fact only exist as a part of something else. (Note: support does not have to be autonomous, but its identity must be.) The users must be enabled to freely associate support and the benefits it delivers. Get a logo. Make sure it appears on everything that leaves your department. Get a house style for printed documents and make sure everything complies with it – newsletters, reports, memoranda, visit reports, and so on. Make sure the support department is involved in and has a representative at any new computing or business initiative within the company; have a positive, departmental opinion how this new project will affect the user community and ensure it is communicated.

Then, how are you going to get that message across? Essentially, this is the same exercise as we covered in Chapter 9. It means a consistent policy of proactive contact with the customer base, where that contact delivers something the customers both want and need. It means plenty of the written word and the ruthless exploitation of the communications channel your newsletter should monopolize. It means constant self-publicity, so that your positive image is always at least twice as big as any negative rumour which could start, because the very size of that image will nip the malicious rumours in the bud and make discussion topics of the more useful ones.

Encourage the support staff to get deeper into their technical specializations. Encourage them each to publicly champion a user-beneficial cause within the company, like improved word-processing software, better training for spreadsheet users, better destruction-testing for new software applications.

12.3 To strive for perfection?

Perfection is an admirable, but intrinsically impossible goal, principally because perfection is an absolute. There are no grades of perfection – something either is perfect or it isn't. Worse still, we abuse the term: if perfection is an absolute, then it is objective – yet we use it subjectively. What is 'perfect' service in one user's eyes may be deeply flawed in another's. First, you will never be able to satisfy the demand placed upon you because the better your services get, the more people will want them and therefore the harder it will be to satisfy the demand; the better you get, the more people you must disappoint. Second, there will always be those who expect more from your services than you are prepared to give. No matter how much you publish your service levels and meet them, you will still get complaints from individuals. Your quality will be flawed. Third, your turnaround will be flawed, because you cannot do everything instantly. This means there will be a queue, which will have to be prioritized, and so some users' queries will have to wait.

Perfection means doing the right thing, correctly, at the right time, every time, for everybody. Clearly impossible, and a waste of time and effort aiming for. Business may be rational, but business is made up of people and people are irrational and imperfect. You cannot be expected to be any better than the best of them. So do not strive for perfection: strive to achieve the highest of your priorities and use your image as one of your tools to minimize the impact of your imperfections.

12.4 Marketing and support

But is all this relevant in the support department? After all, most support groups do not charge for what they do. They are needed and, amazingly, free; what is more they rarely have any serious competition. Support's customers use us because they have to, they have no choice; we do not need to differentiate ourselves because there is no competition which even vaguely resembles us or our services; and we cost nothing, so we can generate infinite demand. So who needs customer service? I heard a technician describe the irrelevance of customer service to his job by stating that he and his clients both worked for the same company – therefore it was pointless to do anything special for them.

Marketing is the science of attracting customers, by the study of their needs and describing and arranging products to give the easily digestible and distinct impression of matching those needs. By using it, one manipulates the market to extract the maximum custom from it. It is inherently an active pursuit. However, support organizations are often more passive in their relationships with customers. Support often sees itself more like the market stallholder, for whom 'marketing' is largely irrelevant; support shall have continuous trade simply because it exists and is available. Use of the helpdesk, for example, is on impulse generated by perceived or actual need, and the cost is so low that there is minimal risk. Put simply, in some companies, support does not have to go looking for customers; the path to the helpdesk is a well-trodden one.

Is all that still true? Most support managers would appear to think so, and with some justification, especially in those companies where they really do hold a monopoly and there really is no competition. But the best Support can hope to have a monopoly on is the particular service they provide. Where the competition comes from is not in the service, but in what the service delivers. In other words, the support team may have the monopoly on providing a helpdesk, but not on providing the knowledge that the helpdesk is essentially only one means of providing.

I'll leave the last word on customer service to the great Noël Coward:

> The customer's always right, my boys
> The customer's always right
> The son-of-a-bitch
> Is probably rich,
> So smile with all your might.

Part Three

Service management

13

Analysing service needs

The complexity of deciding who gets what service is mind-boggling. The number of permutations can be calculated fairly straightforwardly – simply multiply the number of users by the number of different products they will need supporting, multiplied by the number of levels to which they may wish to be supported, and map that on to the number of technical staff you have, multiplied by the number of products each one of them knows, multiplied by the number of levels to which they may know those products. No wonder so many support managers never even broach this question, preferring to let the service find its own natural level and deal with complaints as and when they crop up.

A recurring theme in support and the key to so many of its problems is *lack of control*. A support service in control of its own workload will invariably suffer far fewer problems and bask in far greater client respect than will another support department of similar size and functionality which chooses to deal with everything reactively. One of the first steps in taking control is to decide what services to offer to whom – and making that decision must also involve eliminating some services and/or clients.

Is this possible? Can we actually say to some clients that they will not receive a service or a service they think they need? Of course we can, and indeed we must. Look at this objectively – we already know that we have a finite resource, and in some companies that resource continues to be constricted, in the vain hope that we can continue to do more with less indefinitely. So there are already decisions being made about what services are least important and can be left to drift. True, these decisions may not have been made and communicated formally, but the least important services have indeed been able to find their own level. As support service designers, we should be playing a more active part, and at least recognizing these less-important demands before we consign them to the bottom of the priority pile.

Support resources are notoriously finite – and when they are occupied doing something, *ipso facto* they must be *not* doing something else. Therefore, we have already chosen to ignore or de-emphasize something. I am just encouraging you to be aware of having made that choice. That simple function of making that decision in full knowledge will separate you from so many support 'managers' who frankly fear making that decision just as much as they fear not making it.

> **You can always tell successful support managers from the strength of their handshake – a strength developed from consistently taking the bull by the horns.**

13.1 Where to start?

Given the complexity of services that could be provided, where should we begin to design our service portfolio? Ideally of course with a study of what the business actually needs – note the emphasis on the business, not the company. The needs of the business should be definable by objective study; but the support needs of the company will be so much more nebulous. The company is made up of people, and consequently the first thing we will have to do will be to separate the needs from the wants. So we start by analysing what kind of support the business needs. This takes a kind of objectivity, which will demand an inherent understanding of what the business is trying to achieve. This analysis will probably best be carried out, initially, without involving users or any other potential customer. If others are involved, the objectivity may suffer, as they will naturally try to get their priorities into your thinking. Take interviews with directors with a pinch of salt. Their position on the board may suggest that they epitomize the business and its needs, but it is just as likely that they will be fighting for their division, their budget, their principles, their pension, or their next promotion as the rest of us. And you are not yet designing services to improve any of those ancillary issues (although later on you may choose to).

The business processes will have dictated the existence and importance of certain functions – these will usually be carried out by definable groups of users. Isolate and identify these users and note the sort of services they need. For example, the purchase ledger department may just have the most vocal users or the biggest and most expensive computers, but that alone does not make them a key business function – since when was spending money more important than earning it? Better to concentrate on the sales ledger department first. Another example may be in the sales teams – where one salesman whose figures are down may be complaining bitterly that if he had better IT support he would perform better – he may have a point, but that still does not make him more important than the other sales staff who are already bringing in the big sales, and to whom you will clearly give a higher priority. The computerized production lines may be highly automated, and human inter-action may be minimal – but if those computers fail or misbehave, production falters, and in your business that could be a disaster. Even if there are outside contractors who look after those specialized machines, perhaps the business needs you to get involved. Your study of the business is causing you to prioritize certain clients; for more on prioritizing clients, see Chapter 8.

13.2 Who will fix their own problems?

When designing support services, take into account that some members of the user community will choose to support themselves. On the one hand, these may be the hackers and tinkerers, who far from assisting the support effort are likely to increase it by changing items that they have no authority to, or by hiding significant changes they make. On the other hand, there is a certain type of user who will choose perhaps on occasion to support his own technical needs rather than use the support services; and they tend to be found at a certain level in the organization. Either way, the service designer should be aware of who and where the do-it-yourselfers are, as the level of service and resources to be committed to them will depend on their style of approaching a solution to their computer problems.

Those at the top tend not to fix their own problems. They will delegate the fix, and may even delegate reporting the problem – and this is all very well unless, by implication, they are also delegating even discovering the existence of the problem. Senior staff may feel they do not have time to fix the problem themselves; they may have lost the skills they once had which would have enabled them to fix it; they may not wish to tread upon ground where they feel unsure; they may consider the task too menial or practical (sadly too often the case in western hierarchies); they may see the problem as an opportunity to stretch and grow a staff member; they may wish to demonstrate their power by calling somebody in to fix it.

Those at the bottom of the organization are also likely to delegate the fix, often out of respect for corporate structure because that is how the company works or is demarcated; they may feel they do not have the time to invest in fixing the problem themselves, even if that would mean a faster fix than user support could achieve; they may feel they have nothing to gain from learning how to fix the problem themselves because they have no anticipated future other than one which looks exactly like the present; or because they do not have the self-confidence to anticipate a fix.

The middle layers are those most likely to harbour the do-it-yourselfers. This is where most of the self-starters and enablers are. Often ambitious and practical by nature, perhaps flush with regular success in other aspects of their jobs, they may conclude they do not have the time to wait for a solution, and have enough hierarchical power to attempt a fix themselves without fear of incurring the displeasure of a supervisor. They are probably eager for new knowledge and keen to demonstrate their competence and commitment to those around them. This can produce a paradoxical situation for the support manager – where the concept of *job ownership* is so important in the support department, ownership among the users may hinder the efforts of support to look after them.

The remote offices will often be self-sufficient. Their distance from corporate headquarters means that in general, they do not get into the habit of relying on central services. Where head office staff have to go to the facilities department to requisition paper clips, the remote office staff will nip across the high street to the stationer's shop. Where head office staff call the helpdesk, in the remote office there is a user who has become the local expert because he has an interest and has built a local area network in his back bedroom. Remote offices are used to being out on a limb – so they learn to survive by their self-reliance.

Where the tendency to 'have a go at fixing it myself' differs at various points of the company, whichever way it swings it can be exploited to the benefit of both support and the users. Let those at the top delegate as much of the support job as possible – this is how support can prove its worth directly to the very highest company echelons. At the bottom is where mass opinion is created: let support get a good reputation for taking problem ownership here and the news will spread like wildfire through the most populous layers of the company. In the middle, where the bright-eyed ambitious types wish to demonstrate their ability, engage their assistance and compe-tence to reduce the support workload, encourage them to give their example to those around and below them. The company will be rewarded with a more capable and self-sufficient userbase, solving the simpler problems themselves and leaving user support free to stretch the IT investment to assist in new, more advanced areas.

The only question against all this self-reliance – and it is a big one – is what it costs the company in terms of corporate productivity lost by all those users spending time being surrogate or alternative helpdesks. I look at the cost of that lost productivity in the chapter on cost justification. From there, you can calculate the scale to which it actually makes financial sense to let the users handle their own IT support issues.

13.3 What level of support?

There are several services a user support organization can provide. These may include such things as usage reports, product evaluations, network maintenance, computer acquisi-tion, and so on. But the service for which user support is best known by far is the several levels at which they translate their computing and technical expertise into answers for the user community. This is the support department's main product. It is what users most expect of us, and it is what we are best known for. I call it *knowledge support*.

The level of knowledge support we offer will depend to a large extent on several factors, including who we offer it to, what product or range of products are to be supported and what resource we have available. These issues notwithstanding, there are probably six levels of support we can offer. These are described below. Consider each of your customers and the products they use, and decide which level would be most appropriate for each combination.

13.3.1 Knowledge support level 1: no support

User, you're on your own.

At this level, computer support as a service provider is not involved at all in the relationship between users and their computers. This means users will probably also have a direct relationship with the computer supplier, and will certainly have to get support from somewhere, even if it is from within their own resources. Some users will choose this, notably those who use specialized applications, or perhaps source their computers from outside the company's 'recommended suppliers' or 'supported products' lists. It could be argued that as this means that no support is provided, then we as support service designers do not need to take it into account. However, it is precisely because this service level is an option for both service designer and customer that we have to include it in our list and define precisely what it means and the implications of it.

13.3.2 Knowledge support level 2: pre-sales guidance only

User, you probably need the ABC product from the XYZ corporation.

For the computer equipment supplier (and therefore the external helpdesk) this is the provision of support as a service merely to provide the users with the information they need to be able to choose the product under offer. Cynically, this information, technical though it may purport to be, may equally serve to exclude competitors' products from the decision process where possible. For the internal support service, support at this level may similarly serve to guide potential customers to choosing a product from the 'recommended' list, where they may be considering unproved products. More likely, however, support such as this, provided internally, may well be the only place the user can go for impartial advice prior to selecting a product. Either way, it is entirely and exclusively pre-sales – it makes no offer to support the product after it has been installed. In practice, however, this level rarely exists without some level 3 or level 4 support, no matter how grudgingly supplied, especially where the support is provided by people, as opposed to electronic services.

13.3.3 Knowledge support level 3: product support

Technician, help me, I can't get it to work.

This is the first level where users have a dependency on after-sales support. They may have a number to ring or a card to return to report problems, bugs, or hardware failure. Hardware maintenance falls into this category of support. It is essentially product-oriented and takes no account of what usage a client is making of the product, merely of the fact that they own one. For software problems, this may mean nothing more than the supply of a new copy of the product, using the assumption that the product is faulty. If the product is not faulty, the fault lies with the user's ignorance, the best the user can expect from support provided at this level is a description of how the product has been made to work on another machine or in a 'similar environment'. *Remember the essence of this support is that it is support for the product, not for the user, nor for the usage of the product.* This is also the level of support for return-to-supplier warranty. It has more relevance for commercial support providers than for internal support teams, although that is changing as more and more companies perform their own PC maintenance.

13.3.4 Knowledge support level 4: technical support

Technician, tell me where to find the answer.

Support at this level exists to help the user with product installation and configuration. It will attempt to answer basic technical queries and will attempt to solve problems during a conversation with the user, but it must be stressed that it is not a problem-solving service. The support here will be on a 'try this' level – the user describes a problem, the supporter makes a suggestion as to what the user might try next. This service level assumes the customers will read all documentation and become their own experts in the day-to-day usage of the product.

It is difficult to provide this level of support under some formal control, especially if level 2 support is provided as part of the purchase process – for then the customer finds out who support are and how they are to be contacted. The frequency of user problems is highest when a new product first arrives, and may stem both from installation difficulty as well as new-user finger trouble. That the customer knows who has the knowledge is enough cause for level 4 support to end up being provided by default.

For product suppliers, this can be particularly tricky. They can write off some of the profit against the necessary provision of pre-sales support – but if the profit is a slender one as it can be in some sectors of the IT industry, they may be unwilling to write off further profit by helping the user install the product as well. Some companies get round this by providing pre-sales support for free, but charging for all post-sales support.

Beyond assistance with new product installation, it is at this level of support where users start to ask questions associated with their use of the product. Such questions crop up when users are faced with a new problem, which they suspect their existing technology can solve, but do not know where to start. This is typical of the type of support needed by first-time users and programmers. The support technician cannot read the manual for clients, but can interpret their needs and refer them to the relevant feature of a product or its documentation.

With the exception of hardware maintenance, where an engineer may visit to repair an obviously broken machine, this level of knowledge support and all others below it can be provided remotely, over the telephone. It can also be supplied electron-ically, by question-and-answer technical databases or services which can fax back a document requested by dialling certain numbers on a tone-dial telephone. However, this ability to remain remote is eroded at level 5.

13.3.5 Knowledge support level 5: problem-solving

Technician, solve this one for me.

This is the level at which commercial support providers and internal support organizations begin to differ most starkly. This is the point at which the user can abdicate all responsibil-ity for the problem and submit it to the support service, who take it upon themselves to research the most appropriate solution and implement it. It is less common among the commercial companies for two reasons: first, it implies an intimate understanding of precisely how the users use the product, information that is often simply unavailable to IT suppliers; and second, as it is highly labour-intensive, it is very expensive to do. So expensive in fact, that until the explosion in the late 1980s and early 1990s of outsourcing as a way of providing user support, most IT companies actively de-emphasized this type of support.

To provide this level of knowledge support, there must be a function in place to take user queries, a means of escalation and an expectation of the provision of a solution. In practical terms, this means there must be a helpdesk and a resolver group. The latter will be highly trained and probably mobile, visiting users at their desks to diagnose and solve the problem. All that visiting takes time, and all that ability to diagnose and implement the solution without confusing or intimidating the user takes training and good communications skills – so the people who can do it do not come cheap. That said, this is by far the most popular type of support for corporate computer users, precisely because it is invariably the most appropriate and flexible.

In essence, however, this is still support for what already exists. There is no creation going on here. This type of support will still be a matter of making the computer do what it already can do, by invoking more specialized knowledge and skills than the user has to hand. To make the computer do something new, we have to go to level 6.

13.3.6 Knowledge support level 6: application usage support

Technical specialist, help me invent this.

At this level, users need help not just with the configuration of their computer as a tool, but with the very business output they are trying to extract from the computer. The questions put to user support are not about the computer, but about their work and how the computer may help with it. It is similar to level 5 in that it expects the computer to change to meet the problem, but at level 5 it is a computer expert who is needed. Here at level 6, it is a business expert with computer expertise whose skills will be of use.

The typical output from a query at level 6 will be a tailor-made computer or software system, or perhaps a re-engineering of the business function around what the computer is capable of. Like level 1, this is the extreme that so few will provide in reality. However, queries such as these will become more frequent as new technology simultaneously makes more business solutions available and reduces the number of people who can keep up to date with the technology. The response of some organizations for a demand for support at this level has been to promote from the ranks of the support team a new breed of hybrid technicians. Although coming from a technical background, these are essentially business consultants, with the dual ability to understand what the business needs the computer to be able to do, and then go and make it do just that.

13.4 Assistance levels

The support levels given above can be formalized into individual services and marketed to users or groups of users. They can be looked at another way, however. No matter how formal the service levels are, there will always be exceptions. One group of users wants knowledge support level 4, with the exception of that group of desks in the corner, whose occupants are less computer literate and some of whom have only recently joined the company. Oh and let's not forget Derek, who is one of us but he is also an absolute wizard with computers, so he will expect less from you. It is in cases like this where the formalization starts to break down. It may not be appropriate to go through the hassle of renegotiating service levels for these temporary exceptions – a more practical way may well be to leave it to the discretion of the individual technician dealing with the problem or the user. It must be stressed that such discretion should only be exercised under the auspices of whatever formal agreements already exist – so that the fallback can always be the agreed service level.

That said, the technician will probably choose the level of service to offer to these exceptional users from the list shown in Fig. 13.1. It may look as though this chart accounts for every eventuality except *not* being able to answer the question. (After all, it happens.) Not so – to make that assumption is to get the nature of the problem confused with the nature of the support. Some problems cannot be fixed by the support team; it may require the intervention of the manufacturer who only fixes problems in batches, through scheduled releases – and there is nothing support can do about that. Or it may be that the technology to solve the user's problem simply does not yet exist. In which case, the only possible fix is 'I'm sorry, that problem

Level 1	Ignore me
Level 2	Tell me who to ask next
Level 3	Tell me how to fix it myself
Level 4	Show me how to fix it/help me fix it
Level 5	Fix it for me

Figure 13.1
Assistance levels

can't be fixed' – a perfectly acceptable answer. Not only that, but for the purposes of Fig. 13.1, it is a level 3 fix. The assistance level, and for that matter much of support and customer service is about *how* you respond, not *what* you respond. As to the what, out of professionalism, you would probably find a workaround or a way to render the problem irrelevant until technology caught up with the user's need.

13.5 General questions for support service design

- Company-wide questions

  How many users are there?
  How are user-written systems supported?
  How do we acquire computer equipment?
  Who hooks new equipment onto the network?

- User-specific questions

  How many users are there?
  What are they doing – simple or complex?
  How important is their work?
  How urgent is their support need?
  Are their support needs special?
  How well trained are they?
  How well trained do they need to be?
  Are their systems written in-house?
  Do they have their own support people?
  Do they initiate new users or is that our job?

13.6 Transferring knowledge

The less the customers know about the technology they use, the more they will depend on user support services. This fact alone will have an impact on the relationship between the support department and the users. Some people fear high dependence on a supplier, as that puts them in a weak position – it gives the supplier control of the relationship, and the users have to rely on a service they cannot control for their own success at their job. In some cases, this fear can become resentment. This cuts both ways. The support department also depends on the user's use of those services for the very justification of the existence of the support department and all the jobs and careers associated with it. Where this reaches paranoia, both sides can be pulling against one another: where users are demanding more knowledge in order to reduce their dependency, the support staff are jealously retaining that knowledge in order to maintain a justification for their existence.

As indicated by Fig. 13.2, dependency on the support service increases rapidly at knowledge support level 5 and continues to rise thereafter. This is particularly important where that knowledge support is obtained from an external source, say a computer or support supplier. Level 5 is normally where the supplier can legitimately begin to levy charges for the user of the service, and these charges will be bound to reflect the labour-intensive nature of the job of providing knowledge. Figure 13.2 also illustrates how the supplier tends to provide purely product at the lower knowledge levels, tending to purely support at the higher ones. The 'level of support' axis can have further gradations on it to allow for even higher levels of support offered in some outsourcing contracts, but they are outside the intended scope of this book.

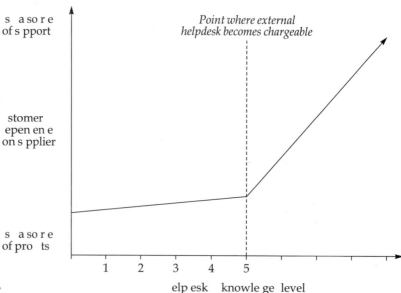

Figure 13.2
Increasing customer
dependence on IT supplier

13.7 I haven't time for all this!

If you balk at the thought of all this analysis, you are not alone. Few support organizations are truly in a position to start with a clean sheet of paper. They usually already have a staffed department, defined users with obvious or suspected expectations, a list of outstanding users' problems, a stern command from above to 'sort it out', and the phone ringing off the hook. Does the 'clean sheet' approach work there? Of course it does: in both cases – a greenfield site or an existing workload – there is always scope for objective analysis and careful design of the form the service offerings will take in the future. For the greenfield site, *recruitment* and *resourcing* will be the means to the end; for the existing team, these will be *change* and *adjustment*.

The job of designing new services will always seem harder to the manager of the existing support department, because change to the status quo is naturally harder than building from nothing. First, there is always the risk of upsetting people (more than are already upset with the way things are?). There may be some difficult decisions to be taken, unsavoury functions to perform – like telling workers who have been with you for years that their present skills and motivations will no longer be relevant.

But put it in perspective – better to tell one worker he is irrelevant, than to find the whole department is irrelevant 18 months from now. The cost to the business could be astronomical if the whole support department was found not to be doing its job because it had not changed when change had been necessary.

Of course, I am not suggesting you stop offering the services while you reorganize them. But I am suggesting that you should be always designing your services six months ahead. But if you need to put something in place *right now*, then the next chapter is for you. In particular, take a look at Sarah's experience (Case Study 14.1).

Putting services in place

14.1 The pragmatic approach

If you are a new manager moving into an existing, troubled department and need to make rapid changes, the process of analysis will be much shorter than that described in Chapter 13. There we looked at the ideal world – and reality is rarely ideal. Under such circumstances, you will need to make your quick analysis of business needs in parallel with an examination of what services you can actually provide given the staff and resources you have got right now. And do not ignore the political pressures: these will be very real. There will probably be some people in positions of power who have expectations that you will be a new broom. Those expectations will probably be mirrored by the support staff. Meet those expectations, like the new broom you are, get some sweeping done – not so as you upset everybody with change for the sake of change, but with immediate improvements that many people will happily conclude are not before time. After all, the first thing you will need in a new position will be acceptability. Get that first and half the battle is over. Make the more strategic, lasting changes over time and in a planned fashion.

In a troubled support organization, gather the staff round you and ask them what they think is wrong. You will achieve a lot by doing this. First, you will demonstrate that although you can make change happen, you value their opinions and you recognize that they have more immediate, 'sharp end' knowledge than you have (presume they too will be expecting a new broom – somebody to make the changes they think their previous manager should have made); second, you will get good-quality pointers to where you should be concentrating your efforts; third, you will give everybody a chance to get their complaining done, so that it will not hamper progress later. Write up your understanding and feed it back to them along with what you intend to do about it, giving them an opportunity to make fine-tuning suggestions. All this will put them on your side and will do a lot of good for your image when your staff get asked 'what's your new manager like?' next time they drop by the water-cooler. But you do not have to be a new manager for this to work – this goes for existing managers of troubled helpdesks too.

One of my favourite exercises at this stage is the 'SWOT analysis'. With the help of the support team, write down a list of the helpdesk's Strengths, Weaknesses, Opportunities and Threats. By each finding, write down what you are going to do about it.

It is too easy to look just at the weaknesses and hope that by eradicating them you will arrive at perfection. Your weaknesses are just that – areas where you are weak, and because of that you will find them so much more difficult to remove. For a quicker benefit, take a look at your strengths. Because they are something you are already good at, you should find it relatively easy to get even better.

Another reason the strengths are so important is they are often underestimated by the pressured helpdesk. In my experience, support managers routinely underestimate their popularity with their customers. The fact is that your helpdesk must be stronger than it is weak, otherwise it would not exist – if it were that bad, the company would by now have reorganized it into oblivion.

As for the opportunities and weaknesses – in effect, they are your potential strengths and weaknesses in the future.

Case Study 14.1: Sarah's experience

When Sarah took over the helpdesk, it was in a sorry state. She had come into support from Development, where she had been a project manager. (Sarah is philosophical about this – with all this shrink-wrapped software, who needs projects any more?) Out of six support staff, she had Mick, a supervisor who resented her coming in, believing the job should have been his; Ron, whose hypochondriac absentee-ism verged on the legendary; Susan, who had already handed her notice in, and was there in body if perhaps not in spirit; Sam, rather older than the others, a hardware specialist who had designed his own job; and Tim and Jean, two of the most knowledgeable, overworked computer whizzkids she had ever come across whose desks looked like the aftermath of a hurricane.

She was not sure if she had been put there to change things or to stop her from having to be made redundant. Her boss did not seem to know what he wanted, except an easier time from his peers, whose numerous and highly vocal complaints about support were beginning to turn into threats. Sarah knew that 'created job' or not, she had to achieve something. Her first attitude had been along the lines of 'they put me here against my will, this is their problem not mine'. After a long soul-search, and it must be said, no sympathy for that attitude from her husband, she decided the only thing to do was make the best of it. Like the theme-park employees who clean up behind the tourists, she would do it with a smile, because the smile would be her ticket to something better.

The first thing she did was tell Mick she would achieve nothing without him, and she asked him to write a brief list of the things he would have done had the job gone his way. She called Ron at home (he was off sick at the time), to introduce herself and start her strategy for him. She needed Ron back, she said, because a little bird told her he might have some useful pointers for her. As well as getting him thinking, this told Ron she was not considering his prolonged absences, at least for now, so he did not have to be so much on his guard. She asked Susan to meet her for lunch, a long way offsite, where they could talk freely – after all, Susan had nothing to lose by giving her frank criticisms that other employees might prefer to keep to themselves. The conversations with Sam, Tim and Jean were cursory: Sam was giving nothing away, preferring to protect the niche he had carved for himself. Tim and Jean were too busy, their heads too full of detail and their perspectives too short to be of any long-term use. She knew that in practice these conversations would provide informa-tion she could use in the long term. The reason she held them before doing anything else was to get the staff on her side. It could have been disastrous if she had come in and started changing her people's working lives without consulting them.

Two weeks before taking over the job, she had started to ask around, to get impressions of the helpdesk's image in the company as a whole. She did not emphasize that she was moving to the helpdesk – that might cause her interviewees to complain rather than inform. By the time she got to her new desk, she knew what she had to do. She realized there must be more success than failure in support, or it would have been reorganized out of existence by now. What she had to do was find that success and focus attention on it. Then she had to pick the helpdesk's dirtiest linen and wash it in public. For both these tactics, the key was going to be communication.

She spent a couple of days watching the way the department worked, identifying its main services and taking measurements of its output. With what she found, she created an alternative picture of success which the company knew too little about. She took that picture straight to her boss, so he had a more positive view of the support department with which to defend himself against his critics. It would give her boss a reason to get on her side, and to get others on it too. She also fed the results of this back to the support staff. The effect on morale and productivity was nothing short of dramatic. By the time Ron got back from his latest illness, the place was humming – and Sarah was ready for him with a nice juicy project for him to get his teeth into. Ron was going to improve the department newsletter – the communications medium she needed. He had to get out a four-pager in less than a week. He complained, but he made it. The department did not miss him from the support effort, and now Sarah had something she could measure him on.

The main complaint of the users had been about the reliability of response to their queries. It had shown up in a number of ways: some thought that from a response point of view, reporting a problem was akin to tossing it into the Grand Canyon; others simply complained about not knowing when or how a problem would be dealt with. When Sarah looked at the way problems were handled, she found that 80 per cent of the queries were ultimately dealt with by the highly overworked Tim and Jean. She gave Mick the job of watching every incoming query to see that there was at least a response to it within an hour, and if not, to ask the technician why not. She left it to Mick to figure out, as he did, that he would have to start to take more control of Sam too, as just watching Tim and Jean quite rightly showed they could not do it all themselves.

The result was a turnaround in the department's performance and their image within around three weeks. Over the longer term, Sarah began to implement the ideas she had heard in her earlier conversations with her staff and the users. The support staff were all the more willing now to accept these incoming changes; they recognized the ideas as their own, with a bit of managerial improvement here and there, and they had clear evidence that Sarah could deliver the goods. Late that summer, on a Florida beach, Sarah congratulated herself on a job well done and a holiday well deserved.

> **If the users don't use the support services, the company fails to benefit from the improved productivity that IT delivers through good user support.**
> **Whatever it takes, *get your services used*.**

14.2 Designing a service

To design a service, first free your mind. There are lots of things making sure that the service you design will be pretty close to the services that preceded it. You will have a corporate culture to adhere to, a set of staff with a certain range of skills and knowledge, some known or rumoured expectations for new services, a few directors' ambitions to satisfy, perhaps a conscious or subconscious fear of rocking the boat. You may have reason to believe that your company may be too conservative to recognize and accept true innovation. When plotting the future, it is too easy to get stuck in a way of thinking, to shy away from certain reaches of change for fear of failing to include some recognizable and reassuring element of the present. This is just fear of change, writ more subtly, and although fear of change can sometimes be an appropriate check on going too wild, often it can get in the way of seeing what is possible, limiting you merely to seeing what is acceptable. It is compounded by the fact that you will have to live with the result.

It is the 'living with the result' that can be so terrifying. There's the rub, and a big one it is too. Suppose the users hate it? I will be a laughing-stock or worse. Suppose the staff hate it? It will take me ages to rebuild their confidence in me. Suppose I am wrong? What will that do for my self-confidence (which is clearly already pretty shaky or you would not be agonizing like this)?

Change the angle. Imagine you did not have to live with it. You have been retained for a NASA mission to map the surface of Jupiter. You fly out the day after the new service goes live, so no matter what you put in place, it will be somebody else's problem. I know one individual who was so convinced by this technique, he went so far as to set himself up with somewhere else to go, looking for another job while designing the new service structure – in the end, he did not have to leave, but while he thought departure might be the only way out, his mind and powers of innovation got free rein. There was no longer any instinct to preserve the status quo.

What the technique depends on for its success is your true professionalism as a support manager. It assumes that you will do what is in the company's interests, even though that may conflict with your personal interests and even though you may have to live with the results. You will not usually leave the company in the end. But the opportunity to leave through the result of your actions will make more innovation possible.

14.3 Stand back . . .

Sometimes, it is impossible to free your mind while staring at the walls of your own office while delving into the experience you already have. You are a designer of user support services. Knowing that will enable you to see the trees. To see the forest, you have got to stand some way back. Sometimes it means that you have to stand so far back that you cannot even see IT from here. To get ideas for IT services, do not just look at an IT function – look at a service function, any service function. Work out what is happening and what lessons you can extract from it. Because you will understand the details less than you do in IT, you will be more able to focus on the processes and results, the more abstract side.

I tend to use the insurance business for a lot of my ideas; it is an ideal model for IT support services. It has a lot of the same problems, but are just different enough, and it sells a product that is highly technical and not everybody understands, but everybody needs, just like IT. Blurring the truth about insurance products are several layers of salespeople with their own agendas, just like IT. The benefits are built on hype and fear rather than plain facts, just like IT. In Section 14.11, when we look at ownership, I'll use an example from the insurance industry.

14.4 Invent what is needed, not what is possible

Ask yourself some pertinent questions about the service you are about to produce. Are you doing it just because you can? Be honest. A common mistake among support managers is to offer a service, or expertise in a certain product, simply because that expertise is represented among the support staff. It is so tempting, particularly for the new support manager inheriting an existing regime, to continue to provide the service with the existing staff and skills profile. (After all, one of the hardest jobs a manager ever has to do is let somebody go, no matter how useless they are.) Not only is this potentially wasteful – in that it risks creating expense and overheads the company may not need – worse, it encourages blindness to what the clients may need. By concentrating on what you can do, you may become unjustly satisfied with that offering and then by default or design, miss what you should be doing.

14.5 Not just a service, but a 'service product'

Never take too simple a view of any service you produce – if you fail to take the service seriously enough, it will have little credibility and will be abused or underestimated. Either way, you risk failing with that service. Your most appropriate attitude is to see the service as a product and the support department as a factory.

Your service has all the features of a product: it takes raw materials to produce (time, knowledge, training, experience), needs a process to manufacture it (client query is reworked in the support office and your people's heads to produce an answer), has a cost associated with its production (salaries and overheads), and a value greater than that of the materials and process that went into it (increased or enabled user productivity). Cost, raw materials, process, added value – four key features of a production line, the main one of which is probably the value produced by the end of the line.

Too many support managers fail to exploit their position by missing that small intellectual hop, and failing to see the production line in front of them. (It is not surprising, after all they are IT people, not production managers. But we will be exploring this concept in a lot more depth in Part Four.)

14.6 Service variety

Another common mistake is to underestimate the number of services the department provides. This in turn leads to under-estimating the value to the clients as well as the latent demand for support services. Worse, it causes the support manager and staff to neglect service offerings simply because they do not recognize them as such – so they under-resource them or fail to perform them altogether. Stop reading right now and write down a list of all the services you provide.

I said STOP READING.

All too often, the list gets exhausted around here:

1 Answer clients' questions.
2 Install desktop computers.
3 User training.

So as not to underestimate our value, the net really needs to be cast a little wider than that. There is potential to make a service out of anything we do for anybody else. Absolutely anything, whether it is regular or once in a while, important or trivial, has value in itself or is done as a consequence of another activity. For example, if we have to tell our senior managers of the work we do, that report is a service. If we have to keep manuals so we can look up the answers to questions, there is a service in our maintenance of the company IT library. If a question turns out to need a hardware repair, our management of that external resource (the repair mechanic) is a service.

We should never consider as one service what may be several. For example, we take questions from our clients. That is one service. Some support organizations actually stop there – I know of a couple of computer retail chains who will take a question from one of their clients, and if they cannot give a definitive answer right there and then, tough luck – the most you can expect is a suggestion about what you should try next. The fact that your support service probably researches questions it cannot answer until it finds a solution, that 'problem resolution' is a service. (A useful thing to take into account if your company ever starts to compare the cost of your support service with external ones – you would not want to be underestimated in those circumstances, because the company would suffer.)

With closer analysis, a more accurate service list would typically look like the one below:

1 Helpdesk – takes client questions, attempts to answer on the spot, makes further suggestions.
2 Problem resolution – problems are researched and passed to experts until solution is found.
3 Management of external resources – control repair technicians and external solutions providers on users' behalf.
4 Emergency taskforce – support team maintains a resource which can move very rapidly to control and deal with an IT emergency.
5 Ad hoc training – clients having difficulty can speak to a technical expert who will guide them through the application, either over the phone or at the user's desk.
6 Desktop computer installation – support technician will install the machine, ensuring it all works, applications recognize printers, and so on.
7 Network connection – support team will connect a desktop computer to the company network, test the connection, provide access to remote computer services and applications, provide an electronic mail address and computer-to-computer file transfer facilities.
8 Network backups – all information stored on the network backed up every night.
9 Data library – Any file once stored on the network will be kept in our tape library for a period of five years, and will be restored to the network on request.
10 User acquaintance – new users coming to the company will be given a brief 'get you started' introduction to the company's computer systems.
11 Computer consultancy – a user with a business need can contact the helpdesk for advice on the best computer hardware or software to meet that need.
12 Product evaluations – the support team is constantly examining products to see which would best suit the needs of the organization overall. (I acknowledge that in some companies, this service is often provided by another group, such as 'office automation' or 'IT strategy' – under such circumstances, the support service here might be 'advice to Office Automation Group on supportability of new IT products'.)
13 Maintain IT library (lending/reference).

14 Reports on usage of support services to IT management.

15 Reports on commonality of IT questions to IT training section so they can see what training is needed where.

16 Monthly user bulletin (and add as separate services the several other communications media recommended in Part Two).

Or whatever services your support organization provides. Other common ones are telephone network management, disaster preparation and recovery, software development, program maintenance. Some also act as the company library and general information desk. Some do procurement. Some are the IT department's administrators or change managers. One helpdesk manager echoed the experiences of many, when she described to me how when her company switchboard gets a request they do not understand from outside, their first instinct is to put the caller through to the helpdesk. 'We're listed in the company telephone directory as "Helpdesk" – it's not uncommon for people to think we can help with anything, not just computers. The fact is, we usually can.'

There are two main reasons for producing this service portfolio. The first is quite simple – if you don't appreciate the scope and variety of services you produce, how do you expect your customers to do so? In my consultancy engagements, I often interview the helpdesk's customers, including the question 'What services do you get from the helpdesk at the moment?' Routinely, the only answer I get is 'I can phone them up if I get a computer problem.' No wonder that helpdesks feel unappreciated, when neither they nor their customers have a grasp of the scale of benefits the helpdesk produces.

The other reason is to do with resource allocation. Most helpdesks decide their staffing levels reactively. They get busier, so after a struggle with the finance director, they get more staff. But they don't actually know what they are busy doing. They have people taking calls and solving problems – oh, and by the way, there's a bunch of other stuff they do, like installations, purchasing, configuration, testing, training, etc. etc. But relatively few helpdesks have even listed these other services, let alone gone any way towards examining how many people are needed to provide them properly.

14.7 Service identity

By listing the services out in this way, we have turned our focus away from the department as one supporting entity and onto each of our individual services. This is tremendously important. First, it gives your clients a true opportunity to choose which services they want and which they do not. That has to be better from a resourcing point of view than employing an army of people to give everybody everything. Second, the clients and the company get several reasons for appreciating you instead of just one – I have lost count of the number of users who tell me that 'the fact that they are there' is the most important feature of their company helpdesk. Third, your manager and the company get something to measure you by: the provision of all these services.

What has happened is that we have given each of the services an identity: the essence of visibility and the most important feature for anything that requires to be recognized. It is not enough to say 'we answer questions' – that is too vague, nobody can relate to it. It is infinitely better to say 'we offer a helpdesk'. The same goes for all the other services you offer – more so because they are harder to recognize. This is because most people know what a helpdesk is, but they may not be so clear on what 'network management' is.

If any one of your services does not have a distinct and credible identity, it will be so much harder for potential clients for that service to recognize it among all the other marketing hubbub they are forced to digest. If they cannot recognize it, they will be less able to take advantage of it. If they cannot take advantage of the service product, it may never realize the company benefits it was invented to produce.

Identity has another importance. I'm a Manchester lad by birth, so a tendency to follow the fortunes of Manchester United Football Club is almost in the blood (with due apologies to Manchester City Football Club, but hey, I was born within walking distance of United's ground). One Saturday while I was queuing outside Old Trafford (back when you could still get in without a season ticket), I was struck by the number of fans wearing the familiar red shirt. They were adherents not just of the club, but of that identity. Manchester United has a reputation for excellence – and people want to be part of that. Take a lesson from United. Get a strong identity for your helpdesk, one that your people will want to belong to, one that they will be loath to damage by performing to any standard less than excellence.

14.8 Value

An important concept in any commercial arrangement, *value* is all too often ignored in the support relationship. However, if we are to see our services as products we produce and users as clients, then the value of the service to the client is worthy of some consideration. Respect for an entity diminishes along with its perceived value. Often, IT support services are perceived by the users to be 'free'; except in companies where cross-charging is used, the user sees no cost in using the support services. And where there is no cost, so is the value that much harder to identify. Of all the trinkets that have dropped out of your Christmas crackers, how many do you still have? They cost so little, ergo they are worth so little. In Part Four, when we study controlling demand, we will take a deeper look at how you can manipulate the cost of support services. For now, suffice to say that if you can increase the cost of using the support service, then its value will rise.

The cheaper, more common or more easily obtainable something is, the less respect it gets. Your clients need to be able to respect your service, or else they will lose confidence in it. Anything which causes your users to lessen their use of your services should bring concern, because if the users do not use the support, the company fails to benefit from the improved productivity that IT delivers through good user support. Establishing the identity of the service is a prerequisite for getting acknowledgement of the value of that service.

Value is also important when considering the support 'production line'. Every service you produce goes through a number of processes within your department, to bring that service closer to something the user can use. Each one of those processes must add some value to that item of work-in-progress. It is that very added value that makes us able to decide whether a process has any point or not. It is that value which we add to a user's request for help which justifies our very existence. If we do not add value, in effect we extract it, because all uncompleted work in the support department is costing somebody money, at least in terms of lost productivity. When designing a service, or the methods which produce that service, always ask where the value is and who benefits from that value. If you are not adding more value than you consume, your support service is a waste.

14.9 Service deliverables

One of the difficulties with getting recognition for a service is the very intangibility of 'service'. This intangibility impedes our efforts to impose an identity, to get our customers to recognize value, indeed even to understand why the service exists at all. The benefit to the customer is not clear. Often, the reason for this confusion is that the deliverable has not been clearly described. What is needed is a change of focus – not to look at the process of providing the service but at the end result. In real terms, this might be to describe a helpdesk service not as a telephone conversation between user and adviser, but as a solution to the user's problem.

When designing any service, always make sure the deliverable is clear. And when subsequently describing that service, do not just tell your customers what the service will look like – tell them what the end result, the benefit, the deliverable will look like. Your overriding concern must always be not what you are going to do, but what you are going to have produced. Remember your customers are always looking to see what they get out of the deal.

14.10 Service production methods

How are you going to deliver this service? What methods need to be put in place? Will these be new methods, or will the service roll smoothly off the production line you already have? The manufacture of any product or service is achieved by the action of a process (say, 'problem diagnosis') on a raw material (say, 'a technician's knowledge'). There has to be a method of control, to make sure all this happens properly. The provision of that control is an overhead. The designer of any service must take this overhead into account. The means of controlling the production of the service when a client asks for it must be in place before the client asks for it. There is no point in offering a service for which there is no method of producing that service. Putting a service into place without having also designed the production methods risks chaos and confusion in the support department when all of a sudden a client takes you up on your offer.

How will you know whether you are succeeding or failing to deliver the service to satisfactory standards? You cannot just wait for the client to complain, after that it is too late. Instead, the production process must have internal targets. It is not enough to have an external target – 'we solved 95 per cent of queries the same day' – because that is after the fact. How will you know while you are doing the work whether you will achieve target or not? Monitor the process to interim targets so you know the work in progress is on course.

14.11 Ownership

Who owns the service? Without ownership, without the responsibility for the production of the service vested in an identifiable individual, it is unlikely that high production standards will be maintained. Ownership is crucial. As I write this, I am locked in combat with a life assurance company, whose grasp of the concept of ownership is suspect. (This book will age, but I'm sure problems with ownership in insurance companies will outlive us all.) The problem is that no single member of that company owns my relationship with them. One chap looks after the domestic contents insurance, another for the buildings insurance. Between them they cannot decide whether one of my house features is a 'content' or a 'fixture' item. The ownership problem is entirely of their making and steadfastly refuses to be solved because nobody owns the overall problem. Several individual departments own a piece of it, but that 'ownership' amounts to no more than each of those individuals enacting their own little process, supporting their own isolated product, unable to change the fact that the entire system of processes is at fault. Until somebody in that company acknowledges that fact, the problem, and my utter lack of confidence in the service provider, will both endure unabated. Think about it: I am the user – they offer a highly technical and necessary service. If they do not know what they are doing, what hope is there for me? The lesson is get the ownership right. And that ownership must extend to being able to redesign the service should it prove to be failing.

Ownership is not the same as responsibility. The helpdesk may be structurally responsible or legally accountable for getting the problem solved, but the ownership must be taken by a warm human being – which means that although the helpdesk is answerable for the service level associated with a particular enquiry, if that enquiry requires that the top of the computer be removed, the ownership must be transferred to and accepted by a technician with a screwdriver in his hand.

14.12 Blanket, ad hoc or premium service?

In many support departments I visit, when, in trying to define the service portfolio I ask the question 'who gets what?', the most common answer is 'everybody gets everything'. This concerns me greatly. Musicians, entertainers, and politicians have all had to learn the hard way that you cannot be all things to all men, and it is a lesson that support managers need to take on board too.

When it is found that the services are much more diverse than just answering the telephone (see Section 14.6) – and that most support departments offer many more services than they have staff – then a scattergun approach like this is dangerous. It could of course stem from a genuine desire to offer the whole company as much service and benefit as possible. If this is the case, it is misguided. It will have precisely the opposite effect. By offering the services in such an unfocused fashion, the risk (and all too often the fact) is that those clients with a real need can at best get a service of diluted quality – a service weakened by the support department's insistence on offering it willy-nilly to other customers who frankly do not need it. Furthermore, this generalization of service is a way of creating more work than you can handle – and as soon as you do that, you risk not being able to service at all some important needs.

I think this scattergun approach stems from a misinterpretation within the support department of the value of its own services (see Section 14.8). Get the focus back. Do not offer every service to everybody. Your clients have to earn that service by their very real need for it. Even more so if you are not going to charge them for it. Show the clients you value the service, so that they may take your example. (But do not refuse to service them just for the sake of it, see Section 14.13.)

Some of the services will have to be 'blanket' services – offered to and taken up by every computer user in the company. PC installation is clearly such a service; so too the helpdesk, but do not take even that for granted – some departments may run their own helpdesks, only needing access to your problem resolvers.

Other users may require occasional services, which do not fit into your 'blanket' offering. For instance, the finance department which always stays until midnight at the end of every fiscal period so as to complete its accounts: they need access to the computers, rapid turnaround of technical queries, redundant equipment in case of failure – but only four Friday nights a year. On those four nights, they are the most expectant, demanding users you could ever expect to meet. The rest of the year they are pussycats, making routine enquiries at a routine level of demand. This provision of extra resources for those four nights is an ad hoc service. You may discover a need for these by getting a telephone call from the user. But my experience is that more often, users who need specialist, short-term services such as this tend to provide them from within their own ranks, muddling through and hoping the worst does not befall them.

The support manager has to have her ear to the ground to identify and offer to service these needs, but service them she should – after all, she has the best staff for the job, and users should use, not support.

Still other users may find your blanket services have too low a service level. The services themselves look OK, it is just the service level they are worried about. For example, the resolvers may undertake to respond to all queries within one hour, and for most of the company, that is more than adequate. But say your company is a television station and the computer which maintains the videotape library suddenly fails. Unless you want a couple of million blank TV screens and advertisers pulling their investments, you had better be able to react to that instantly. Another example: your free, overworked helpdesk is so popular that most callers get the engaged tone – but there are some users out there who really need to be able to get through first time, every time. These are examples of *premium services*. Part of their value is intrinsic to their exclusivity, the higher service level which separates them from the mass market.

The benefits of structured services such as these can be immense. By separating the services out, you can prioritize them against one another much more easily. The services have a clearer identity which makes them easier for the clients to take up. You can ensure that those clients who truly are the ones most important to the business are receiving the highest service level. You can use the responsibility for providing certain services or service levels as a staff motivator or recognition tool. Having services which need defining in this way gives you good cause to keep in contact with your clients to ensure they are getting the best from your service catalogue. You can rotate staff between services to increase the variety (real or perceived) in their job.

14.13 Handling a new service request

So often, staff numbers and resources are at a premium in the support department. This comes from the department's financial status in most user companies as a cost centre, a necessary overhead which eats into the company profits rather than contributing to them. If the support department is approachable enough to earn a request from a user for a service which currently does not exist, the way that request is received is crucial.

A common reaction is to look immediately at the resources, asking oneself 'Do I have the staff to provide this new service?' At this stage, the question is probably pointless. Most support departments are either already overworked or will believe themselves to be: the answer will invariably be a resounding 'No'. When that refusal is passed to the client as starkly as that, there is as much damage done to the support manager's career as is done to the user's support need. Some managers enter into a negotiation at this point, requiring a headcount increase in order to provide the service. This is a perfectly legitimate response, but not at this stage in the negotiation. To respond to a general request for additional service with an immediate 'not unless' may suggest to your peers and customers that you see problems rather than opportunities and prefer a negative to a positive attitude. It may be true that you do not yet have the resources to provide this as an additional service – but to open a negotiation with this stance risks your losing support from the outside; furthermore, it could limit the development of your career.

When any new service request comes in, the support manager's first priority should be to receive it willingly; in fact such requests should be common, and ideally solicited in the support department's publications, e.g. newsletters and bulletins. The request should be taken seriously, and this positive attitude conveyed to the customer making the request. The first consideration should not be whether providing this service is possible, but whether it is desirable; which it probably will be, especially if the user is significant enough. Next, look at this service in the light of all the others you already provide. Is this an opportunity to do something new, which will yield greater benefit to the company than some of the existing services? Can an existing service be de-emphasized to make room for this new one? Is there a newer support team member for whom the responsibility for this new service would be an ideal opportunity for personal growth?

The new service should never be viewed as impossible without new resources – the support manager who holds this view risks getting a reputation for negativism and empire-building. The new service is an opportunity to deliver increased benefit to a user and to the company as a whole, a chance to reduce the drudgery of the support workload by introducing some variety. Only when all the possibilities for positive approach to this request have been exhausted does the time come to consider increasing staff. However, even at this stage, the manager should be looking to see whether he should take on new staff then offer the service, or offer the service and take on new staff to maintain some of the older services.

At the service request stage, one idea is to offer the service immediately, on a small scale, without any other adjustments to the department or its service portfolio. This will at least provide some feedback as to how much new resource the new service is likely to require. It gives the staff a chance to experience providing this new service and to make recommendations for improving the way it is provided. It may even be that the support workload naturally adjusts to accommodate this new requirement; that in the end, no structural changes are needed at all. People like to do new things – give them the chance to try.

As a matter of procedure, always put the demand for a new service through a proper change management process. It may mean that new staff have to be hired, the service level agreement must be redrafted, new financial investment must be sought. These things have to be approved, planned and carried out, and that requires change management.

14.14 Launching a service

When the time comes to launch the service, we have a choice, namely whether to go for a general, specific, or trickle launch. A general launch makes the service available to everybody, and brings with it certain problems. Chief among these problems is sudden, massive demand. You must be ready for this sudden demand. It will be created by the hype which accompanies your launch. Potential customers will be intrigued by the new offering and will want to try it out. They may be looking to see how much of an improvement it is on what went before. The service must be and be seen to be an improvement on its predecessor. The demand will almost certainly tail off once the users have explored the novelty, and will most probably find its own level, where predicting the resource required will be considerably easier.

A launch of a service specific to a certain set of customers would usually require the same type of preparation as a more general one, but clearly not to the same scale. However, one must consider what makes the service so specific. Niche market products, as this would be, have a tendency to be more focused on quality than mass-market ones; so although the burden of initial demand would be less in terms of quantity, here quality is likely to be more of an issue. A matter not of just getting the work done, but of getting the work done to a measurably high standard, even at launch time, when demand may be unusually high.

One way to curb this initial demand is to avoid making an announcement altogether and to 'trickle' the service out to the customer base. The service launch is kept deliberately low key, customers are allowed to hear about it by word of mouth rather than through official channels. This has the advantage of making the initial demand a little less instant – but there are some disadvantages. First, there is the risk that by not announcing, some potential clients who could gain great benefit from the service may fail to hear about it. Second, some clients may voice disappointment that they were not told of this new service, which might damage the relationship with that client. Third, the speed with which word of mouth travels is unpredictable – where the service is likely to be popular to a mass market, they may come to hear about it more quickly than you had prepared for, with all the risks that a highly hyped launch could bring.

In any case, any service which survives the initial launch and becomes a standard service product will probably sooner or later begin to go stale. Customers and staff come to take it for granted, initial excitement and enthusiasm pale, competition for the service increases. This is the time to consider relaunch or replacement. The concept is commonly used in marketing to rekindle customer interest in a product or service. The basic structure of the service and the way it is produced by the support department may still be sound and customers may still be benefiting from it. However, their interest and appreciation of the benefits they gain has dulled over time and they need to be reminded. A repackaging of the service, a renaming, a slight adjustment of the service levels to bring them up to date with changed customer requirements may be all that is required to bring this service back up to the standards of output and benefit it once enjoyed. This is the concept of the 'mid-life kick'. It requires less marketing effort on the support provider's part than a complete redesign would but can achieve much the same effect.

> ## Case Study 14.2: the overhead of working here
>
> Phil had run the helpdesk as a reactive unit for years, and although it had not been smooth, somehow they had muddled through. Then within a week, two of his staff turned in their notice. After a bit of soul-searching anxiety and some discreet enquiries, Phil had established their

reasons for going were genuine and not part of a more deep-seated mutiny. So he stopped worrying and set to figuring out how he would replace them. This caused him to take a long look at the department's services, which he had never done before. But if he was going to get new staff, he would have to be able to prove he needed them.

He took his list of services to Maria, his boss. She was immediately suspicious. 'You've never done this before, and always managed up to now. Are you sure you're not just trying to show me you're doing more than you are?' Phil assured Maria the list was absolutely genuine, but her suspicion continued. 'What is this "General Enquiry Desk" service? I can't pay to have you take 25 calls a day with no support content!'

On the face of it, Maria had a point. Any examination of the call-log would yield a large number of call-reports reading 'Derek called – can Mark call him back', or 'Query wrongly put through here, should have gone to development'. But Phil was not going to give up that easily. He had done what he could to reduce these calls, but they kept on coming. Wherever he improved communications to stem the flow of one type of irrelevant query, another would crop up. Eventually he concluded they were part of the 'work overhead'.

As he explained to Maria, any organization produces an overhead on the working day of the individuals within it. All those people have to interact with one another, sometimes for commercial reasons, sometimes for purely psychological ones. This was the unseen force that ate so much into the working day. His final way of proving it to her was to bet that if she measured her day, she'd find an overhead too. (When she did, she scared herself by finding an overhead of over 30 per cent of her time spent apparently non-productively: so it is with managers – so many people want to get the decision-maker's attention.)

Eventually Maria capitulated. Phil was only replacing staff he'd had, and she was only trying to grab the opportunity to reduce her costs. She accepted the fact that Phil's 'General Enquiry Desk' was a genuine service. But as well as signing Phil's headcount request, she started to take a long hard look at who was getting a service from her without her realizing it.

15

Excellence in support service

Excellence is the art of surprising the customers every time they use you. As we established in Chapter 7, it is not enough to do just what the customer expects – you have to add value to your service, and not only should this be taken on board by your staff who have to deliver the service, it should be woven into the very fabric of the service itself. Services have to be described internally (to the helpdesk staff) and externally (to the customers) in a way that makes excellence natural, both in the way the service is produced and as part of what the customer gets.

It should be a high priority in all service organizations to build excellence into the operation or provision of any service. Without excellence, the competition becomes too strong, nowhere more so from the do-it-yourselfers, most of whom could support themselves, their peers and their colleagues to a level of mediocrity. But as discussed elsewhere, it is not in the company's interest that users should do their own support – it is a job for the professionals. So logically, the support organization should compete against and effectively nullify this mediocrity by making excellence part of the standard provision.

All too often, the natural reaction from support departments is that there is not sufficient time, resource, headcount, whatever to put that kind of effort in. Of all these excuses, lack of time seems to be the most popular. When we study time as a resource in Part Five, I will contend that 'lack of time' is a meaningless phrase, even in the most overworked support organization. On the principle that if a thing is worth doing it is worth doing well, then if there is not enough time to do it well, there is not enough time to do it at all.

On the one hand, excellence is a high priority – on the other, time is a limited resource. So providing excellence in all services may mean that some services may not get provided at all. *This is acceptable*. I must stress this point. It is perfectly acceptable to be unable to get round to doing poorly something that is unimportant, because you are doing everything else excellently. But there is a caveat: your customers must see what you do as being excellent. For if they do not, then all you are seen to be doing is providing a service level which is mediocre at best and non-existent at worst. So in every function you perform, your success at being 'excellent' must be measured in your clients' terms, not yours.

> **It is perfectly acceptable to be unable to get round to doing poorly something unnecessary because you are doing excellently everything you should be doing.**

Demonstrating excellence has an intriguing impact on your customers' behaviour. Excellence in service provision will attract customers who desire excellence, feel they deserve and can afford excellence. After all it does not come cheap. Your mediocrity may be the reason that a high-profile department in head office has not used you yet – they may feel they deserve better, so the service is not for them, nor will it be until you start to provide what they see as a good-quality service. At the other end of the scale, there are some who may feel intimidated by excellence – that they or their service does not need or deserve it – but these are in a minority. After all, what professional person is too intimidated to shop in London's famous Harrods store?

That your customers can afford the excellence you provide is a key point, even when there appears to be no cost involved in using your service. There is always a price to pay for using your support service, even if it is as low as, say, the amount of time your customer has to spend picking up the telephone. Customers are prepared to pay more for excellence. It allows you to put your prices up – perhaps as high as insisting that the user be computer literate, or that the caller knows the asset number of his or her computer (more of this in Chapter 16). Where you are supporting external customers – e.g. the end users of a computer supply company – excellence and its affordability are even more important. Then the excellence of support is a value directly added to the sale of a computer and essentially part of the price in dollars and Deutschmarks. Then support excellence and its ability to attract high-spending clients can be translated directly into higher cash revenue earned (a fact the support manager should continually and tirelessly point out to the sales director and her peers).

Excellence begets excellence, not least by the force of example. The behaviour of one service department becomes a benchmark for others. Logically, a culture of excellence, where it is initially strong enough, should spread through the company. The excellence of support will beget excellence among users. For example, there are those who are willing to pay the higher price of knowing more about their computers, in order to get the best from support. They will become more competent in their use of the technology, making them more competitive in the open market and thus delivering greater commercial benefits to the company as a result.

Excellence appeals to the staff member. There are few things more frustrating to the true professional than being unable to act professionally because of the constraints or negativism of their employer. Management attitudes like 'I cannot deliver excellence because I don't have the staff' are often used as a kind of appeasement to the staff, as well as being a weak excuse for mediocrity. The staff do not wish to be appeased – they desire to be enabled to do their jobs properly (more of this is peppered throughout Part Six). To most professionals, 'properly' means 'excellently'.

You, the support manager, take the opportunity to design and manage the services in such a way that the customer either stifles or emits a 'Wow!' every time they deal with one of your staff. This will convince the staff that the work they do is more truly worthwhile, a reward in itself for the effort and professionalism they put in. It will convince the users that a high-quality service is genuinely your aim. And it will convince the managers and those who measure you that your intention is to benefit the company through improving the lot of the IT users.

15.1 But my company doesn't want excellence . . .

It is a perfectly legitimate business strategy to limit the quality of a product or service precisely because that is what the clientele wants: a low-cost product dedicated more to keeping costs down than to keeping quality high. And under such circumstances, the support manager's attempts to provide excellence in service may appear to be thwarted by the actions and policies of higher authorities. Typically, this manifests itself as the company resisting the support manager's attempts to recruit new staff in order to maintain a high standard of service. So the little things that get you a reputation for excellence, like personal attention, giving the bit extra, taking a bit more time, and so on, they are what suffers as headcount and expenditure restrictions bite. I've been there. And boy, did it hurt until I realized that I was the one out of step – I didn't understand the company's strategy. Served me right for believing the marketing rather than seeing the truth.

The provision of excellence is a matter of attitude, not just a result of the resources to hand. It is a matter of doing the best you can with what you have got – as opposed to doing precisely what you can with what you have been given. Excellence is best produced by knowing and managing your clients' expectations and then exceeding them, just enough to make them realize how valuable your services are. You can only do that if your department's attitude to their collective output is a positive one. A typically negative support operative's view is that they are struggling to be 'excellent' despite the company, against the odds, and so on. A typically positive one is that the company, of which they form a part, has set the support service market parameters – and within those parameters, through the professionalism of all concerned, all services are delivered to an appropriate standard of excellence.

Your company's directors are not IT support experts and at best can only offer educated opinions as to how IT support should be run. They are unlikely to be trying to thwart excellence, and more likely to be attempting to avoid waste in effort and materials. Where your company appears to be thwarting you, the problem is more likely to be one of mutual communication than it is one of deliberate constriction. And as we have established already, the board constitutes one of the support desk's customers. So as with any other customer, find out what they want and give it to them.

16

Service level agreements

The key to providing a 'satisfactory service' lies in satisfaction as much as it does in service. It is no good providing a good support service if your clients do not appreciate the service as being 'good'. They will measure the service, either against benchmarks or against their instincts (the latter is far more common) and draw conclusions based on that measurement. The fact that they use their instincts as a measure introduces all kinds of emotional and experiential variables that, on the face of it, you can do little or nothing about. Logically, if you want them to measure your service accurately and favourably, you must manage not just the service but the clients' *expectations* of the service. It is for the support provider to give the client the benchmarks by which the service is to be measured. By formalizing the measurement in this way, there is less room, less credibility and less acceptability for the more instinctive and emotional ways of measuring and appreciating the service.

This is where service level agreements (SLAs) come in. They are the ultimate in formalizing the service relationship between provider and client.

16.1 What is a service level agreement?

An SLA is a formal, written and signed contract between a service provider and a service client. It lists and describes the services to be provided, by whom, with what frequency and to what standard. It will usually also describe what the service provider is to receive from the client in return. Once compiled and agreed, the SLA forms the sole terms of reference against which the effectiveness or otherwise of the service provider is measured. The SLA satisfies two main needs in the service relationship. First, it sets expectations on both sides. The client has a concrete description of what the supplier can be expected to offer; the supplier has a description of the client's role in the relationship, e.g. how technically competent the users are supposed to be, what level of diagnosis should have been done before reporting a fault, what information should accompany a service request, and so on. Second, the SLA sets in stone the parameters under which the service provider should operate: not only what they should provide, but also what they should not – and these restrictions make it easier to forecast resource requirements, budgets and so on.

The benefits of an SLA can go beyond the control of client expectations, however. By forcing users and support to discuss the services required and the consequences of providing or not providing them, the support department is brought that much closer to the real business reasons for having IT support. In other words, the process of setting up SLAs provides the starkest possible description, if one were needed, of the fact that support is not needed simply to support the computers – but to support the way the company's staff use the computers in order to produce turnover and profit. The SLA can and should also show what is over-provision, so that the support department does not waste effort giving the users more than they need (as I have seen some helpdesks do in the thick of a newly born customer-service ethic). The SLA must necessarily stand up to objective analysis – after all, its prime intention is to bring some objectivity to the service relationship. This enables it to be understood by outside onlookers, such as board directors and others who have a financial or managerial interest in the service provision but take no part in it. The SLA can make the job and benefits of the helpdesk more easily understood by these interested onlookers.

16.2 Where SLAs work

Service level agreements are at their best in an environment where the amount of work is predictable and the type of work similar. For example, they are invariably the backbone of a relationship between a company which uses computers and the company that repairs the computers: 'all calls will receive a response within one hour, a technician will attend within eight (working) hours, 85 per cent of faults will be fixed on the first visit', and so on. The SLA is most suited to the computer repair environment because of the relatively safe assumptions which can be made about the type of fault: that the users will understand their computers well enough to tell a mechanical breakdown from another functional aberration; that it will be an item of hardware which has failed; that the failure will either be instantly obvious or will be isolated by standard diagnostic techniques; that a repair can usually be effected by replacement of the faulty part, and that part will be one of a standard catalogue. The SLA is less effective where the root of the problem is more nebulous – for instance, where the fault lies not with the machine but with the user's misunderstanding of the machine; where the evidence for a fault is circumstantial; where the fault is a software one, due to circumstances the programmer did not foresee and requiring not a replacement but a rewrite to fix; where the speed and efficacy of the fix will depend on the ability of the user to grasp the implementation of the fix rather than depending on the ability of the service provider to describe the fix.

Case Study 16.1: the ignored helpdesk

The computer department had existed for years before the helpdesk was conceived of, and helpdesk manager Charlie had always known it was going to be difficult to persuade a company this size to start using a helpdesk when for so long the users had been used to a direct line to, well just about anybody. It had been the arrival of the PC that had made the helpdesk necessary. To some of the more cynical computer staff, the average age of the users had suggested that this new technology would present a few problems; some of those guys had been out there for 20 years, and they had been used to having it all done for them by the mainframe. They were not going to take to downloading data into Lotus that easily. Sure enough, the number of calls to the computer department had gone through the roof. The developers could not get anything done for being interrupted and when the complaints started to damage the IT director's Friday afternoons (golf with the chairman) the helpdesk was hauled, kicking and screaming into existence.

It made no difference. The users had their habitual routes for support and the number of interruptions did not even slacken. User training was brought in. No difference. Common attitude – why go on a two-day course just to hear something, half of which I already know and the other half I can get when I need it just by picking up the phone? Something, the computer department managers mused, had to be done. Looking at the problem objectively, the users would benefit from the helpdesk if only they would use it – which they would not by choice. Similarly, they would benefit from training, if only they would take it – which they would not by choice. Drastic action was needed – but not for ever, just to change the habits of the world outside.

It began with the IT director pulling a few strings, and it has to be said, hooking and slicing a few shots to get the Old Man in a good mood. That did the trick – the order came down from the board: section heads would now be measured on the computing competence of their staff. Training took off like a moonshot. Over in user support, Charlie was busy drafting his service level agreements, which stipulated, among other things, no support for undertrained users. In the development department, changes to telephone numbers and hunt groups accompanied a reorganization to make the developers less accessible while implementing a long-overdue plan for improving PC software development.

The SLAs were eagerly awaited. They contained detailed descriptions of the helpdesk service, concentrating on the benefits of a centralized service and the reliability of a dedicated service over that of a favoured contact in the development team. It had been thought that marketing consultants would have to be brought in to sell the new support structure, but in the end it was not necessary. The initial hunch had been right. Once the culture shifted onto using the helpdesk, only determined effort would ever shake it off again. Later on, the bureaucratic grip of the SLAs was slackened – they had brought about the change they were meant to.

SLAs work in large organizations which are committed to tight control of costs, especially those in service departments. SLAs work where there is sufficient resource and management time to manage the agreements, for there is a considerable overhead to maintaining them. SLAs work where the relationship is essentially two-way, e.g. where there is a financial charge for services provided. SLAs work where bureaucracy does; that statement is not meant to be judgemental, though my feelings on bureaucracy are certainly biased – but in those companies where bureaucracy thrives, SLAs will usually fit well. SLAs work where there is the authority to design and represent them.

16.3 Content

What needs to be in the SLA? There is no prescribed format – it is a matter of what best suits the relationship you want between the users and the support department. Certain things are clearly vital to the SLA in order to set the terms of the service relationship. The agreement should contain the following:

- Names of the departments or groups in the relationship.
- Names of the representatives or authorities within those groups.
- Descriptions of the services to be provided, frequency and service level; this can go to several levels of detail, from a simple statement of the minimum level acceptable through to describing what would be 'over-provision'.
- Business reasons why the services are needed, outlining relative priorities of the services and of individual members of the user group.
- Outlines of the business risks as a consequence of a service target not being met.
- Allowances for peaks and troughs in demand.
- Details of 'special' coverage, e.g. outside normal working hours.
- Descriptions of the role played by the users in the provision of these services, e.g. minimum level of technical knowledge users must attain, troubleshooting to be tried and information to be gathered before reporting a problem.
- Descriptions of the methods of monitoring measuring performance against these target levels, format and frequency of reports and review meetings.
- Acknowledgement of who polices the SLA, who arbitrates disputes.
- Change control methods – how to update the agreement to allow for change, such as new technology, user staff, or needs – for change both within the life of the agreement and while negotiating a new or additional agreement.
- Descriptions of what is not provided, especially if there are some services which have been perhaps unreasonably expected in the past, or if the support department has a range of services, some of which this user has declined to take.
- Procedures for changing the SLA to keep it up to date and in tune with the business and the actual services demanded.

The format of the SLA will depend entirely on who is using it and for what. At one extreme there is the almost legal document, there to describe in the most formal terms the relationship between two departments who might otherwise be virtual strangers. This may be necessary in the case of extremely large user groups or where numerous remote sites are to be supported. It may be a feature of the culture of the corporation that formality is the usual way of setting standards of practice. Such an SLA will be large, detailed, and designed to cover or control every eventuality. These more formal SLAs are not meant for general consumption, and if they or their content are to be communicated to ranks other than those who negotiated the agreement, then they will usually have to be reworked into a more digestible form. Such SLAs will usually require more management time in maintenance and performance measuring. The risk with them is that they will be inflexible, and that the challenge of renegotiating them in the face of a change in circumstances will be too daunting. This may in turn cause future service opportunities to be lost in favour of keeping control of the present.

At the other extreme, there are SLAs which use the minimum of formality. They are designed to be communicated to staff at all levels, on both sides of the agreement, with the minimum amount of effort in preparation, negotiation and maintenance. Such less stringent SLAs can be more flexible; but this can backfire. Where the circumstances generate too many exceptions to the SLAs, this can result in constant renegotiation to deal with the exceptions. So either with a formal or an informal SLA, the parties must both commit their time and their priorities to regular reviews, discussion and maintenance of the document in order that it stays useful. This commitment should be stated in the agreement – after all, the maintenance of the SLA is both one of the services to be provided and part of the price the client has to pay for the service.

16.4 Managing the SLA

All SLAs need managing. Issues of management include monitoring: who keeps an eye on the provision of the service to make sure that it always complies to the stated agreement? How often should this monitoring take place, or if it is continuous, how often should it be examined? It is impractical to have the client's representative deeply involved in the day-to-day performance of the helpdesk – he or she will have their own job to do. Even a monthly examination of figures might be too time consuming. The solution many organizations arrive at is to report on exceptions only, dealing with the exceptions as they crop up. Ideally, the monitoring system will be automated to throw up where the targets have been missed. Most commercially available helpdesk management software packages now have a means of setting target response times and reporting on a failure to meet them. However, this only covers helpdesk and resolver responses, and is less likely to cover the other services a support department might offer.

There is the issue of policing: what happens if the service department fails to meet the agreed service targets and who polices that? In a user company, where the service provider and the client both get their budgets from the same place, policing such as this can be especially difficult. Certainly it is hard to saddle the support manager with a financial penalty, as that could merely result in making it even harder for the helpdesk to meet the targets it is already failing to meet, thus harming the very users the desk has been put there to help! In the end, this will come down to the professional commitment of all concerned, and especially the support team. They will attempt to meet targets not because they are under some financial pressure to do so (although some companies do 'incentivize' helpdesk staff), but because they are professionals who have been made aware of the consequences of their success or failure to the success of the business which employs them.

16.5 SLAs in user support

As we have already seen, the SLA is a very effective way of managing and measuring the service relationship where the work is predictable and the company culture amenable to such formality. Even where such formality is not the company norm, where the support department is under particular financial pressure, or where user expectations are completely out of control, an SLA may still be an appropriate measure, even if only for a short period of time, of getting the service provision back onto an even keel. Once SLAs have been accepted as the means of doing this, it will usually become clear that there is a tendency of most consumers of the service to leave the responsibility of deciding the service level to the support department. This abdication represents an opportunity for the support manager to set the service levels unilaterally in effect. But because the SLA has to be agreed, this one-sided draft becomes the basis of, rather than the result of, a negotiation.

However, in user support, it is rare that the work is predictable enough for an SLA to be workable. In the computer-repair environment we are dealing with failures of machines; in the user support department we are often dealing with the failings of more nebulous entities, such as people's skills, organizational systems and software suites. Often the diagnosis is not a matter of running a utility to indicate where the failure is; it is a matter of interpreting an individual user's way of working to find out where they have a problem with the technology, rather than where the technology itself has failed. Often the solution requires some change in skill on the part of the users themselves, which they may be momentarily unwilling or unable to do. Often the solution is in two parts: first, to get the user productive again, then only second, to address the support effort to the technological problem at hand. All this vagueness, inter-pretation and inexactitude make the service level very difficult to define, often too much so to make an SLA effective in such an environment. Where the circumstances look like this, the SLA which started life as a tool for managing client expectations can come to distract us from that very purpose, so we end up pursuing the SLA for its own sake rather than for the benefit we intended to derive from it. SLAs have their place in a user support department – but only where the service is appropriate to such a control and measurement methodology and only as one tool in a more varied kit bag.

Case Study 16.2: the support SLA at the Department of Fiction

Like the name of the organization, the story of the service level agreement between the user support section and the 2500-odd users of desktop computers at the UK's State Department of Fiction is a complete fabrication. Here, the SLA is laid out precisely like a legal contract. This establishment went through the SLA process at the very highest level: senior managers negotiating with one another, based on detailed statistical information supplied to them by the service department. Figures of helpdesk usage, average response times, query categories, numbers of staff, average time to fix, and so on were all taken into account. Undermanagers were asked to consult their staff for input. It must be said that some of these undermanagers did perform something of a consultation – but many did not, either realizing that they knew too little about what their staff did to make an intelligent contribution, or having neither the time nor the communications channels to talk to 150 people.

The SLA, when it was written, was an extremely lengthy document – over 200 pages – and no user below section head ever saw it, although they all knew the process had been taking place. Of course the appropriate government minister was sent a copy, which of course she never read. That is not to say that she did not make use of the SLA; it was waved in front of the Opposition Benches on at least two occasions, as concrete proof of how the DoF was labouring hard to control overhead costs and sharpen up management practice, by taking such a hard lesson in contractual stringency from the private sector; at a stroke improving services, controlling headcount and limiting the DoF's demand on the Public Sector Borrowing Requirement. And all this in the computer section, showing how switched on the minister was to information technology.

The impact on the quality of user services? Uniformly agreed to have been negligible. The exercise had the worst possible effect: raising user expectations, then dashing them immediately after. In addition, it was deemed to have severely alienated the users, both from their own managers and from the IT department. And the Minister? Less than a year later she was promoted to a prestigious Cabinet position in the highly spendthrift Department of National Medicine.

16.6 SLAs and authority

When drawing up the SLA, one of the main considerations should be whether the provider and client representatives have the authority to make an agreement which will impact those whom they represent. In this case, the one with the 'authority' is not necessarily the most senior manager of either side. Authority, although often assigned, needs also to be invested by those whose interests are represented – and a senior manager, speaking purely with the authority of her post in the company, may not be the best representative of her staff's needs. She may not have enough knowledge at a low enough level. She may never have been a computer user in the department she manages, so she will be ignorant of the real, day-to-day problems and difficulties with which real users need frequent help. Putting somebody from the top of the management pyramid in charge of the negotiation for services needed mostly at the bottom of the pyramid is extremely dangerous. A very likely result is that the wrong set of expectations will be represented in the resulting SLA – and the inevitable consequence of that is that even if the terms of the SLA are met by the service provider, still the users remain dissatisfied with the service. In such a case, the main purpose of the SLA – to set the users' expectations – is negated.

The user representative, drawing up and negotiating the SLA, needs authority lent not by position, but by the equally important qualifications of (i) in-depth knowledge of the users' true needs at the very lowest level; (ii) a full comprehension of the relative priorities of each of those needs; (iii) the confidence and complicity of the users themselves with the chosen representative; and (iv) proven negotiating skills. The representative of the service provider also needs to be a good negotiator, and here the other necessary authority comes from (i) complete understanding of what is possible given existing and obtainable resources, and (ii) as complete a comprehension of the users' true needs as they have themselves. Once these authorities have been exercised, then the senior managers can play their more appropriate role of formalizing the agreement, and agreeing the usually considerable sums of money which must change hands.

Case Study 16.3: the wrong authority

'The costs of general support services in this company are out of control', said the managing director. 'We must get some control over which department uses how much of what, or by this time next year our staff budget will go haywire.' The result of this apparently simple philosophy was profound. All over the company, service departments like personnel, accounts, facilities and marketing suddenly had to invest more time and effort than ever before in justifying their contribution to the sales effort, deemed by the board to be the only one which brought any money in.

Nowhere was this more profoundly felt than in IT. The developers did not have it so bad, because they did everything on a project-by-project basis in any case, but the helpdesk was seen as an overhead which now had to control the amount of service it delivered. The received wisdom was that service level agreements were the way forward. Nick, the support manager, was sent on an SLA training course – and what he learned there made him suspect all the more that SLAs were not the way. Still, ours is to do.

Nick had done much of the groundwork anyway – he knew which users needed what and who the most senior person in each department was. He began by drawing up sample SLAs and putting them out to the department heads. Meanwhile, he had to provide accounts with several figures they would use to calculate how the cross-charging of the SLAs would be done.

There was not much evidence to convince Nick this SLA business was really workable. Most of the department heads did not reply to his draft SLAs. They were often too busy with all the other SLAs to deal with Nick's, and as long as Nick's people kept answering the telephone, the helpdesk SLA was a low priority. In the restaurant, Nick bumped into Cheryl, a heavy user of the Sales Ledger Records and Forecasting system. 'Has my boss replied to your SLA yet, Nick?' she asked. 'The agreement he made with the warehouse just showed how little he knows about what my team does. I've been all afternoon trying to redraft it, and even then I'll have to get it past the boss without showing him up.'

Over the next couple of weeks, Cheryl's boss turned out to be one of the hardest to come to some agreement with. He was never in his office, then he kept changing his mind about what he wanted; finally he said 'You tell me what I want, Nick – I'll trust your judgement.' This annoyed Nick – not only was it an abdication of the SLA process, but it meant that the whole affair was a waste of time and effort, because guessing what the user managers wanted was what Nick had always done. But Nick was even more annoyed at himself for doing what he was told to do even though he had known in his heart it would not work. By the end of the quarter, the whole SLA thing had been quietly forgotten.

16.7 In conclusion

If pressed, I have to say that I find that while SLAs are a sound framework in themselves, in most user support departments (i.e. where the SLA exists for the helpdesk alone) to be at best a sledgehammer to crack a nut, at worst a nightmare of excessive bureaucracy and management overhead. They are usually implemented with the best of intentions: to set user expectations, to control support costs, to define service parameters, to enable accurate support resource forecasting. But more often than not, you can do all that in a much more user-friendly way and with much less bilateral effort than is the case with many SLAs. The SLA can be the logical conclusion of a project to try to do everything right in one go. That is why it does not work. Nothing is ever right first time, you invent something and then improve it once you see how it works in real life.

A major flaw in the SLA concept as regards helpdesks is that an SLA has to be two-sided. Two departments set out the rules that only one of them will have to comply with. The provider ends up being restricted; the client ends up in a negotiation about which he or she is essentially ignorant. Then these two have to meet again and again, to make sure everything is going smoothly. In my opinion it is a recipe for conflict. For managing external suppliers, excellent. For relationships between two members of the same company, potential disaster.

The work in the average helpdesk or user support operation is just too non-standard for SLAs. An SLA is at its best where the work is repetitive or formulaic. The problem-solving ethic of most support departments means their work is certainly not repetitive; and every six months, new technology causes much to change.

Rationally, there is a need for a statement of what the support provider will provide. He or she will need such a thing for laying out the internal objectives of the support department anyway. Support managers will have to know or have a pretty good idea of what their customers need anyway, or they are not doing their job. So they can describe pretty accurately the services their clients will need without necessarily getting user managers involved. They can make and publish that list of services. I call this approach the *service level statement*.

The users will often prefer this approach. They do not want the hassle of designing support services when there is somebody there to do it for them, more accurately than they could anyway. And any user who sees the statement and thinks it is not enough for his or her needs; well maybe he or she needs a private, little, manageable SLA for his exceptions to the company norm. What about policing? No problem. The support manager is a professional – he or she will make sure the service gets delivered. They know the risks to their company if they fail.

> **Why force somebody to negotiate an agreement –
> when a simple statement may do?**

16.8 SLA Template

The following paragraphs have their own numbering, outside the format of the book. They constitute a skeleton of one of my favourite formats for an IT support service level agreement. I have deliberately used a different font to separate it from the rest of the book. Be aware that when you sit down to write this from scratch, including all the measurement and analysis and IT-internal agreements you may have to get, and negotiations with the client, it can take three weeks or more. This template will only save you time by offering the main headings in the SLA.

SERVICE LEVEL AGREEMENT

1.   INTRODUCTION

Outline description of contents

1.1   Purpose of this agreement

E.g. to set client expectations, define mutual responsibilities, describe service catalogue, etc.

1.2   Scope of the agreement

E.g. what's included, what's excluded – covers the helpdesk but not network support and so on.

1.3   Terminology

Glossary of any special jargon or terminology used in the document.

1.4   Authorities

Description of role and duties of signing authorities; client-side manager; supplier-side manager; review body, etc.

2. SERVICE PROVISION

2.1 Supplier services and responsibilities

List the services here, what they do, how they work, what purpose they serve, how the customers obtain them. Note: do NOT describe the actual service levels – they appear later in the Schedule. This part is your catalogue, so you can offer the same SLA to several clients but differentiate the actual services delivered by only making the Schedule specific to a given client. This may mean that not all clients get all services – but from the SLA, they then know what's available and can come back and ask for more services if they need it.

2.2 Client responsibilities

All the things the customer has to do as part of the service relationship. So if they have to attain a given level of technical competence, use only the helpdesk for reporting problems or be available when your second-line technician comes to fix their machine, say so here.

3. SLA MANAGEMENT

3.1 SLA administration

Who ultimately owns the SLA; who administrates it, produces the reports, etc.

3.2 Review process

E.g. how frequently the reports are compiled, who they go to and what happens with them. How the 'performance review meeting' is constituted; what should be the output of that meeting and what actions may be taken as a result. Who signs off the reports and meeting minutes.

3.3 SLA change management

E.g. how the agreement may be suspended in the light of any external circumstances affecting either party; how that suspension is documented and what effect that has. How the agreement itself may be changed in the light of any significant alteration in demand, how that alteration is authorized and how it links into the change management process.

3.4 Performance reporting

E.g. processes, names and purposes of various reports coming out of the SLA process.

181

3.5 Breach of agreement

E.g. process invoked as a result of any breach by either participant. How the breach is measured, acknowledged, recorded and actions to be taken.

3.6 Termination

How the agreement should be terminated (but not when – that's in the Schedule).

4. FORMAT OF DOCUMENTS

Copies of (or references to) templates of all the documents pertaining to or produced by the SLA relationship, e.g. reports, sign-off sheets, change documents, meeting minute formats, change request forms, project initiation documents, equipment procurement forms, etc.

SCHEDULE OF SERVICE PROVISION

S1. SCHEDULE ADMINISTRATION

S1.1 Client details

S1.2 Period of validity

S2. SERVICE LEVELS

A table like the one below. Remember to allow for changes to service levels based on increase or reduction in demand.

Service name	Service level	Exceptions	Comments
As per the list in 'Supplier responsibilities' but this time only for this client	*How much of it they get, how quickly – response and fix times, etc.*	*Any particular exceptions, e.g. user departments that do their own thing and don't want this service*	*Anything relevant*

S3.   Anticipated demand level

E.g. number of users, pace of growth in user population, expected number of moves, installations, training course requests, etc.

S4.   Supported products list

Table: it may be handy to put a note here to refer reader back to the third section for instructions on how to add or remove products to or from this list.

S5.   Agreement acceptance

We the undersigned . . . .

APPENDIX

GENERAL TERMS AND CONDITIONS

Where the legal bit goes. Useful if you have general Ts & Cs pertaining to all intracompany agreements or all client contracts.

17

Support from outside

This chapter is about those support functions and resources that come from or are used outside the 'support' department. We support professionals certainly have no monopoly in the market for support services – in fact we do not even have an equal share. Most user support is actually done by people employed outside the user support function. And I do not mean that bit of support that we buy in, like hardware maintenance or network changes, although that is relevant too – I mean the bulk of IT user support, which is performed by those who, although professionals in their own field, are amateurs in the field of IT support.

Nor is this external support necessarily in harmony with our services. For the most part, it is in vigorous competition. It includes users operating their own support services, unofficially or otherwise, such as the accounts clerk whose avid digestion of the computer magazines has made him or her the local computer expert; the secretary, so famed for her copious knowledge of word processing and her helpful nature that she regularly provides her technophobic peers with hints and tips; the specialist department using a niche software package which the IT helpdesk has refused to support, either because it is non-standard or because to support it would need specialist, non-IT knowledge; the financial forecasters whose spreadsheet queries tend to be more about business than about computers, and so need financiers who understand spreadsheets more than they need computer specialists who understand finance; the large and self-important group of users so fed up with what they see as inadequate service from IT support that they prefer to support themselves; the department head who buys his Microsoft Windows training from a private source; the curious user who, when not issued manuals by the support department, picks up one of the numerous self-help volumes from her local bookshop and starts to write her own programs.

The key operating principle here is competition. We face it from inside the company as well as outside. From the users' point of view it is a matter of choice among several sources they can go to to get the type of support they need. They may be wrong of course, but that is not the point – we all know examples of customers who are blindly loyal to a product or service, which to objective eyes is patently wrong for them. While this competition exists, we need to acknowledge and compete with it. For as long as we ignore it, it continues to grow in its ability to outperform us.

User support as supplied by the official 'support department' accounts for only a small proportion of all the actual support that gets done: some sources suggest this figure is less than 10 per cent. This means that the management effort invested in the support department, although vital, is seriously wide of the true target. Support managers should be spending more of their time figuring out and probably taking control of all this other support the rest of the world is doing. They need to do this for several reasons, not least to ensure that all this external support gets done to a satisfactory standard, i.e. such that the interests of the users and ultimately the company are best served. All this amounts to yet another reason why support managers need to spend more time away from their own desks, visiting their customers. It is a sad truth that all too many 'managers' in our profession are content to stay inside their departments and wait for the work to come to them. Work will continue to come to them only while the service stays relevant, while the department stays in touch with what is relevant, while the competition continues to have less to offer than the incumbents.

However, what the itinerant support manager discovers may suggest that bringing support in from outside is the most appropriate strategy. It may be true that your users' specialist use of computers requires more expertise in the business usage of the application than in the workings of the box the application sits on. It may be that your helpdesk has been so consistently run down that the investment required to bring it back up to speed is prohibitive. It may be that your IT strategy is so leading-edge that you need constant changes in expertise so as to stay flexible. It may be that you consider outsourced support to be cheaper than internal support, or that you desire to focus on your core business strategy, from which providing your own IT support would only be a distraction.

17.1 The users' 'local support'

Figure 4.1, 'Who supports what?', at the beginning of Chapter 4 and the consideration of the 'user group representative' in Chapter 3 have already looked at this topic in some depth. From the support department's point of view, there are three main issues we have to worry about. First, is the support conducted to a standard with which we are happy? Remember that the user representative may well look after that user's demands, but are those demands being adequately serviced? Put simply, when the users ask their local support for help, do they get the right answer? Second, are the demands the users place on the local support in the interests of the company as a whole or just in the interests of that user? Is that local expert being asked to help out with the desktop publishing of a manager's monthly report or with the installation of a non-standard package that will swamp the computer network? Only the central support department can truly be in possession of the big picture. Third, are the communication channels between central and local support doing their job? Do you have ways of making sure the local representative has the knowledge he or she needs to provide the best support possible? And in the other direction, can you be sure you know how much support effort is being expended for that user, and is it enough or too much?

Some companies are worried about the escalating costs of user support and have chosen to combat this by making these costs more accountable. This has led to user departments having to make budgetary contributions to user support, and in many companies, individual heads in the user support department are directly sponsored by the user department. You can point at a person and say 'that's my techie'. By and large this puts the headcount issue in a nice, neat pigeonhole, but if that user's techie is a Lotus genius and what they need is an Oracle magician, then focusing on headcount alone can entirely miss the point – you hired him to support the users, not so you could manage his headcount allocation.

It is not uncommon to have these sponsored technicians managed by the support department. This raises the issue of which master they serve. Do they do as they are told because the user is paying their wages or because the support manager is motivating them in that direction? And what happens if there is a conflict of interests – whose interests are served then, and will the company as a whole benefit?

17.2 Software written in-house

One place users often help themselves is with in-house software. There are two types of this: the software written by an official development department; and the routines, macros and sometimes whole systems written by particularly knowledgeable users. This is a knotty problem which is rarely solved entirely satisfactorily. Software written by the development department has its problems. It is expensive and time-consuming to create, sometimes taking so long that it is obsolete before it goes live. Because of the expense, corners are often cut, increasing the support workload and inconvenience to the users. 'Official' software is written by somebody who is an expert at writing software, not an expert in the job of the person they are writing it for – so often it does not precisely match the user's ideal, which again can create more work for support.

The approach of some support teams to this challenge is to pass problems with the software back to the development team. This is riddled with difficulties: the developers would rather the helpdesk took on all the support to leave them free for the next development, and that is understandable – but often it was the shortcomings of the original development which caused this situation. Chapter 3 looked at the user support centre as a response to this. But user support centres can only be instigated by acknowledgement at the very highest corporate level that this is a real problem, and invariably there are empires and snugly fitting niches to protect, getting in the way of fundamental change. The quickest and often the only practicable way out of this dilemma is to remove the influence of 'outside' altogether. If the software simply has to be maintained, then support should start looking for ways to maintain it. Even if the developers are protecting their empire, they may well come round when they realize they are less likely to have their development projects interrupted by a user needing a bug fix in a program they all forgot about a year ago.

Consider how the user could be recruited into this. In the end, the support relationship is between the user and the supporter, and if the developers wish to be part of that, all well and good; if they do not, they are passing up an opportunity to get closer to the business, which I believe will damage them severely in the long run.

The other type of in-house software has exploded in recent years with the growth of desktop computing. It had to happen. It may be too expensive for one department to have its private routines developed to run on the network, and MS Access, Lotus Notes *et al.* have become the easy way out. The programs developed here have often grown up organically, in ignorance of good programming technique and usually without documentation. Often, they are unmaintainable. They work either until circumstances make them obsolete or the person who wrote the program departs the company. Of course by then the system has become so vital to that user's business function that the obsolete system gets replaced by a more robust, often commercially available product. The decision to maintain or replace such software will ultimately lie with the user. Even if they have not supported the system up to now, this is the point where the support department should get involved so as to make sure the replacement is as 'supportable' as possible.

Whether it is the old package or the new one which needs supporting, written in-house or ultimately bought in, the issue is the same, and that is the difference between support for the application's technology and support for the application's use. Somebody who uses any computer package as part of their job will invariably know much more about that package than any technologist ever could. It will always be impractical for a computer specialist to also be an expert in the business use of applications – there simply are not enough hours in the working day to acquire that amount of experience. So there will always be a need for users to do some, if not most, of their own support. And the people who do this support will be users with a computing bent, not the other way around. The best the support manager can strive for is some control over the standard of that support, making prompt identification of these local supporters and good communications with them the prime support objectives.

17.3 Outsourced support

Some IT products lend themselves readily to support from outside the corporation altogether. They fall into two main categories: *commodity support*, such as that provided by a maintenance company, and *niche product support*, where the product is so specialized that experts are difficult to find or create. Both are arrived at by commercial considerations. Commodity support is widely available from a competitive market, not difficult to do but expensive to get into. However, this last factor is changing – desktop computing is becoming so cheap that hardware maintenance contracts are beginning to make less sense: why keep a stock of spare parts when it is easier and cheaper to replace whole machines, which with the speed of technological change are obsolete by the time they break down anyway? Computer maintenance is a low-value form of support, with little or no business relevance, stemming from the fact that it is the machine which is being maintained, not the user.

Niche product support is the way the so-called 'vertical markets' are supported. The product in question is too far away from the mainstream and services too small an installed base to have created a competitive market in post-sales support. Examples of this are computer aided design and some accounting packages. The product is complex and expensive enough to require specialist user support, but the support needs to be for the use of the product rather than its technology. The user will invariably need to talk to a supporter who understands the business the product is used in rather than the computer it is running on.

To these two common forms of outsourced support, we now need to add the growing trend towards contracting IT support services out to external suppliers. This is often hailed as providing several benefits, including reducing headcount, predictability of support costs, tighter control of service levels, access to increased support resources, enabling the host company to focus on its core business, and so on. The movement is epitomized by the currently fashionable tendency for some governments to test how competitive and efficient their public service IT departments are against commercial offerings. In the United Kingdom this process is known as 'market testing', and has ultimately led to the awarding of some enormous contracts for IT services to private companies. This has caused some worrying discussions – for example, would there be security issues at stake if the taxation records of the British population were held on a computer managed by a non-British company.

Where any form of outsourced support is retained, the role of the support manager is substantially changed. On the one hand, he or she may be ignored altogether, as is the case where users take these contracts out direct with the supplier. On the other hand, the management becomes biased towards monitoring rather than providing the service. This requires a different type of support manager, more bureaucratically inclined and less of a team leader.

There are examples of this kind of support being taken to its extremes in the so-called 'virtual' support department. The only person employed in support by the IT department is the support manager. All other services, including helpdesk, problem resolution, training, repair, even the newsletter, are outsourced and the manager manages not the staff but the commercial relationships. The company would need no computer expertise, merely buying it in from computer experts. Costs and service levels would come under the control of formal contracts. Let me point out though that this is a commercial solution to a people problem. This extreme would give absolute control over support expenditure – but at some considerable cost to the user needing some one-off flexibility. There are many things which can be effectively supplied by mail order: this writer is not yet convinced that user support is one of them.

Where the relationship with a provider of outsourced support is managed at all, the most common way of achieving this is via a service level agreement (see Chapter 16), and understandably so. The SLA becomes the basis of the contract between provider and client, setting out benchmarks against which performance will be measured. Because the relationship is essentially a commercial one, it has to be two-way – money will change hands in both directions, depending on whether the service is a success or a failure, and this is a powerful incentive. However, when considering the flexibility or otherwise of the outsourced SLA, I am compelled to recall the words of an IT manager in the British Civil Service: 'all this Market Testing and Service Level Agreements', he said, 'I remember a time when "working to rule" was a way of withdrawing your labour – now it is becoming normal business practice'.

17.4 Support from IT suppliers

Beware computer suppliers offering 'support' with their products. It is not that supplier support is intrinsically bad, but neither does it follow that because they supply (or write, manufacture, or distribute) the product that they will necessarily be better at supporting it than you will.

It is probably true that a manufacturer will have people on its staff who are technically better informed about the product than your people are. But where will those people be? Probably in R&D, programming, or production. Their working-day priorities will be dedicated primarily if not exclusively to those functions, and not to post-sales support. It will be an unusual (and probably small) manufacturer who will not have ranks of other people whose job it is to face customers, and who by default if not by design will keep the end users away from contact with the truly knowledgeable.

Even if you could speak with the product designer, would you want to? It is unlikely that a designer will have much experience or training in dealing with customers, let alone communicating with the occasional fraught and confused end user. The ability of a manufacturer's technical developers to effectively deal with end-user queries is not guaranteed. In truth, you may be better off dealing with the manufacturer's support team, even if they do fall short of your expectations.

17.5 Support from PC distributors

When you come further down the distribution chain, the problems can get worse. Think of all the products supplied by Compaq. Imagine how difficult it must be to support all those. Then imagine you are a PC distributor, who handles Compaq, Hewlett Packard and perhaps IBM, plus Microsoft, WordPerfect, Lotus, Sage, Novell, Mountain, several brands of Ethernet card ('and by the way we also sell photocopiers'). What kind of support can be expected then? For many PC dealers (and several manufacturers) the closest their support people will come to being acquainted with much of their product range will be to read the back of a shrink-wrapped box. The manufacturers go some way towards helping with seminars, and so on, but in practice, the sheer weight of knowledge to be acquired means that some products in their range are simply not supportable.

17.6 The rules of supplier support

1 Only provide support if necessary.
2 Support the product only.
3 These rules are not cynical, they are objective.

If you are dissatisfied with the support you get from your suppliers, do not be surprised. The principles under which they operate differ from yours in two ways, both of them highly significant to the support relationship. The first is that the supplier only does things in order to sell and to continue to sell their products to you and others they consider to be like you. The complexity of the product may be such that without passing some knowledge to the market, customers may not have the information necessary to be aware of how the product may benefit them. After the sale, customers may need assistance with integrating the product into their businesses. This means that technical knowledge becomes a necessary part of the selling process, so it is as important as the box the product came in. By the same token, the provision of technical knowledge is as open to reputation as is the product itself. So they do it because if they do not, they will lose future sales.

In conclusion on this first principle, remember that you buy the product to extract some benefit for yourself, and your user support is dedicated to that end. But the supplier sells you the product for their benefit, not yours, and the support you get exists chiefly to serve the business goals of the supplier. This is a flawed, but perfectly legitimate support relationship, and it is probably exactly the same one as your company has with its own customers.

17.7 User or product support?

The second principle is a matter of what is supported. You support the end user, and in that sense, you support the usage of the product. Your job is intertwined with how that product is exploited to the benefit of the business. Your job is user support. However, the manufacturer sees things an entirely different way. Their job is product support. The manufacturer cannot be expected to support your users, and certainly cannot be expected to understand precisely how your business applies their products. So when your query goes to a supplier, it is just one of several to do with that product. They will answer the question from a product point of view, and it is your job to translate that inherently general information into the specific information your end user needs.

And if it sounds like they are doing their level best to look after your users' specific business needs, thus eroding the second principle, remember that the first principle applies.

In the end, the only support service truly qualified to support your users is your own. It should use the supplier service only as a resource, for that is the best it can be. If you depend on supplier support, the best you can hope for is an accidental or actual coincidence of purpose. Hope or engineer that the two widely differing sets of goals (those of your support supplier and your end users) coincide somewhere, so that your company can extract some real benefit from supplier support. But do not expect too much. Even if they wanted to provide real user support, they probably can't afford to these days anyway, there is just not the money in computers any more. And that is why they are all getting into outsourcing, so they can do support properly. But we have already been there in this chapter.

18   The international dimension

There are many examples of companies who have begun to operate user support on an international scale. It makes sense, especially where the userbase is international. Two distinct types of international support have emerged. The first is the single centre, where all customers make their queries to a single, central point. The second is the multiple centre: several support desks, in different time zones, attempting to provide out-of-hours (even 24-hour) cover as well as to solve the problem of supporting users in different time zones. In both cases, they are a form of centralization. The single centre is obviously centralized; the multiple centre may still be centralized as far as customers in that time zone are concerned.

One of the key drives behind any centralization of support is cost. It will always save money to gather the resources in one place or in the minimum number of places: critical mass is more easily reached, duplication of effort can be reduced. On the face of it, internationalization is cheaper. Cheapness matters in computing. The price of a product can make the difference between the world benefiting from a wonderful new technology or losing out on it because we were not prepared to pay for it. But wherever money is saved, we should always be on the lookout for what balances that saving. In this case, one risk which counterbalances the saving is reduced quality of support from the user's point of view.

18.1 Does internationalization mean poor quality?

Personal attention has always epitomized quality of service. And as there are few things less personal than a centralized telephone query desk, it looks easy to conclude that centralized telephone query answering is intrinsically poor quality – but that would be rash, for at least two reasons. First, quality is a subjective concept. If the type of service to be offered meets (or ideally exceeds) the expectations of the user, then the quality is more than adequate. Note that I did not say that it has to meet the needs of the user – only the expectations.

Second, there may be little to be gained over a telephone-only service by adding the personal touch, such as putting experts on the ground wherever there are users. Experts on the ground are enormously expensive, for which the user will eventually have to pay. Local experts may be wasteful; no matter how local they are, they always spend some of their time travelling, so you do not get as many solutions and as much service out of them as you would like – what you get most from them is miles covered, where what you wanted was problems solved, users placated.

In the packaged product industry, internationalization and extreme centralization of user support make a lot of sense. The expectation of the user may be for a low-cost form of support: after all, if they only paid a hundred dollars for the package, they cannot reasonably expect on-the-ground experts providing a premium quality service. So a telephone service across international boundaries will do the job just so long as the service they deliver does not drop below those already conveniently low user expectations.

Arguably, internationalization can mean improved quality of support, both for the customers of a manufacturer helpdesk and an internal user helpdesk. Internationalization means that the regional users are put in touch with central support. Economies of scale, brought about by supporting remote countries from the country of manufacture, can mean that the regional user can have recourse to levels of technical ability that would be way too expensive to provide at a regional level. Escalation routes are very rapid: the user's problem is delivered right to the heart of things, where the user support technicians are, and where the product designers are just down the corridor – and all this for the price of an international telephone call.

However, it does not always work out that way in practice, especially if the userbase is a big one. Then the product designers are only too aware of the international masses itching to bang at their door for a discourse with the people who really know the answers. Centralization of international support in this way is as likely as not to make the real experts even less available to the actual users. When did you ever actually get to speak to the man who wrote Microsoft Exchange?

18.2 Internationalization and alienation

However, centralization will always have some problems even producing a good telephone service. The more you centralize, the more you alienate the service from the people it is supposed to serve. Where the support is aimed at a product rather than the actual user, this alienation is taken as read. In essence, it does not matter that the support desk has no rapport with the user, if the desk only really exists to support the user's product. Alienation is an intrinsic part of the relationship and does not really need to be worried about separately.

It is worth exploring alienation a little more deeply. On an international, centralized helpdesk, the next issue to be addressed is what the helpdesk will do if it finds itself unable to solve a problem – for example, if diagnosis is impossible without visual contact (after all, the user may not have the vocabulary to describe accurately what is going on with the computer at the time of his or her query) or if the user is unable to implement the solution the helpdesk describes. If the problem is a hardware one, usually this will be taken care of by local hardware replacement – but for software problems, remote support is always more difficult, international or otherwise. The user is effectively on his or her own, with a computer that steadfastly refuses to do what is expected and a problem that steadfastly refuses to be a simple hardware failure. This form of user alienation is as perennial as support itself and where the support is international, is taken to extremes.

The other form of alienation is cultural. Any language student will confirm that it is not just the words you use, it is the way and the context in which you say them. The polite humour of the English can sound patronizing to a German. What the American hears as blunt and aggressive is reassuring self-confidence to a

Scandinavian. Mediterranean calmness can come across as vagueness or ignorance to the English, and so on. These barriers to communication cannot be broken down by crash courses in languages, they can only come from an understanding of the culture of the language. You may know how the words translate, but that does not mean you understand what is being said.

18.3 An alien experience

Let's pretend . . .

I'm a computer user in grey, rainsoaked Newcastle upon Tyne, England, stuck with a really knotty problem with my desktop. My company BMW gleams in my personal parking space, icons of my drive and ambition. This drive and ambition have just been jerked to a shuddering halt by the failure of the computer on my desk to perform. I call my support helpdesk, based in the company headquarters in some distant land. The place I am calling sounds more like somewhere I'd take the kids on holiday than expect any work to get done. Nevertheless, that is where I've got to go, because it's their computer, their software and their tune I'm dancing to.

I am greeted by an accent I have difficulty following, from a technician to whom ambition and urgency are foreign concepts and whose choice of words seems facile and groping because of his, in my opinion, flimsy grasp of my language. I cannot get close to this person. He clearly is nothing like me, cannot see my problem from my point of view and probably cannot understand half of what I am saying. The *mañana* of the whole, sorry experience leaves my stress at an all-time high, my confidence in the company at an all-time low and the desktop computer on a one-way trip to the nearest elevated window.

This is alienation in practice. It is the sort of thing that gets some head offices a deservedly bad name. They must have been conscious that the service was needed, so they kept it on. But they clearly did not understand how badly it was needed. Typical head office, don't care a fig for us out here in the regions. They ask us to perform and then give us lousy tools, and clearly they don't know the first thing about computer support. They have kept costs down so much that now, not only does the service not meet the needs of the users, it actually causes more damage to morale by being there than it would if they got rid of it altogether. What little they spend on computer support now is utterly wasted. At least if they did it properly, some of what they spent on it would only be partly wasted.

Now I am not saying that people from Newcastle upon Tyne are any more or any less xenophobic, jealous, or unreasonable than the rest of us. What I am trying to do here is illustrate how distance and cultural difference can mutually alienate the user and the support provider; and how that alienation, real or imagined, can corrupt what might otherwise be a fruitful and productive service relationship. It happens, you know it does; for example, I was in an ethnic restaurant last night and I had a real problem getting my order through to this chap behind the counter, who appeared vague and not concentrating. Now I know and like that restaurant; the staff are usually diligent, kind, generous, cultured people who never fail to impress with their linguistic skills and their magnificent cuisine. But if that chap had been the first of their employees I had met, in my desperation for service (I was hungry!), that experience might have given me a bad impression and done nothing to boost my confidence in his restaurant's ability to meet my service needs.

This is the risk you run by internationalizing helpdesk and support services – it is not racism or xenophobia you are up against, it is cultural differences which subtly alter the priorities of communication. And remember, this alienation can exist within nation states as well. Are there cultural differences between Chicago and Dallas? Vancouver and Montreal? London and Leeds? Hanover and Munich? Milan and Naples? Sydney and Melbourne? Madrid and Barcelona? Paris and Toulouse? Calcutta and Bangalore? Edinburgh and Glasgow? In my experience, the answer to all these is a resounding *yes*.

18.4 What are you supporting?

There is no doubt that where the product only is to be supported, alienation can help – it keeps users at arm's length and expects users to gain some expertise themselves. The support issues get narrower, so easier to deal with, and easier support means cheaper staff and potentially more rapid reaction to change. On the other hand, it can also mean a lack of flexibility: if the query cannot be fixed by a stock answer, it may have difficulty getting a solution at all.

The other end of the scale is to support not the product, but the user's use of the product. This is extremely difficult to do from a centralized helpdesk and virtually impossible to do across international boundaries, simply because user support tends to be more face to face. So support people have to move around – and internationally, the distances are just too great.

In conclusion, I would feel compelled to advise that although product support can be provided effectively across international borders, user support usually cannot.

18.5 Choosing locations

Back in the 1990s, when Quarterdeck were considering how to support Europe, they had to decide on a location. Without needing to put staff on the road, the actual location they would choose within Europe would need no geographical bias: if you do not have to travel, it really does not matter where you live. What matters at this point are three things: the indigenous population, in terms of their abilities, availability and salary expectations; local telecommunications technology, in terms of the cost and accessibility of international communications; and the local government, in terms of their tendencies either to discourage or assist immigrating international companies. In Ireland, Quarterdeck found an educated and available work-force with language ability. Despite that, salaries tend to be lower there than in many other countries in Europe and Quarterdeck are on record as complementing the telecommunications offerings.

Other companies wishing to support the whole of Europe choose Germany. Despite a strong local culture and rich language, Germany freely accepts English as the lingua franca of IT. Germany is also attractive as an international base because of the size and wealth of the home market, plus the proximity of other German-speaking markets (Austria, Switzerland, parts of eastern Europe) and the emerging economies east of the erstwhile 'Iron Curtain'. What I am describing here however, is a product support tendency. Quarterdeck based a focused product support helpdesk in Ireland; whereas other product-oriented companies have moved to central Europe for commercial reasons, to sell to those big markets, and the support desk has sprung up there as an arm of the product distribution function.

18.6 International politics

If you have ever heard anybody say 'it wouldn't work here', you will understand what it is like negotiating international implementations of anything, let alone an international helpdesk. Nations are innately protective of their indigenous cultures, and this is an emotional and political movement that has been gaining momentum ever since the Berlin Wall came down. Corporations may believe that they have the expertise in head office to show the regions how to conduct their businesses, and within the relatively limited scope of their organizations in their country, they are probably right; but it does not necessarily follow that what works in the US, New Zealand, or Holland will work exactly the same way in France, Argentina, or Singapore if we choose to attempt to impose it there.

There are too many considerations, and what you do not want to do is to install a user support service which consistently annoys people by blithely sinning against local sensibilities. They may be providing an excellent support service, and the local population may be willing, on the face of it, to allow for these cultural gaffes. But deep down they may resent the unspoken insult of having their sensibilities disregarded for the sake of exploiting them as a market commodity, and this will eventually erode the support relationship. After all, we helpdesk professionals need our clients to believe in us for the professionals we are.

The international helpdesk may be rendered irrelevant by local rules – some countries insist on a certain percentage of local employment, and some are just plain corrupt enough to expect a rake-off. But these are the extremes. Local employment may become necessary not just out of financial considerations, but out of practical necessity – the central helpdesk just may not be able to come to terms with the remote culture, methods of working, expectations, or language, and putting in a team on the ground may be the only way to support those users.

In the end, however, it comes down to what the local user community wants from its support service and how much it is willing to pay for it. If the multinational corporation has a local manager who insists on having her own IT function, she may have to explain this to the central board or take an increased business target to pay for it. If the IT manufacturer is under pressure from his international market to put support in locally, he may have to charge more in that market for his product – but that opens up a whole can of worms called 'grey importing', where the market buys its product cheaper from a market next door, then gets the local company to support it, pushing support demand up to inordinate levels which they have not paid for.

18.7 Helpdesk globalization

Throughout the last decade, globalization of corporate activity grew in importance, until now it has become part of everyday life. Indigenous markets and home bases do not necessarily have the attraction they once had. Now the rule is 'manufacture it where it is most cost effective, sell it anywhere'. Some companies go global through growth and deliberate strategic investment in chosen markets. Others do it by buying an established company in a target region of the world. The growing company may take its IT standards with it – the acquisitive one may have to impose those standards as an alternative to the existing methodologies of the acquired office. Either way, sooner or later the corporate IT standard arrives in all significant locations and with it should come the corporate IT support process.

Broadly speaking, there are two types of support globalization – one is establishing helpdesks in international regions or larger offices, the other is what's known as 'follow the sun'. I have advised clients in both systems, and neither could be said to fit all companies or to be 'better' than the other.

'Follow the sun' is the concept of IT support, more or less central to a set of time zones that is roughly eight hours wide. So when one helpdesk closes down, any users working late that evening can call the next one in the chain, which is just starting its working day. It is difficult to make that work absolutely, because there are too few major cities in advanced, industrialized nations that are exactly eight hours apart, and the breadth of the Pacific always seems to mess things up in my experience. But it can be done, often by extending helpdesk availability by an hour or two either side of 9am to 5pm. But there are practical difficulties. The availability of specialized language skills may not be guaranteed, accents differ, second-line support may be impossible and high bandwidth for computer remote control is still not universally available. Faced with this challenge, many helpdesks end up acting locally – they give their local second-line technicians retainer payments so they can drag them from their beds if the network or batch jobs fail in the middle of the night.

One alternative to 'follow the sun' I·tend to use is region-alization. This means establishing a main helpdesk to serve a group of countries and operate in a limited range of almost-local languages and a narrow group of time zones (say around two hours either side of the usual working day). Second-line support can be installed at the relatively larger remote offices – say beyond about 30 users. For fewer than that, a well-equipped triage desk with good remote control software and a deal with an outsourcing company to occasionally send a technician to the smaller offices will usually do the trick. It's not cheap, but if the business needs a small remote office, the price of maintaining its productivity must be paid.

Part Four

Workload management

19

Reactivity and proactivity

The apparently diametrically opposed concepts of reactivity and proactivity are at the heart of organizing and managing the workload of the user support function. Reactivity is the tendency of the support team to deal with its workload by reacting to situations as they crop up; what the *Oxford English Dictionary* calls 'acting or operating in return'. Proactivity is the state of anticipating the workload, relating to it and controlling it in a way that allows for innovation; a tendency to make things happen, as opposed to reactively dealing with them after they have already happened.

For most IT support organizations, the ability to be reactive is vital. Emergencies will crop up, accidents will happen, machines will fail, users will forget their training, deadlines will exist, directions will be changed, opportunities will arise, mistakes will be made – and somebody has to be there to pick up the technological pieces and get the computer system back on track or shifted in the new direction. Many of these instances cannot be forecast – so even if you were proactive, in some areas it would not do any good. You never really know what is going to happen next.

However, that does not matter, you do not need to forecast what will happen, just estimate how much resource it is going to take. And if you have been taking measurements of how the department performs and what work it gets through, you will have a pretty clear picture of how much reacting to emergencies you are actually going to have to do. The key to proactivity is controlled reactivity – and to control reactivity, you have to measure it. More on measurement in later chapters. At this stage, suffice to say that if your support department has a history of needing to be reactive, then it is likely to need to be reactive in future.

19.1 The benefits of reactivity and proactivity

The company and the users benefit from both ways of working. As we have already seen, there is a need for a reactivity. The company benefits by having the confidence that it can cope with most things that befall its computers and users. The users benefit, not just because they have a resource to call on during an emergency, but because they can call on those staff at any time they can persuade the IT staff is an emergency (even when, in a corporate perspective, it is not really an emergency). The technical staff benefit too. When they are asked to react and do so, they are seen to have dealt with the crisis at hand. This raises the technicians' standing and often confers upon them the warmth of human gratitude, which is always nice.

However, the benefits of reactivity are bound up in the present, and when reactivity becomes the only way of working, often the benefits are far outweighed by the damage done by just reacting. To simply react to what crops up today is to fail to invest effort in what may crop up tomorrow. The point of solving any given problem is lost, when a few hours later the same problem is solved again, albeit by a different technician, albeit for a different user. The fact was, the work had to be done again. The first couple of times may be inevitable – the next time should have been anticipated and proactive steps taken to prevent it or at least prepare the world for it.

Reacting, although necessary, is always bound up with damage done. If you are having to react to a problem, then the problem has already occurred, it has already caused production to cease, it has already become part of the backlog that is costly work-in-progress. Only if that problem had never occurred can it be said that it never caused damage.

The benefits of proactivity are considerable. First, there is the self-respect due to all proactives for being sufficiently in control of the workload to be able to anticipate it rather than lurch uncontrollably about in pursuit of it. In order to be proactive, you must have created space in the workload to examine the job to see what you would do next. In proactivity there is the choice between options, a choice which is not there when you are simply reacting to whatever needs doing next. In proactivity, there is the opportunity to invest resource to make change and real improvement instead of just firefighting. That said, however, reactivity in extreme may be a product of a choice made – a choice to do the heroic problem solving rather than the future-ready but boring planning.

Proactivity can bring a real benefit to technical staff, in that it can be used to inject variety into the work. Variety can be a key to solving the perennial problem of the support helpdesk, that of burnout. Working on a helpdesk can be enormously stressful; it can look as though the computers are always failing the company or that the users are too incompetent to use the machines correctly. Then once a problem is solved, the following day it crops up again somewhere else and has to be solved again. All this can make the helpdesk job seem rather pointless, and can wear down the enthusiasm of the most committed user support professional. Well-directed proactivity can create different types of work in the support department, work with a point which actually delivers a tangible benefit. From this can come renewed motivation.

19.2 Staffing for reactivity

With the need to be reactive proven, then clearly that need must be adequately resourced. But a reactive need is unpredictable – you cannot say when an emergency will crop up, although you will know from a study of your own work history that emergencies have always cropped up in the past. If you could precisely predict an emergency, it would not be an emergency, because logically, you would organize yourself to stop it happening in the first place. This is the paradox of reactivity: the need to cater for emergencies is obvious, and you know how many staff you have needed to deal with them in the past, but the nature of the emergencies is obscure until they happen. Emergency is at the same time unpredictable and predictable.

So because it is unpredictable, and because you must be ready for it, you must necessarily have resources ready to deal with the emergency when it does come in. Logically, you must have idle resources; that is to say staff who are, if not exactly twiddling their thumbs, then at least, involved in less than perfectly productive work until that day or hour comes when they are suddenly 110 per cent involved in work that is so vital that the cost of them doing it is irrelevant.

Can the accountants out there hear me? All the short-termist cost-cutters who laid off technicians during the recession? I am saying that for the good of your company and your continued profitability you have to have some element of waste on your IT support staff. People you are paying to do nothing! They must be there – ready to react – just in case the balloon goes up, as it surely will. We do not begrudge the city firefighters their game of pool and hand of cards, a couple of hours of paid inactivity prior to the catastrophe they will inevitably have to cope with; nor should we distrust the computer network genius whom we happen to catch reading a lowbrow computer magazine in the calm between storms. His time is not being wasted – it is the very fact that he is there that makes him so valuable.

19.3 Examining the 'over-reactivity' problem

As a helpdesk consultant, one of the conditions I am most frequently asked to deal with or comment on is the tendency of some helpdesks to be 'too reactive' – as if that in itself were the problem. What tends to happen is that the reactive work appears to swamp all opportunity for proactivity. In problem environments like this, 'lack of staff' is often cited as being the root of the problem. It sometimes is, but more often it is not – the root lies elsewhere.

Many helpdesk managers see their own reactivity as a weakness or failure, especially when that reactivity has swamped every-thing else. They feel that if they were more in control of their workload, they would tend to be less reactive and more proactive, or at least achieve a balance between the two. A lack of control contributes to reduced self-respect, which contributes to reduced confidence, which in turn reduces the ability to take control. This is a common vicious circle in helpdesks which have lost control of their workload, and in such situations I have found it not uncommon for the blame to be placed elsewhere, such as on the lack of sufficient staff; it cannot be the fault of the manager or technicians, after all they are working like Trojans just to keep their heads above water.

It is in this tendency to overwork that the clue lies to the real solution. That they are working at exactly 100 per cent of capacity to deal with exactly 100 per cent of the tasks set them is just too precise to be likely. By some percentage, they must be either overachieving or underachieving. Are they working at less than 100 per cent? Could they in effect do more? Or are they working at 110 per cent? In other words are they spending too much time at the office and not enough in those other activities that keep them balanced and well-adjusted human beings with a full outlook on life and a happy and harmonious domestic situation?

Another question is are they actually achieving 100 per cent of the goals they should? Or are they so wrapped up in the stuff they deal with now that they have missed an unknown number of other goals which no longer get counted as needing to be dealt with?

When I am assessing an apparent problem of over-reactivity, I try to see the whole picture – maybe they are reacting because they like reacting. Maybe they are reacting because reactive work is easier, less challenging, quicker to yield results, more self-gratifying, less regimented, less formal, less boring, less measurable than other types of work. Maybe they have become reactive because they have lost touch with how IT is deployed in their company, so they do what they are asked to do rather than what needs doing. Maybe they have become reactive so they do not have to think about the implications of their work, because if they did they would be overwhelmed by guilt for what they are not achieving on their users' behalf. Maybe they are reactive by design, clandestine or otherwise. If the warmth of human gratitude is on offer to anybody who can solve a user's problem, how about letting the problem occur so it can be solved? (There are some cynics who would say this is a politician's tactic: do nothing about a known problem, cynically let it fester until it reaches crisis point and then suddenly throw your weight into the problem, say three months before an election. Win your support not from having caused the problem, which you did, but from having solved it, which you did. Simultaneously the perfect deception and the perfect justification of your own existence, while deliberately manipulating and exploiting the users, oops I mean the electorate, in the process. But that is another story.)

Maybe they are reacting simply because their priorities have become confused: they deal with an urgent problem simply because it is urgent – without stopping to consider whether it is important. In other words, there is some work that gets done by some support teams that frankly does not need doing at all, but because it is urgent and time critical, it gets dealt with right now. This is a waste of effort and in the long term clearly serves neither the support team, who waste their own resources, nor the user population, who lose support effort that could have been better invested, nor the company, which pays for that waste straight off the bottom line.

In dealing with a reactivity problem, be suspicious! Some technicians might secretly be glad that it is so difficult to measure the value of their reactive work. See it from their point of view. Let us say I am a problem-solving technician; in comes a problem from a user and like the dedicated chap I am, off I go to solve it. The user may be on the other side of the corporate campus, or on the other side of the Bay of Biscay but that makes no odds, this is my mercy mission. At this stage, the support manager may not even have been involved in the decision, as the responsibility to resolve is quite rightly fully trusted to the resolver. And now the resolver has disappeared, the manager is presented with a *fait accompli*. The decision to attend has already been taken, whether the manager would have disagreed or not. And while the technician is away, the manager has no real means of assessing the value of the work actually being done. Asking the technician on his return is an option, but such a discussion risks generating more heat than light – the technician will want recognition for a success achieved, not an inquisition into the value of the achievement.

In departments suffering from extreme reactivity, often the manager has, perhaps even subconsciously, shied away from challenges such as this – the manager's technical knowledge is no longer strong enough to engage in complex discussion of the nature of a technical problem, or the challenge might be seen as detrimental to departmental harmony. But this avoids dealing with the root problem of reactivity.

19.4 What does helpdesk proactivity look like?

Proactivity in a user support department takes many forms. One of the most common of these is a regular study of user problems encountered with a view to preventing them in future. Another is the creation of an inventory of user equipment to help with diagnosing and solving problems the users may have. What these forms of proactivity have in common, however, is that they are all actions now in order to influence the future; whereas reactivity is some action now in order to have some influence now.

Logically, it could be said that extreme reactivity is the result of a denial or at least ignorance of the future. However, in business, and certainly in computers, the future is inevitable and so close as to be blinding. Change is happening all the time. And if the users, the technology and the problems all change, why doesn't the support department? A challenge I almost always make to the support managers who attend my seminars goes as follows: 'Hands up all those whose support services look different now than they did three years ago. Now, hands up all those whose company's use of computers looks exactly like it did three years ago.'

For the first part, few hands go up. For the second part, almost all hands go up, usually falteringly, because by the second 'hands up' they have guiltily twigged what I am getting at. Finally, I ask if they were really that sure three years ago that they had organized well enough to meet the future, and how sure they are now.

To design yourself proactive services, one of the first questions to ask yourself is what else your department could be doing that would deliver a real, additional benefit to the users. Then compare the potential value of that benefit with the actual value of the benefits you are currently delivering. Where the potential value of a new activity exceeds the value of a current activity, stop delivering that cheap current service and start delivering that valuable new one. Nobody can challenge you, because you can clearly justify this change. All you have done is adjusted your priorities. If they wish you to carry on with the old service as well, it is that one that must be resource-justified, not the new one.

Real proactivity comes from changing the reasons why people need you now, so they cease to need you for those reasons. If the users have problems with a piece of software, what can you do to change the software or the users so that problem goes away and stops doing the damage it is doing now? If you have users who do not use one of your services, what can you do to start them using the service? Conversely, if there are users who are using your service the wrong way or for the wrong reasons, what can you do to change that in the future?

One of the reasons some support teams shy away from proactivity is because it changes things. That is the essence of proactivity. Meeting real and potential changes with changes to ourselves or the market we operate in. And as I have said elsewhere in this volume, technicians are a conservative lot. Many of them do not like change. Better just to wait for the telephone to ring. To change the present is to introduce risk: if I reduce the users' present need for me, how can I be sure they will continue to need me in the future, thereby justifying my salary and my gung-ho, problem-solver-extraordinaire image?

Helpdesk proactivity can and should be enshrined in specific services, which just like the helpdesk service have to be continuously delivered. This entwines proactivity into the day-to-day work of the support function and makes it that much harder to stop doing. Specific services to maintain proactivity might be as follows:

- Formalized analysis of the last fortnight's helpdesk queries, identifying user groups who seem to have a lot of the same type of query, contacting those users and designing mutually acceptable solutions to plug knowledge gaps.
- Producing reports on changes made to the computer network, how the company/users benefit from those changes and how to make use of them.
- Compiling and maintaining a directory and regular reports of computer usage, company department by department, as a report to senior management of where their IT investment is being used and perhaps where it is being wasted.
- Maintaining a register of equipment in use, so you can identify which workstations are becoming obsolete and can thus advise the user when to replace their equipment and what with.
- Keeping a central catalogue of macros, batchfiles and datafiles in use by user location, and offering that catalogue to the users so they can share programs and data.
- Producing a monthly newsletter of hints, tips and goings-on on the computer system and in the IT support population.
- Monitoring the performance and learning rate of new company employees for advising the employees' line manager or perhaps the personnel department; how about recommending changes to the corporate induction process as a result of what you discover?
- Analysing new technologies as they arrive on the market and offering reports to the users; topics could be 'how our company could implement this new product and what benefits we could gain as a company', 'how usable the product is in practice', 'how the product differs from the hype', 'what support queries this product is likely to raise'.

There is a thread running through these 'proactive' services. Every single one of them adds value to you as a user support department. In almost every proactive service, you have had to look at what your users could make use of, and create a service to satisfy that potential demand. With these services, you are doing much more than just answering the telephone and putting out fires – you are producing new value, making new use of your unique position halfway between the users and the computers.

19.5 Staffing for proactivity

Moving from a reactive to a proactive base may require you to re-examine your staff and structure. If you currently have a Support Department that looks less like a slick, creative, and analytical machine and more the Legion of Superheroes, then going proactive is probably going to be tricky. You are going to need more of the stay-at-home type, people who are motivated by studying data and drawing conclusions, people who like writing fluent and readable prose, people who like taking risks and inventing new services from recognized opportunities. You are going to need less of the reactive problem solver who prefers doing to writing about it, fewer independent types who like visiting people.

The people are only part of the problem – if your support department is divided along the conventional helpdesk–resolver split, then the structure will not lend itself to proactivity. You will have to dedicate resources to your new proactive services and this will mean structuring the department to cater for a non-reactive function.

Case Study 19.1: Derek makes the change

Derek came to realize only slowly that his team's reactivity was hurting both him and the users. It was the recognition that the last three computer systems that had been installed in the company were being supported by external companies. He had not thought much of it at the time, as the computers were all specialized so-called 'vertical' systems: one for accounting, one for running a production line and another for monitoring the delivery fleet. But now he had thought about it, all those systems could have been run on the existing computers. Had he not missed out on the system specification stage (too busy fighting fires at the time, as usual), he could have influenced the purchasing decision. The company had three departments rebelling against the corporate IT strategy, and four different standards of user support. Derek vowed it would never happen again.

In the support department was Lisa, who had been a technician for years and who had clearly had enough. Her motivation was slacking, and although she had no difficulty keeping up with the new technologies, her heart was no longer in it. Trouble was, there was nowhere to promote ex-technicians. Derek wanted to keep her, but how to make her useful again?

The new need for proactivity was Derek's opportunity. He put the case to his boss, who was also worried about the potential fragmentation of the IT strategy if the user rebellion was not curbed. The only problem was persuading the boss to part with a respectable salary increase for Lisa, but once he was convinced and Lisa heard the plan, it was plain sailing from there. Lisa's new job would require her to be with the users as much if not more than she had been before. But now her role was to learn as much as she could about the way the users used the computers, what their business problems were now and what they were likely to be in the future.

She would come up with two types of response to what she learned. One was to use her technical knowledge to make adjustments to desktop computers to make them more usable from the user's point of view. The other was to keep examining the market to see what new products were becoming available to address the users' changing needs. This meant regularly reporting back to her old colleagues in technical support about the new products they were going to have to support.

Lisa stayed technical, and stayed with the firm. The users got better support and assistance with buying new IT products. The IT department got control over what the users were buying and the support department got a chance to prepare for the new products that were coming on board. Nice move, Derek.

20

Managing the queue

The queue is a perennial feature of almost all forms of service management and none more so than user support services. Queues exist throughout user support – an engaged tone is a form of a queue, it means that the caller is going to have to wait until a helpdesk telephone comes free. The stack of outstanding problems the resolvers still have to solve also form a queue. The heap of work you will, as a department, 'one day get around to' is a queue. The stack of papers in your intray are a queue. The promise you made to the user that you will 'get to him just as soon as you've finished what you're doing right now' means that he is now standing in line – he has joined a queue to wait for a window in your day. Look at the calendar – the days ahead are all forming a nice orderly queue, waiting for you to deal with them, one by one.

Queues are unpopular. Taken at the extreme, they are an insult to anybody who has to stand in line. The logic of service need is simple: 'I want, you provide, so give now! Why should I have to wait?' The reality is different but also callously simple. The queue says to all those in it that we cannot or will not service your request right now, even though it is our business to service your request. This is where the insult lies: the implication is that the service needs your custom to survive or justify itself, but it does not need your custom so desperately that it cannot afford to make you wait at their convenience. The extreme customer reaction to this insult would be to shun the queue and the service altogether, as some supermarkets have found to their cost, and go to a competitive service which appears to value customers more highly by offering a shorter queue.

The user support department cannot afford such a risk. If it is an IT supplier helpdesk, the loss of a support customer can also mean the loss of a product customer, so it is in the vendor's interest to offer a short support service queue. If the helpdesk is a company-internal one, failure to provide an efficient and quick service (from the user's point of view) causes lost user productivity, which eventually finds its way to the corporate bottom line.

20.1 The cost of a queue

Queues cost money. As pointed out so eloquently in Eliyahu Goldratt's *The Goal* (in my opinion a must read for all user support managers), queues mean inventory not shipped, resulting in a cost in work-in-progress. When a request comes in, it immediately starts to consume costs. There is the cost of the support department's response to that request in time and knowledge, the response of the user's lost productivity and work which she cannot do until the request is satisfied. That request goes on running up that bill of costs all the time it stays in the support department, right until the request is resolved to the user's satisfaction and normal service is resumed. These are the costs of work-in-progress, and they can be calculated.

In Fig. 20.1, the cost of the outstanding queries in the helpdesk is calculated. Take any technician currently working on a query. Work out the hourly cost of the technician, including all the on-costs like use of desk space, telephone, heating and lighting. Multiply that by the number of hours this query has been open for. Add to that the hourly cost of the user, again multiplied by

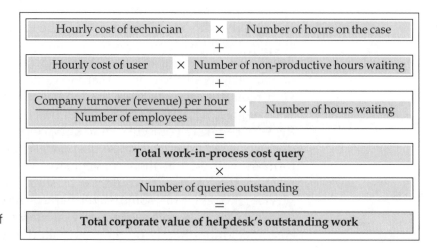

Figure 20.1
Calculating the cost of the queue

the number of hours the user has been non-productive – if the user has something else he can be doing, you can leave out this figure. Next, add in the lost user productivity, which is the turnover that user could have been making if he were working properly; you may have to adjust this number by a percentage, to allow for the fact that the user is not completely idle. What you are left with is the cost of that query so far. It will probably be an uncomfortably large number. Now for the sake of completeness, multiply that by the number of queries the whole department has outstanding. You had better be sitting down at this point, and think long and hard before you tell the board of directors about this number.

One helpdesk I worked with was part of a company that had a turnover of around £140,000 per employee per annum. The productive time of a user was about 7.5 hours per day, 220 days per year, meaning that each user contributed to around £85 of sales every hour they were working. The average salary plus on-costs was around £18,000 so for the sake of simplicity we used that figure for both users and technicians; it comes out at about £10.90 per hour. Our typical queue had about 50 outstanding queries in it at any one time and a typical fix time was, conveniently, about one working day. Each technician fixed about seven queries a day, so they would spend just over an hour on each problem. So the average value of our work-in-progress was an hour of the technician's time at £10.90, plus any time the user was idle for, and as they were rarely totally idle, they were still earning their pay so often there was no addition for this. Next to calculate the productivity cost. We made a 50 per cent allowance for the user doing something else while he or she was waiting for a solution, so the lost productivity cost comes to £318.75. Add the salary costs to make £329.65 *per query*. Multiply that by our typical 50 outstanding queries to get a total of £16,482.50 – just invested in our ability to keep users waiting for an answer. What could the company do with that free capital?

20.2 Why queues are needed

If users are insulted by queues and if queues cost money in work-in-progress, then why have queues at all? All this sounds like a compelling case for the eradication of queues. But it is not so cut and dried. The cost example I gave earlier shows a pretty extreme case, I hope, and there are two sides to this story. The cost of work-in-progress is a capital cost, not a revenue cost.

Although it is related to revenue figures, it is entirely one-off. So if you were to eradicate the queue I described above, you would release £16,482.50 as a one-time-only contribution. Once it were spent, that would be it. Compare that with the cost of eradicating that queue and keeping it eradicated. That would mean deploying some resource to stop the queue ever building up again. That resource costs money. What we have here is a straight trade-off between the financial cost of the queue (disregarding, for the moment, the emotional or political cost) and the cost of avoiding the queue.

Queues are needed to save money. They are also needed because of the nature of work, in the way it arrives. There are plenty of sayings to describe this nature: 'boom or bust' is one, 'glut or drought' is another, 'it never rains but it pours' is another. Work does not come at a steady trickle, it comes in waves of relatively high and low demand. Furthermore, the resources we have to deal with them are never totally idle, they are working on something else at the moment a job comes in. So the queue forms naturally – either because there is a sudden high demand which we will get through eventually, or because we have to drop something else to deal with a new problem, in which case the 'something else' goes into the queue. Queues are inevitable.

The key issue here is dealing with sudden demand, as this is the essence of what the helpdesk does. This is how the emergency arrives. Let us say that we have a resolver group which between them can handle three queries an hour. If the queries do not come in at three queries an hour exactly, there will either be an idle technician or there will be a queue. And the queries will not come in that regularly, they will come in twos and fours. But the only way to be able to deal with everything would be to predict peak demand and resource to meet that, rather than resource to meet average demand. In this case, we would need an extra technician to deal with the occasions when there were four queries an hour. The cost of the extra technician, which would be a continuous one year on year, would eventually outweigh the capital saved by eradicating the queue.

20.3 Making the queue work for you

Queues cost money, somewhere along the line. You can be said to have mastered queue management when you have passed the cost of the queue onto somebody else who is willing to accept that cost. As we have seen, a queue is caused when demand exceeds the ability to service that demand. This is called a 'bottleneck'. If the bottleneck exists somewhere inside your system, then you, as the queue owner, will be carrying the costs of that queue. However, if the bottleneck is outside your system, or at the head of it, the queue does not cost you any money. Instead, the costs are passed onto those jobs which are waiting to get into the system at all; so far they have not used any of your resources or materials, only their own time.

You know how many jobs your system can handle at any one time. To maximize the efficiency of your system, arrange a bottleneck at the entry point of your system so that precisely that many jobs enter the system. To do this, you have to have a backlog, but for the queue not to cost you anything, the backlog must be outside your system. The British Post Office appears to have realized this. They may deny this, but they appear to manage their queues in precisely that fashion. In any Post Office I have ever visited, I have always had to queue to be served. The Post Office reduces the number of service windows available, not when the backlog has gone, but when the queue gets down to a certain level. If they did not have that backlog, they would have staff sitting idle at service windows, so to avoid this, they always make sure there is a queue. This means they can free up staff for other functions. It keeps their staff costs down and passes that cost onto the customers queuing for service.

This technique, if that is what it is, can be used by helpdesks also. However, it is probably of little use to helpdesks inside corporations, as keeping their own users waiting would constitute a cost to the corporation somewhere. However, those who are supporting external clients, minimizing the workload inside the support operation is merely a matter of narrowing the bottleneck through which all incoming work must pass. That is obvious. But it also means that those queries which do get through will get a far better service, as once they are in the system, they will not have to queue behind anything else. If this is what you wish to do, you can accomplish it simply by reducing the size or availability of the helpdesk.

In practice, it means making the difficult decision of which queries to service and which to discourage, and how that should be carried out. One way of ceasing to service certain queries is to simply take the helpdesk telephone off the hook. Crude, but effective; however, that is a little extreme, because then no queries can come in so the helpdesk loses its purpose. However, a variant on this may be a possibility. For example, have the helpdesk available for limited hours only, let us say you close between 11am and 1pm; this will enable you to catch up with the backlog you accrued in the morning. Beware that limited-hours opening can also have the effect of making the times you are open that bit more chaotic. However, you will lose some calls, typically the ones you want to lose; those casual callers who only call you because it is easier than opening the manual.

It would be better if you could distinguish at source between the calls you want to take and those you wish to discourage. Ideally, that distinction should be made even before the query arrives at the helpdesk, which usually means having to discourage not only types of queries but perhaps certain classes of user. Later I suggest splitting the helpdesk up into several helpdesks with different numbers offering different service levels to different user classes.

20.4 Eradicating queues

First be sure that your real desire is to eradicate the queue at all. As discussed above, there may be sound commercial reasons for the queue being there. If that is the case, then your problem is not one of queue eradication, but of marketing, so that the queue assumes its rightful place in the customers' list of priorities and is not seen to be more destructive than it is. Sometimes it takes the helpdesk to make the commercial argument, especially when users demand a level and speed of service which they do not make enough money to pay for.

Decide if your queue is a natural one, like the Post Office example, where the queue exists in order to make your support organization operate at maximum efficiency and maximum resource occupation. On the other hand, if the queue is just a plain old-fashioned backlog, then perhaps it is time to get rid of it. It is easy to tell the difference between a queue and a backlog: a backlog keeps growing, a queue remains more or less the same size for considerable periods of time.

If what you have is a backlog, then perhaps temporary staff or contractors are the answer. This will take some analysis of the work in the backlog first, and what you are looking for are 'commodity knowledge' problems – the sort of problems which anybody with the right level of knowledge could deal with. Once you have identified these, all you then need is a technical specialist in that area. However, do not start to deal with a backlog unless you know you have already eradicated the causes of the backlog.

Find out what sort of work is in the queue. Is it all work that you should be doing? If your company is like many others, then every department is doing work that is really the priority of another department. For example – a small one, but one that drives me round the bend – when you are filling in your expenses claim, do you have to calculate the purchase tax or Value Added Tax and put it in a separate column? Are you an accountant or a computer problem solver? Get the accountants to fill in their own forms, you are no tax expert and you have got better things to do! For another example, do users call you as an alternative to reading the manual on their desk? You can help them use the computer, but let's face it, you cannot use it for them. All this work is somebody else's priority – identify it, and get them to take responsibility for their own priorities instead of using your headcount budget to do their work.

If a queue is caused by a bottleneck, the simplest way to eradicate the queue is to widen the bottleneck. However, often there is more than one bottleneck. Widening them all may often be either impractical or impossible. However, all the bottlenecks must be considered; not just for how narrow they are, but where they come in sequence to one another.

A bottleneck capable of admitting three queries an hour will at times cause a queue of at least one query an hour if it is preceded by one capable of servicing four queries an hour. However, swap these two round and a different story emerges; a bottleneck servicing four queries an hour will sit idle sometimes if it is preceded in the sequence by a bottleneck admitting three queries an hour. So the simplest solution to this queue has been to alter the order of the bottlenecks so that the next bottleneck or process is always more capacious than the previous; the first bottleneck or process is the narrowest, the last is the widest.

Look at the flow of work through your support operation as a series of demands or queries which have to be dealt with by a sequence of processes leading to a completed job. See the problem-solving route as a production line. What constitutes a production 'process' in your support operation? What is the capacity of each of those processes in terms of jobs done per unit of time? How does work move from one process to the next? What else could earlier processes do to reduce the burden on the later ones, thus making later processes effectively able to handle more work?

A typical sequence of support processes might be: user diagnoses problem; user reports problem to helpdesk; helpdesk allocates query to resolver; resolver visits user to diagnose problem further; resolver builds test environment; resolver tests possible solution; further diagnosis; further testing; resolver visits user to implement solution. There are a lot of potential bottlenecks here; for example, so much diagnosis, could it not be put right at the head of the sequence by having the user or the helpdesk do most of the diagnosis? Also all these visits, with the frustration of matching a technician's timetable with that of the user so they can meet to discuss the problem; could that sequence of bottlenecks not be eliminated altogether by remote diagnosis or implementation?

20.5 Controlled queues

If the queue is inevitable, then you have to live with it. The main way of dealing with work that is already outstanding is to prioritize it. It is easy to do this once in a while, but that will not manage your queue – this is more of a backlog minimization technique. Queue prioritization has to be continuous and automatic.

The most successful queue prioritization method I ever saw deployed in a helpdesk was entirely computerized. When a query came in and was passed on to the resolvers, it had a priority of 60. This number was unseen by anybody in the support department – only the computer knew about it. This 60 was increased or decreased by the name of the user and the type of fault being reported. So the system had to maintain an accurate record of which user was which and how commercially important that user was to the corporation (a database which had to be constantly updated, having the fringe benefit of keeping the support manager in constant close contact with the users). The system also increased the priority of every query for every unit of time the problem was outstanding. And of course, nobody could look at the outstanding database without seeing it sorted in priority order. To top this, the standing instruction to the resolvers was that they always take their next job from the top of the database; and the computerized prioritization system had already seen to it that that was the next job that needed doing.

This is an example of prioritization after the query had come in. However, you can prioritize before the query comes in, offering certain users a 'fast-track' service. You need to identify those users to whom you wish to give a better service and offer them a different, wider route into the support service. In effect, this splits the queue into several queues, so the problem of waiting is lessened for commercially important users and perhaps worsened for those less commercially important. This has the effect of reducing risk also – without a 'fast-track' for VIP users, you risk losing a VIP in a longer queue with a low level of service.

21

Delegation and escalation

If the art of management is achieving results through the efforts of others, then a central skill of management must be delegation – the process of passing responsibility for carrying out a task from a manager to a member of staff. The core of this is the transfer of responsibility, much more so than the direction along the hierarchy that the delegated task takes.

There are several excellent works on the topic of delegation. I do not intend to repeat them here, and some of my favourites are listed in the Bibliography. However, some examination of the process of delegation is necessary in this book, because it is at the heart of a key concept for any user support organization; that of *problem escalation*.

For effective delegation, there are two key considerations: why delegate and how the delegation is conducted.

21.1 Why delegate?

Managers delegate – up, down, or sideways – for several different reasons. The obvious ones are resource or priority related. Quite simply the manager may have neither the time nor the skills to carry out the task herself. The manager exists to take responsibility for a group of tasks which would easily overwhelm one person – so she negotiates for more staff to help her with the burden. Those staff will probably be more specialized or technical in their skillset, as opposed to the generalist skills of the manager; thus the manager's priorities move towards the co-ordination of the efforts of those more specialized and more numerous staff. Her skills become more co-ordinative and less technical – thus her priorities come from a wider perspective than the solving of individual problems or attention to smaller detail.

A less obvious reason for task delegation is to stretch the staff member's skills, to challenge him or to expose him to a problem he may not have tackled before, so that he will gain valuable experience.

Having seen why one delegates, it is clear to see what should be delegated: a task which falls outside the manager's current skills; a task which requires an attention to detail; a task which challenges a staff member.

21.2 How to delegate

The delegation will fail unless the staff member takes ownership of the task at hand; this is a key concept. Never merely delegate a task, delegate the responsibility for the task. It is a much more powerful motivator to have the staff member conduct the task because he or she wants to rather than simply because he or she has been told to.

Never delegate something that in other circumstances you would not do yourself. The act of delegation should be a positive one, so no 'it's a lousy job, I know, but I hope you wouldn't mind doing it'. Similarly, stress not the task but the achievement. You want your delegate to focus on the end of the task, not on the process of it. Therefore, never delegate a task – always delegate an objective, which is something specific and worth doing, to be done by a specific time and reviewed in the interim if that specific time is more than a week away.

Never delegate a job simply because it is important and urgent and you don't have time to do it. You are setting your delegate up for failure. If the job is important, then the benefits of success are as notable as the damage done by failure. But if it is also urgent, then your delegate only has one, immediate chance to either get it right now or not at all.

The best type of objective to delegate is the important one that is not urgent. This gives your staffer a chance to succeed at a goal that has a real corporate or personal benefit, but because the job is not urgent, the worker has the time to spend getting it right – he can make mistakes with impunity and still have chance to correct them.

Delegate something that encourages the staffer to grow – in skills, experience, wisdom, knowledge, self-esteem, character, self-confidence, usefulness, strength, breath of vision, perspective, power or status. Don't be worried that your delegate may have to go through a little bit of pain in meeting the objective you have given him – he may have been limiting his own growth by avoiding pain such as this – but make sure you acknowledge the improvement he has thereby made, not just to the company by completing an important task but to himself by learning something. By delegation, give your staffer yet another opportunity to add to his internal catalogue of past personal successes. Don't just turn your people into better employees – turn your employees into better people.

21.3 Problem escalation

What happens if your support team cannot solve a user's problem? The problem gets escalated – you pass it on to a higher or more competent authority. Problem escalation is delegation writ large. The same concepts are in play, the same forces govern the success or failure of delegations and escalations. Escalation is delegation in action, for it is entirely in keeping with a goal shared between you and the delegate, which is to see the problem solved. Logically, the authority you escalate to is just another one of your resources. At this stage, the possibility that the resource may report to another manager is a separate issue. Here more than ever, the concept of *transferral of responsibility* is absolutely central.

There are two types of escalation – I call them 'resolution' and 'authority' escalation. Resolution escalation is moving the query between technical resources, different specialists who might be better able to solve it. More of that later.

21.4 Authority escalation

Authority escalation is passing not the problem, but awareness of the problem up through the corporate ranks. The idea is that the longer the problem remains unsolved, the more serious it becomes and the greater its potential impact. You would use authority escalation to keep an increasingly influential management stratum apprised of the problem. You would do this partly out of courtesy and partly to get other resources involved, if that is what is needed.

Authority escalation is no less important than resolution escalation. Hell hath no fury like an IT manager embarrassed in front of his or her peers because the support group forgot to mention that the accounts department server has been down for two days ('but we're working on it'). But as well as keeping the political wolf from the door, authority escalation has more practical purposes. Assuming your superior has more clout than you, he or she may be able to bring more resources to bear on your problem than you have authority to do. In practical terms, the boss may be able to put more pressure on the boss of the person you sent your resolution escalation to.

So authority escalation has two purposes: first to keep your superior apprised; second to get the problem solved more quickly.

21.5 When to 'authority escalate'

But be careful of apprising – especially do not overdo it. As well as running the risk of crying wolf, you may annoy the boss. Have you ever been in the position where a member of your staff insists on telling you everything they are doing? That does not look like information, it looks like sucking up – or worse, fishing for praise. And it gets no respect, either from above, below or beside the one doing the fishing.

As a rule of thumb, your superior should be made aware immediately of top-priority problems (system unusable, several affected); when medium-priority problems (system unusable, few affected/system usable, several affected) become critical or are likely to miss resolution targets; and only statistically of low-priority problems (system usable, few affected) after, not before, you have fixed them.

Escalate top priority problems by voice. Go and see the boss, confident that the problem is urgent, important and worth an interruption. After all you are both on the carpet if you do not solve it quickly. Consider escalating medium-priority problems by electronic mail. Low-priority problems need no authority escalation, save for being included as a mere statistic in your performance reports.

21.6 Resolution escalation

This can be a minefield, especially if you are escalating to a group outside your control. There is a real probability that these resolvers will not have the support of your users as their main priority. They are pulling in a different direction from you, under another manager with other goals in mind. The best you can hope for is that your intended results will coincide.

This goes for internal as well as external resolver groups. The development team are measured primarily on their ability to deliver new systems within budget. Their ability to allow themselves to be distracted from that goal, by helpdesk or user solving problems with existing systems, must necessarily be a secondary concern. So whatever priority the problem takes in your intray, it is safe to assume that it takes a lower priority in theirs.

21.7 Back to the supplier?

Escalations passed to suppliers may fare a little better – but the priority mismatch still exists, even though it may be more subtle. Here the difference stems from what is being supported. You support your users, ergo you solve the users' problems. Software manufacturers support their products, ergo they solve the products' problems. Usually the end results coincide – but where they do not, the result can be exasperating.

This subtle but important difference is what gives rise to the perennial software support excuse, 'that version is no longer supported – you'll have to upgrade (and see if the problem goes away)'. Yes, we both know that they do that because it is easier than solving the problem, but we cannot prove it and it would not make any difference if we could.

21.8 When escalation fails

Sometimes, the escalation simply does not work. A problem sent to development gets ignored because of the mismatch of priorities between the helpdesk and the resolvers. Check first to find the real reason for the failure. Perhaps this is the wrong resolver group for this problem and consequently the problem is bouncing around and finding no one to whom it is relevant. In which case, you must elect a resolver to whom you feel the responsibility must pass and take it up with them directly to get them to assume that responsibility. Be careful – do not cross corporate ranks in any such negotiations, respect the hierarchy and deal with your peers.

Perhaps the escalation was so vaguely worded that it is simply unclear what is required by way of a solution or from whom; so again it bounces around looking for ownership. To be effective, any form of delegation must contain the imprint of an objective – a specific result to be achieved by a specific time to a clear purpose. If your escalations lack this clarity, you may need to do a little more work with the helpdesk to improve their communications of escalations.

Perhaps the resolver group simply does not have the skills to solve this type of technical problem. In which case, consider why your department may have thought the resolvers had those skills in the first place. Do you perhaps misunderstand the duties and abilities of the resolvers? Or have you perhaps found a skills gap, where the needs of the users cannot be met by the IT function at all? Being an entrepreneur, I like finding gaps in the market. It is an opportunity for me to fill them, making me just that bit more valuable and indispensable. Is there not scope for you to set up a subsection of the helpdesk as a resolver group for this tricky problem type?

Could it be that the resolvers do not understand the users and their use of the computers well enough to understand why such-and-such a problem deserves immediate attention? Some resolver groups, by their very specialist and technical nature, can lose contact with the users. It is not that the resolvers cannot solve the problem, it is just that they do not understand enough about the users' ways of working to grasp what all the fuss is about. Remember that the position of the helpdesk, simultaneously and constantly in touch with both the user population and the computer systems, is unique among IT functions. If this is your problem, then maybe you have an opportunity to represent not just the computer systems to the users, but the users to the rest of the corporate IT functions and people. You could become a kind of two-way go-between, with your unique mix of knowledge and understanding the key to improvements all over IT and the way it is used.

If your final conclusion is that mismatched priorities are solely to blame, combat this by co-ordinating authority and resolution escalation. I do not mean that every time you send an urgent problem to Development you get your boss to jump on their boss – that will be counterproductive in the long run. Nor do I mean waving the threat of lost business over your suppliers – some would genuinely prefer to live without the threat than keep the business. So do not overdo it.

Find out what really are the mutual goals of you and your resolvers. Get the bosses to sort service levels out between them in advance, rather than crisis by crisis. Discuss how you and the resolvers can contribute to one another's needs. Maybe you can help the resolvers to help you, perhaps by formulating escalations differently, or identifying problem patterns.

In an ideal world, we would not need external escalation. Systems would be reliable and developed with our assistance so as to avert future support problems; support would have its own maintenance programmers so we would not have to interrupt the developers; and the helpdesk would be staffed by highly motivated, technically competent and friendly wonders who fixed every problem first time.

Case Study 21.1: a better service for all

The helpdesk in Georgina's charge consisted of three middle-aged women who had been with the company since the late 1960s. Delightful, friendly and helpful though these ladies were, none of them had been particularly ambitious; they had started in the data entry pool, dabbled in operations, returned to data entry and had been threatened with redundancy in the mid-1980s when what were then called 'microcomputers' had made key-to-disk a redundant technology. They all retrained as secretaries, but their enormous knowledge of the needs of individual mainframe applications still came through and they found themselves being asked questions by other users.

The need for help for the users was clear, and it was a determined Georgina who had championed the formalization of this help into a helpdesk in the late 1980s. The women were delighted, motivated, professional and astute in their new job. However, their knowledge just could not keep up with emerging technologies – and although between them they knew every mainframe application inside out, the rapidly changing PCs left them behind. When networking appeared, they were lost. Georgina tried retraining; some of it stuck, most of it did not. To support these products needed a depth of technical expertise which just was not there. By and large, over half the user queries had to be escalated, either to the network design team or to program development. This annoyed the users, so often having their queries passed on to experts; now they were losing the point of the helpdesk. It annoyed the network and software developers, who looked down on the helpdesk as being technically incompetent and not doing the job of keeping the users away from the developers. And it annoyed the managers, who could see that having every query dealt with by at least two people (helpdesker and developer) was too expensive.

Georgina knew something had to be done to raise the technical competence and image of the helpdesk. She recruited a graduate, straight out of a computer course at the local college. This chap knew microcomputers and networks inside out and had an almost magical approach to solving problems. The graduate sat on the helpdesk and took some of the queries. He liked the technical stuff, but not the telephone calls so much. He was very good technically – so much so that within a year of joining, he had been recruited into the network support team. Back to square one.

Georgina concluded that she was only meddling with the escalation issue. Training and recruitment had not worked. She decided it was time to look at the problem strategically. She convened discussions with several users to find out what kind of support they wanted. She was not surprised at the answers. 'Single point of contact', 'transparent escalation', and 'solve my problem' were phrases that kept coming up. A need for a clear support strategy had emerged. The current methods of problem escalation helped nobody.

Georgina started to design a new type of support, with smoother problem escalation and solution delivery. It involved a self-sufficient helpdesk, with its own problem solvers. It took a lot of selling. At first, development were dead against the plan, because it meant sacrificing some headcount to the creation of this new support service. But the developers realized that support was important, that escalation had to be rapid, and that choosing between solving problems and writing code often meant that problems had to wait. In the end, they relented, though it has to be said that the two programmers they lost to the helpdesk were the least productive and lowest paid ones: there was still a long way to go to get rid of the 'technically inferior' image of the helpdesk.

Georgina had more luck with finding a network support specialist. She got her graduate back; the young chap had found the design and maintenance functions of network support a little too routine, and ached for the more stimulating environment of problem-solving.

Georgina's new team could now handle most problems thrown at it. They still had to go to development and network design for some problems. But Georgina was now in a better position to negotiate – she could directly influence how much pressure she took off those teams, and they showed their appreciation for this by dealing with Georgina's few remaining escalations with all possible speed. Everybody benefited, and the turnaround in the helpdesk's image was startling. Georgina now formalized the internal escalation procedure. She made sure that there was a record of every call, every diagnosis and every solution; this had been almost impossible when the resolvers had not reported to her, and now it became standard practice.

Georgina's only remaining problem was with escalations to external suppliers; they would never have her sense of priorities for her users. She was philosophical about this and just made sure her team could handle as much as possible.

To smooth escalations, she made sure that everybody spent some time on the helpdesk, so they could better understand the users' view of the systems and the problems they were likely to incur. While resolvers were occupying helpdesk chairs, the helpdeskers were spending hours immersed in the applications software they had to support, using it in real life, helped on their way by the very users they would eventually be assisting.

21.9 The 'operational level agreement'

Throughout this book, we are looking at the relationship between the service provider and the service consumer. We have seen that service demand flows from consumer to provider, while flowing the other way is expectation management and service delivery. By default, we have viewed the provider as the helpdesk and the consumer as the user. But in truth, the relationship between the user and the helpdesk is the same as that between the helpdesk and the resolvers.

Which means that if the managers of your second-line resolving departments are as adept at service management as you are, then they should be treating you in pretty much the same way as you treat your end-user customers. But if that doesn't happen, don't be surprised and don't think of them as being any less of a service professional than you are. In the second-line departments, the culture is different – they are less focused on supporting people and more on supporting machines than you are, so the rules, ethos and priorities are different.

Earlier we discussed the service level agreement as being one way of governing the service relationship between provider and consumer. If, as I have contended, the relationship between the helpdesk and the user reflects that between the second line and the helpdesk, then perhaps a service level agreement is as appropriate here as you may feel it is between your helpdesk and your customers.

Where an SLA is drawn up between components of a service delivery mechanism, it is called an operational level agreement (OLA). But for any such mechanism to govern the process, something else has to be in place first. Just as in your preparations for the SLA, the OLA must be preceded by a catalogue of who provides which resolution services and how that provision is made.

Ideally, once compiled, that catalogue should sit in your helpdesk system. It should define:

- Each resolving agency.
- The technical functions or product areas for which the agency is responsible.
- On what topics they are willing to accept escalations.
- What user information is needed.
- What pre-diagnostic questions the helpdesk should ask of users enquiring about this product area.
- Which enquiries the helpdesk should be able to solve without escalation.
- Known problems and solutions (put them in the knowledge database if you have one – see the chapter on knowledge).
- How, and to whom, enquiries should be escalated.
- The nature and service level of the response coming back from the resolving agency.
- Who is responsible for communicating with the user about escalated enquiries (ideally this should be the Resolver – see 'Dealing with the pops' below.
- How, when and under what circumstances authority escalation should take place on enquiries (resolution) escalated to this agency.
- Who writes what and when, in the enquiry's record in the helpdesk software.

The bullets above essentially define the process to operate between the helpdesk and the resolving agency. As a matter of course, definition of process should always come before choice of tool, because if you don't know what you're doing and how to do it, automation will just make things worse.

Once all those processes have been agreed, then one option is to enshrine them all into a suite of operational level agreements. Then you can monitor, measure and change the process in an ordered, managed fashion.

But there's a problem with this.

How many resolving agencies do you have? Because that is the minimum number of OLAs you will need. And do you and the other agency managers have the time to draft, implement, manage and police so many agreements? That sounds daunting enough, but it gets worse.

Let's take, for example, a typical user enquiry, 'My printer won't print.' The helpdesk is baffled, so it escalates to desktop support (DTS). DTS suspects they could resolve it, but discovers there are two issues – the printer drivers need updating in any case, but there appears to be a problem in the network addressing of the printer. So DTS escalates the network issue to the networks team, to get that resolved so that DTS can then download the new drivers. And that means DTS needs an OLA with the networks team.

And networks needs one with communications and development needs one with operations and on and on it goes. Soon, there are so many OLAs floating around just to handle incoming helpdesk calls, that the whole OLA thing becomes unmanageable. How many OLAs do we need? Is it the square or the factorial of the number of resolving agencies? Neither. It's ONE.

The helpdesk manager draws up a single OLA and gains the signature of all the resolving agency managers. The relationship is a global one, ultimately owned by senior IT management. The reason the helpdesk manager does it is that in effect, he is responsible for the relationship with the user. The resolving agencies only receive escalations because the helpdesk has subcontracted that portion of its work. If the problem is not solved in a timely fashion, the responsibility still lies with the helpdesk, even if it was the networks team that moved too slowly. It is the helpdesk, quite rightly, that will get the blame. So the helpdesk is the instigator and owner of the OLA relationship, gaining the same service level commitment, in terms of response times and enquiry updates to be placed in the helpdesk software from each and every resolving agency.

'But no!', cries the development department. 'You cannot measure us the same way as you measure the networks team because our work takes longer!' Doesn't matter. Just because a program takes longer to write than a TCP/IP address takes to assign does not preclude the courtesy of responding quickly to the user, claiming ownership of the enquiry and setting the user's expectation of what will happen next and by when. And the OLA can certainly govern how quickly that response takes place, and the helpdesk software can and should monitor whether that happens.

The reason one OLA can work is that the process is left out of the OLA. All that matters in the OLA is the service level commitment. The process can be agreed separately and can change.

21.10 Skills-based routing

Skills-based routing (SBR) is an automated process by which the technical enquiry is passed to the most appropriate resolver (in terms of responsibility, authority or technical skills) for the job. The routing can be made at two points.

The first is at the telephone system, where that system is fronted by a response unit. The unit offers the caller a number of options and asks the caller to select one either by voice or by entering numbers on the tone-telephone keypad. You know the sort of thing – 'If your enquiry is about a hardware failure press "one"... For software enquiries, press "two".' A survey of UK consumers in March 2001 found that 61 per cent of people would prefer to avoid Interactive Voice Response (IVR) systems if they could. Nevertheless, they are a reality, and in fact the caller benefits by having the call routed quickly to somebody with the right skills to tackle the enquiry immediately.

The other point for skills-based routing is in the helpdesk management software. The system has been populated with the names and skillsets of the most appropriate teams or individuals to take an enquiry escalated from the helpdesk. All the helpdesk operative has to do, more or less, is take the call details, including the products or technologies affected by or involved in the enquiry and press the 'Assign' button. The helpdesk software does the rest, parsing the details of the enquiry with a look-up table to find the most appropriate resolver, then automatically assigning the enquiry and advising both the helpdesk and the resolver that it has done so.

SBR is another of those examples where the processes and procedures are already in place before the automation is implemented. It can fail for all sorts of reasons – not least of which is that the resolver has to be willing to accept the escalation. It is often problematical when escalating enquiries to development departments, whose individuals may not often receive escalated enquiries and as such so not run the 'notifier', which is the software routine that monitors the list of out-standing enquiries and notifies an individual when it finds a job for them to do. When that happens, the automation is worthless, for the helpdesk technician then has to do it the old-fashioned way, calling or visiting the resolver to advise him to look in the helpdesk database.

21.11 Dealing with the 'pops'

I was engaged by one of the UK's accounting/management consultancy firms. They had a procedural problem. 'When an enquiry is escalated by the helpdesk', the IT services manager told me, 'it can "pop" up all over IT.'

We fashioned a statistic out of this, the 'pop rate', which is the average number of changes of ownership of an escalation before it is closed. Given that at the time of writing, the average rate of helpdesk enquiries fixed at the first contact is 53 per cent, then the pop rate should ideally be a shade under 1.5; half of the calls should be dealt with by one person (1 'pop'), half dealt with by both the helpdesk and the second line (2 'pops'). So for a hundred calls, 53 get fixed immediately and 47 get dealt with twice. 53 + 47 + 47 makes 147, divided by 100 calls is 1.47.

For this client, the pop rate stood at about 3.2. We realized that every one of these pops constituted a manpower cost, so if we could reduce the pop rate, we could significantly reduce support costs. The reason the pop rate was so high was that the escalation process simply did not work properly. The call came into the helpdesk and was escalated more often than not. First solution – get the first-time fix rate up. Next, if the resolver felt that the escalation had come to him in error, rather than finding the correct resolver, he would pass the call back to the helpdesk – 'Here you go helpdesk – try again.' Second solution – if a re-escalation must be made, the current assignee makes it, which is cheaper and quicker from the user's point of view. But that wasn't the only problem. To be honest, there was a disconcerting number of staff who were in the habit of keeping their personal workload down by re-escalating any problem they didn't like the look of – too boring, don't like the user, too difficult, etc. Third solution – either reassert the process, or give a few people a metaphorical good slapping (professionally I tend to recommend the former, but instinctively, I favour the latter – I have little patience with people who will not take responsibility).

At another client, they have invented the role of the job co-ordinator (JC). This person is a helpdesk administrator to whom the call is escalated if it appears that solving it will require the efforts of more than one resolving agency, and thus she retains ownership through the life of the enquiry. The JC is technically highly skilled – has to be to understand all possible technical aspects of the problem. She is also a bit like a project manager, identifying component tasks and ensuring they are dealt with by the most appropriate resolver group. She also has a huge amount of authority invested in her; if a job arrives on your desktop from the JC, you had better have a very good reason for refusing it.

Not only does the job co-ordinator role prevent these unmanaged changes of ownership of complex problems, it also offers a career path to your more competent first-line helpdesk staff.

22

Measurement and reporting

> **Maxim One:**
>
> *There is only one reason to produce a report[1] – and that is to be able to make a decision. If the report cannot do that, then at best it may be 'interesting' but otherwise useless.*
>
> **Maxim Two:**
>
> *Data (numbers) are not information. Think not what the 'data' say, but what they mean – only then do you start getting to 'information'.*

How do you know if there is a problem in the way your support department is run? You may suspect there is an administrative or service-delivery problem; your staff, superiors or customers may complain about what they see as a problem. But until there is hard evidence that the problem both exists and is doing some damage, it would be foolhardy to do anything about it. Without gathering evidence first, you may end up reacting to something that turns out not being a problem at all. Even when you start gathering evidence, if you do not have enough of it how will you know whether you are under- or over-reacting? How will you know where precisely to focus your efforts, so that you do not either waste time and effort or perhaps even make the problem worse?

---

[1] Except of course where a report has to be produced just because your auditing procedures say it must – but that serves the auditing procedures rather than serving you.

Your strategy for dealing with problems should first be to gather data, then analyse them to produce information. You act upon information. We have just discussed one reason for taking measurements, that of assessing the existence of and damage done by operational, logistical, or managerial incidents or problems. Clearly, we should be measuring these, as they are the exceptions to the smooth running of our support operation.

This raises another question, however. How are we to know what to recognize as an exception unless we have a clear picture of the norm? The argument for measurement, therefore, is not just to control the exceptions, but to understand normality. Without this, we cannot really react to the exceptions either, because we do not know for sure how far they differ from the norm, therefore how much they should concern us.

Without measurement, the best you can hope for is that circumstances and incidents will control your support operation. You will occupy a stressful environment, buffeted by one challenge after another, unaware of whether the challenge is a dragon or a pussycat. Or you may be blissfully unaware that you are being challenged at all; totally ignorant of the opportunities passing you by, of the withering decay of your popularity, of the mind-numbing irrelevance your Support Department is increasingly seen to have.

It was a wise man who said 'what you cannot measure, you cannot manage'.

> **Without sound methods of measurement, user support is just a pinball; being jerked around without purpose, making a lot of noise, possibly quite entertaining, certainly costing good money and eventually disappearing down a hole.**

22.1 Taking measurements

In any user support operation, there are several measurements which can and should be taken. It can be easy to do: in most support offices, computer expertise is easily come by, so the computers can be made to take several measurements automatically. However, I would not recommend taking measurements just because you can. There is always an overhead to come from taking measurements, from preparing the measurement methods, gathering the data, converting data to information, deciding on actions, analysing the impact of those actions, archiving the data, and so on. If you are not prepared to invest the time and people in this overhead, then taking measurements will become just another burden on what is typically already an overstretched service (but do not forget that taking measurements can reduce the pressure on you by highlighting those areas where you are wasting effort).

One of the most demoralizing demands a manager can make on his or her staff is over-bureaucratization – asking them to collect data which are then never used, or at least never seen to be used. If you do not reward the effort in information-gathering by then using the information, next time the staff may not be so diligent. The moment your data-gatherers start to shirk is the moment the integrity of the data is lost. And because you do not know how much integrity is lost, all the data and expended effort are wasted, because you know the data are inaccurate but you cannot be sure by how much, so you cannot allow for the inaccuracy. Thus the data are worthless, and by then they have cost money and trust to obtain. The simple maxim is that if you are not going to use the data, then do not bother collecting them; it is much too risky and too costly, not just in money, but in credibility.

The results of user surveys produce valuable information which measures the effectiveness or otherwise of the support operation. If these are structured in such a way as to provide some constants, trends over time can be calculated. Providing these constants is relatively simple: simply ask the same questions in the survey, with the same choice of replies and see how these change over time.

It is so easy these days to produce statistics. Push a button in your helpdesk software or telephone system and the printer will vomit the lifetime product of a small tree. But the data coming out of the helpdesk software are only part of the story. All they can tell you is quantity – how many of this, how many of that. In itself, this is meaningless. Look at all those calls! See how many we fixed first time! Look at that speed of response! Is that good or bad? Or is it just 'many'?

Those quantities have to be put into some context, for which we need other statistics. When we compare a quantity with a preset target, we may call the comparison 'performance'. So now we know how well we did, but only after a fashion. The combined statistics of quantity and performance may look good –

especially of we exceeded our target – but they don't tell us whether that was the right target in the first place.

So we take another measurement, namely quality, which we can measure from the random telephone survey of customer satisfaction described in Chapter 9. This gives us the important qualifier of whether the customer liked what we did, and thus applies some meaning to the targets. But that doesn't tell us whether it made business or financial sense to deliver that level of service.

So another statistic is needed – value – against which we can compare the cost-effectiveness of the helpdesk, and there are some algorithms for calculating that later in the chapter on cost justification.

Quantity alone is all very well, and usually all you can expect from your helpdesk software. But it is supervisory, rather than management information. For true management information, you need all four statistical measures:

QUANTITY – PERFORMANCE – QUALITY – VALUE

Without them all, you cannot be absolutely sure that it is worth the company's while to have you investing all that money, effort and time in the service level you currently produce.

22.2 Statistics are not everything

Statistical data gathering only really provides measurement of one type of activity, namely repeat tasks. Statistics are good for measuring the norm, as well as highlighting trends away from the norm. They are less good as a means of identifying a sudden exception – precisely because that would be construed as a statistical blip. Blips have little or no statistical significance unless they highlight or conform to a discernible pattern.

For measuring exceptions, other methods have to be used, and these are the methods which make the manager a manager and less of a supervisor. It is at this point where the professional relationship between the manager and his or her staff (or supervisors) is important, because exceptions will be picked up by people much more quickly than they will be identified by statistics. Of course some of the exceptions will require measurement to prove or disprove their veracity or significance; however, alongside your statistical measurement it is always advisable to have good incidental and formal communications.

One method I like is the weekly *operations management meeting*. This meeting is open to managers and team leaders in the support function. It happens at the same time in the same place every week. Attendance is by default not by invitation, by expectation not compulsion. There is no agenda, but brief notes of the discussions, conclusions reached and actions delegated are taken and circulated to all department members as soon as possible after the meeting. The lack of agenda means that a time limit (I usually use 40 minutes) must be imposed on the meeting. It is chaired, often by the most senior manager, whose job is to offer the floor to all attendees. Prior to the meeting, all attendees are expected to have gathered together topics for discussion. The manager will have spoken to users for information, the supervisors will have spoken to the staffers for their opinions on what current issues are worthy of managerial discussion, all parties will be aware of the latest operational statistics and may have comments about them. The objective of the meeting is to arrive at as wide as possible an understanding of how the support service is currently faring, what issues are of departmental concern, what if anything should be done about those issues and who should take that action. The meeting is not a talking-shop – it is purely operational, there to measure the department's performance and to mandate responsive action. The minutes of this meeting are as much a measure of the department's productivity as are any statistics.

22.3 Using helpdesk management software

A good helpdesk package will provide you with lots of data, usually much more than you need or can use. It is a common failing of many, if not of most, of the commercial packages that in their default incarnations they are stiflingly bureaucratic and insensitive to the need for speed and ease of use; nor do many of them seem to take account of the rebellious dislike some technicians have for any attempt to shackle them.

Worse still than all these weaknesses is the virtually universal inability of the helpdesk software industry to distinguish between a call-log and an incident report. In almost every package I have used or seen demonstrated, every single incoming message to the helpdesk is treated by the software as though it were a reported technical problem. This is a real and dangerous failing. In my experience, somewhere between 40 per cent and 95 per cent of calls to the helpdesk will not be problems requiring solutions or incidents requiring responses, but will be requests for information or assistance. These requests will not require an incident report – so often, usually because it is too much bother to fill in the form, they do not find their way into the helpdesk management system. Support Managers are therefore deprived of the single most important measurement they can ever take: the number of times their customers use their services.

In defence of the helpdesk software authors, many of them do allow their packages to be customized, and thus much of this damage can be minimized. Furthermore, many helpdesk managers fail to take into account the resource overhead they will have to carry simply for designing, installing, maintaining, archiving and querying the often massive usage database such software can create. It is a common error by support managers who, realizing they need to take more control over their departments, seize upon a helpdesk package as a panacea. They think they have found a cure to their problems, but often they have just found another problem. To go from no or little measurement to a professional helpdesk management system is a monumental leap which should more often than not have been taken as a series of controlled steps. I have seen many helpdesk package implementations which have simply proved the old maxim that if you computerize chaos, all you get is faster chaos.

In choosing your helpdesk package, look for one that provides you as much as possible with information, not just data. The reporting system is crucial – it does not matter one jot what data there are in the database if meaningful conclusions cannot be drawn from them. In the face of the infinite variety of report types required by different helpdesks and the sheer amount of data which may have to be trawled to get information, many commercial packages have gone for a mixture of standard and custom reports. Others offer interfaces to database or spreadsheet analysis packages. Again, setting these reports up is part of the overhead the support manager must allow for. Once set up, however, they can become an almost hassle-free and automatic way of extracting the information you need to make decisions.

22.4 Key helpdesk and support statistics

Your key statistics are a direct result of the critical success factors imposed upon you by senior management. Whatever they are measuring support against indicates a need for data. This may require you to count installations performed, problems with a specific piece of software, the level of service to a given customer, the level of service overall, etc. These will be specific to the commercial environment in which you operate.

However, there are some statistics which I feel are important in all user support environments. These are the statistics which measure the norms of general user support, in the form of providing information and solving user problems. First, my favourites:

Statistic	Description
Calls taken per helpdesk operative	Productivity of first-line heads.
Spot rate	Number of calls fixed by a first-line operative during the initial telephone call (see below).
Pop rate	Average number of changes of ownership of a logged enquiry (see previous chapter).
Fixes per resolver	Number of escalated enquiries fix per man per day per second-line resolver (see below).
Man-hours available	A 'value' statistic – number of staff man-hours available to the helpdesk in the reporting period – i.e. are we getting more, or less efficient?
Quality index	Customer satisfaction as measured by a random telephone survey (see Chapter 9).
Lost-user productivity	The dollar value of potential corporate productivity enabled by the speed at which the helpdesk resolved user problems (see later chapter on cost justification).
SLA compliance	Performance of the support service as a whole against targets set out in the Schedule of the service level agreement.
Operational compliance	Performance of individual staff members against targets agreed with support manager.

Usage rate – the number of times the users actually called on your service, for whatever purpose. This will mean taking account of all contact made with user support. The most practical way of doing this is to log all incoming calls. For statistical purposes, divide this by the number of active users (calls per user); by the number of helpdesk people (calls per helpdesk station, users per helpdesk station); and by the number of support people overall. Some of these calls will be incident reports, requiring diagnosis and fix. Some will just be requests for assistance with a given piece of software, and so on. Some will be administrative calls; nothing to do with supporting users, but more to do with the running of the helpdesk as a department of the company. Another way to work it is by user department – are fewer departments using you, are some departments using you less often than they used to, and if so, why? Are they getting more technically competent, or are they getting their support services elsewhere?

Still another type of call is what I term the *overhead* call; these come about merely by virtue of the fact that the department and its people exist at all – questions like 'Is Vic there, and if not can you get him to call me?'; or 'This is Barry's wife, I've locked myself out of the car, can he meet me at lunchtime?'; or 'Have you solved my problem yet?'; or 'There's a delivery for you in the loading bay.' There may be no immediately apparent need to record the arrival of non-technical calls – except that not to know exactly how many calls you get is to risk underestimating the number of staff you need for the helpdesk. Every single call to your service, technical or not, user or not, is a demand on your resources and you must therefore have staff to meet it; so you must measure their frequency. I would recommend you also need to measure specifically the incidence of these 'overhead' calls. You may find, as I often have, that the number of overhead calls is justification alone for a member of staff; maybe there is something you can do, once you have a measure of these calls, to reduce them.

The next key statistic is the *spot rate*, the percentage of calls taken which require no further action. This little-used statistic is crucial, yet I have still to find the helpdesk package that measures it by default, and the current market leaders in both the US and the UK require you to devise custom reports to get it. Sometimes, I have to resort to comparing the statistics from the telephone system with those from the helpdesk system to calculate the spot rate. When coupled with other measures, the spot rate tells you which packages you can support and which you cannot, how many resolvers you are likely to need, and what level of immediate service the users can expect. These numbers are essential. Measure them technician by technician to compare the effectiveness of individual knowledge, or user by user to see who is posing the trickiest problems.

Another important statistic is the *response time*. Some users are happy to expect a fix to their problem when it comes; all they really need is constant reassurance that somebody does actually own the problem and is working on it. For them, response time is more important than fix time. This is a measure of how well you communicate with the users, how well you keep them informed or whether the users are left to make all the running. So take a measure of how quickly you got back to the user after the query had come in (to make this truly effective, you have to give that first response some meaning, e.g. to tell the user who would be working on the problem, what would happen next and when to expect a fix).

The *fix time*, how long a query stays with you before being solved, is also an important statistic. Compare it with the total number of outstanding problems and try to separate cause from effect. Often, if a problem is not fixed immediately, it goes into a pile which if it had a label on it might read 'too difficult' or 'too boring'. Not fixing a problem straight away can and does encourage procrastination – keep an eye on that by watching the fix time. Anything over a week old should be discussed at the operational management meeting, to look for a cause for the delay and action its removal.

Measure too the *fixes per resolver*. This number tells you how many staff you need in the resolver groups, and is especially important when the group does nothing else but solve support problems. In some groups, where other activities are also carried out, this figure can be as low as three per person per day; in others, where the problems are not particularly tough and all fixes are done over the telephone, I have seen this figure as high as 25; in a typical resolver group, I would be looking for something like seven per working day.

Couple 'fixes per resolver' with the 'spot rate' for some very enlightening results. Let us say the number of calls per day is 100, at a spot rate of 55 per cent. That means that 45 calls are getting escalated, and at three fixes per resolver, you will need 15 resolvers behind the helpdesk; at £16,000 annual salary, that will cost you £240,000 a year. Get the spot rate up to 70 per cent, and that expenditure drops to £160,000 or a saving of £80,000 per year. If you had £80,000 to spend, do you think you could increase the knowledge level of your helpdesk people by 25 per cent in a year? Of course you could, if not by training, then by recruitment. That is why the spot rate is so important to measure. The alternative, of course, is to get greater productivity out of the resolvers; however, by influencing the spot rate, you only have to change two people on the helpdesk (all you would need for 100 calls a day); but to improve the resolvers, you would have to influence 15 people. Clearly the helpdesk would be the easier bet, and think of how much happier it would make the resolvers to stop getting so many 'easy' problems to solve.

22.5 Reporting

In order to extract or offer the most appropriate reports about any process, first we must know why reporting is necessary. If you do not understand the need for reporting, then there is a strong possibility that the reports you create or use will not have their intended effect. The essential purpose of reporting is to communicate results to those who need to make decisions about those results (regardless of who the recipient is – it may be your boss, your staff, even yourself). However, often this is not the actual purpose of reporting, which may in reality be more Machiavellian; take the example of the boss who feels he needs to 'keep an eye on' his staff, so asks for reports simply in order to check that they are working a certain way; or the report that goes to your boss, so that he has a weapon with which to defend himself against more senior critics. It is essential to determine the true purpose of any report before designing or submitting the report – and beware this is one occasion where the direct approach ('hey, boss, do you want this report just to cover yourself in the boardroom?') may not be the most appropriate.

Like anything else you produce, reports take resources to create. You will need to take this into account. Never produce a report that has no eventual payoff for you – if the payoff is for somebody else solely, then it is their priority to produce the report, not yours. If there is no direct payoff, then engineer an indirect one; for the report the boss asks for 'just to keep an eye on you', look for some way of exploiting the fact that this report has the boss's attention, it is a communications medium through which you can convey information and priorities you need the boss to notice. Be aware that without a payoff to you, there is a risk that the report may one day not get produced in the face of all the other demands on your resources. Check that the reports you send out are used – if they are not, discontinue them to stop you wasting time and effort. Be prepared to negotiate with anybody who then complains at the loss of the report; if they were not using it, why should you produce it? Is there scope to produce the reports ad hoc, rather than regularly.

As well as being a means of communication, reports are a service to your customers in their many forms. This implies that as you would for any service, you should always be looking for new possible recipients of this service. This increases your range of customers, and along with it the number of people in the corporation who benefit from your existence; and along with that, let us be frank, your personal and departmental value to the people who measure you.

Who are you reporting to? Do they actually need a report? Some middle managers send a report to their boss more as a way of calling for recognition than just to satisfy the boss's stated need for information. Also consider the needs of the helpdesk and support staff; they really do need reports so they can see how they are doing. Without some kind of feedback, there will be no way for them to improve their service, and you as manager will lose an opportunity to motivate them by shining their own light back on them.

Consider whether there is anybody missing a report who would have a use for one. There may be user groups who would dearly love to know if their computer problems are unique or whether they are experienced by other user groups. There may be user department managers who need reports on how their staff are using the helpdesk. The personnel department could perhaps use a report on the performance of all the new recruits. What about equipment suppliers? Could you produce a report that would tell them how difficult or easy the users are finding their products?

As for any communication, the report's message will get through all the more clearly if articulated in the language and style of the recipient. Never produce a report that states purely what you think the reader should know – always put in copious helpings of what the recipient wants to hear or know. Be aware that some recipients are suspicious of reports, especially glossy or overly graphical reports, wary that the glossiness of the presentation disguises a lack of truth or substance. Use graphics for clarity, not for obfuscation.

An effective report will probably also contain your conclusions about any figures you present. This saves your reader the effort of thinking – which is not patronizing, it shows your awareness of the fact that you are the specialist in your trade, and cannot expect the reader to understand your results as quickly or as fluently as you would. A good guide for contextual style in a report would be facts (presented graphically if need be) followed by conclusions about what those facts mean in the context of your reader's environment, followed by recom-mendations, if any, of actions to be taken as a result.

User Support Dept.				
Weekly Report #125		**7th to 11th February**		
From:	Noel Bruton		Helpdesk Manager	
To:	A.N.Other		IT Director	
cc:	All Helpdesk and Support staff Company library for archival			
Key statistics		This week	Last week	Same week last year
	Calls taken	434	365	429
	Spot rate	82%	83%	74%
	Fixed same day	12%	12%	7%
	Fixed in two days	4%	3%	15%
	Over two days	2%	2%	4%
	Fixes/resolver/day	5.2	4.1	4.5

Conclusions

The number of calls made came back up to normal levels following last week's big drop due to the network being down for the day. We're still making more or less the same number of calls as this time last year, which I'm watching, seeing as there are so many more users. No cause for action yet; I'm examining the calls piecemeal to try to assess whether the users have got more sophisticated.

The key figures are more or less constant now. But that is with two fewer staff in the Resolver group compared with last year. This means the users are getting at least as good a service but for less money. I intend to find out if they agree with that conclusion by running a user survey around Easter.

Key events

Sarah has now completed her network training and moves from the Helpdesk to Resolvers, to replace Malcolm who leaves at the end of the month. We will have a contractor on the Helpdesk until Sarah can be replaced; I'm expecting the figures to get worse over the next few weeks.

The network branch over at Accounts seems to be giving more problems. We have it under control through rerouting, but I'm going to have to bring the whole system down next Friday (18 Feb.) to run some diagnostics. I need your signature to pay overtime over the weekend – slips attached.

Figure 22.1
A sample weekly helpdesk report

Be aware that the report has to be read and understood quickly, so brevity is important; if possible, get it all onto the psychologically important single sheet of paper (see Fig. 22.1, for example). Remember too that the report may also be archived, and read in time to come by people who never knew or have forgotten how things were done in those days; the report may have to be understood by aliens, so make as few assumptions as possible of prior knowledge.

Controlling the workflow

The need for control is a point already made in the previous chapter – essentially that if you do not control the workload, it controls you, to the benefit of nobody. Measurement provides an indication of what is happening; this chapter looks at the issues of controlling and managing workflow and considers some of your options.

23.1 Procedures and standards

As in other parts of industry, formal procedures and standards for helpdesks and technical support offices have become increasingly fashionable in the last few years. One notable influence on the movement is ISO 9000. Under this standard, formal procedures are required to be fully documented and accompanied by a *quality manual*. Evidence must be produced from time to time that these procedures are being adhered to, otherwise the company risks the loss of its accreditation of compliance with the standard. Another standard, aimed squarely at IT, is in use at an increasing number of IT support desks in the UK Civil Service as well as non-governmental and private sectors. These are the methods described in a set of manuals known as the *Information Technology Infrastructure Library* (ITIL), published by the UK government's Central Computer and Telecommunications Agency (CCTA). ITIL has been taken a stage further, by becoming the subject of training programmes leading to academic qualifications, which are themselves recognized by some companies.

There is no doubt that much benefit is to be gained from formalizing procedures, and ISO 9000 offers a way to measure standards of management regardless of industry. Compliance with ISO 9000 purports to be an indicator of professionalism and completeness in the way the business is run, and this can imply that the work done by a holder of ISO 9000 accreditation is of high quality. However, the standards advisers do not tell a company how to do its job; it cannot, the standard is too general and applicable to too wide a range of industries. ISO 9000 offers an opportunity to set in stone the current standards of your work and document them to ensure strict compliance. Ostensibly, this ensures consistency of work; and if a high quality were documented at the outset, then compliance to the documented and accredited procedures would apparently ensure consistent high quality. That means, however, that the opposite is also true – that if the documented procedures oversaw a low quality of work, then what would be produced would be a consistently low quality. At the time of writing, a new version of ISO 9000 is gaining ground, which deals admirably with this criticism by implementing in a standard a process of continuous improvement – thus compliance with the standard will now imply an improvement in the quality of the product or service.

ITIL differs from this in that it purports to show support and other IT managers how to do their job; it describes techniques and methods. Personally, I have some strong differences with ITIL; I find it inward looking, uncommunicative, not customer-oriented, and too focused on technical issues to be considered a complete operational guide for a helpdesk or IT support service environment. ITIL does not do enough to inculcate into the helpdesk the fact that there are real people out there among the user population. The result is that it worries too much about staffing and knowledge, and not enough about user expectations, communication and motivation. Do not misunderstand my views on ITIL – it has much to recommend it. On matters of internal organization and workflow control in a user support department, it is unsurpassed. Its volumes *Helpdesk* and *Problem Management* are recommended reading for all support managers. However, I have stated often in this book that I feel these issues are at best of equal importance to the marketing of the helpdesk. ITIL has in the past been decidedly weak on anything to do with client management, and I see this weakness to be fundamental. However, ITIL too is in good hands – and reviews of its methodologies and philosophies are constantly taking place.

Having read my thoughts, should you ever have cause to study ITIL as well, you may find some of my reasoning at odds with much of theirs; that is good, you will have the opportunity to make up your own mind.

It is this opportunity to make up your own mind which leads me to my conclusion on external standards such as ISO 9000 and ITIL: that they can never be absolutely right for anybody. The firmness with which ISO 9000 sets procedures has trapped some compliant firms; they have not allowed for enough flexibility in their procedures, so they have restricted their options for change in a changing world. The dilemma of some ISO 9000-compliant firms is either to remain compliant, thus possibly missing market opportunities by being unable to change fast, or to risk losing accreditation by failing to remain compliant, thus becoming less attractive to those clients for whom ISO 9000 compliance is a main requirement in a supplier. Either way it is clearly a loss of flexibility and the only way to deal with it is to build into the formal procedures the anticipation of change. Change management procedures are notoriously difficult to document; after all, ISO 9000 strives to maintain consistency, and so I find it inherently at odds with change. If I may be momentarily flippant, I have yet to see in an ISO 9000 procedures manual the procedure 'In the event of rapid and unforeseen market change, this procedures manual shall be consigned immediately to a swiftly forgotten pit in a distant corner of the company car park' because that would probably be judged to be a non-compliant procedure.

In the absence of an external demand for you to formulate and abide by procedural standards ordained by an external authority, the best procedures for you and your own customers will always be the ones you design for yourself. By all means take advice in the design of your procedures, but in the end they should be yours. If they are not yours, the risk is that you will find them difficult to comply with, and very difficult to sell to your staff. Computer technicians are notorious for their resolve to retain their freedom of action. And if your procedures and standards look to them like unnecessary imposition – then somebody else's procedures may look like an occupying foreign army. Imposition incites resistance.

23.2 Designing support procedures

It is unfortunate that in some cases, the very real benefits of operating to some extent under formal procedures have been hijacked by the often self-serving motives of external consultants peddling this or that 'corporate standard'. This drive to comply with ISO 9000 and other standards can become a burden on the department rather than delivering true improvements in the quality of work. Procedures do bring about benefits, but not where one assesses the compliance of the procedures to the standard rather than assessing the benefits that the procedures deliver to the business. My advice is: never lock yourself into any management methodology unless you can categorically prove that it is doing some good to your support department or its customers. So the first rule of designing your own support procedures manual is to ask yourself what benefits you want the manual to deliver.

This could be an opportunity to adjust some ways of doing things. There is a temptation when constructing procedures to make the improvements you know are needed, and procedurize the new rather than the old as a way of making the new way stick. This is a temptation I would recommend you avoid. You can get trapped into a vicious circle of each event waiting on the other: we will make the procedural change when we write the procedures but we will write the procedures when we are ready to change the way we do things. Procedures ensure things happen. They force you to analyse where the cracks are, and by formalizing the procedures, you are then forced to plug the gap. For the sake of completeness of service, if the procedures are worth writing, they are worth writing now. If it is important that a job gets done, documenting the fact will go a long way towards ensuring that happens. This may mean that you end up formalizing some of the old and replaceable procedures. Do not let that stop you – if you have written the procedures well enough, changing them when the time comes will be a piece of cake compared to writing them in the first place.

Not everything will be worth documenting as a formal procedure. The nature of problem solving in a technical support environment will mean that you may not, for example, be able to formalize or even describe some of the things you do. Take problem diagnosis: how would you procedurize the network technician's brilliant flash of lateral thinking that produces an answer from exploring an unlikely avenue? To even try to formalize this would bog you down. In general, unless you are striving for external assessment, only document formal procedures for what has to happen, not necessarily for everything that actually does happen.

When composing procedures, take into account the amount of effort that will be needed to keep them up to date and to make sure everybody who needs to know has the most up-to-date copy. Procedures manuals fail by being unmaintainable as well as being irrelevant.

23.3 Chart the workflow

A good place to start is to draw up a chart of how the work flows through the support department. At the points in the chart where a decision has to be made and a specific action results, these are where formal procedures may be needed.

Figure 23.1 is an example of the sort of flowchart one might use to document part of the work in a user support environment. This chart shows the workflow as seen from the problem resolver's point of view. A number of queries have arrived at the helpdesk and, answers being unavailable, the queries have been escalated. The resolver examines the resulting queue of outstanding queries and this flowchart describes the way he or she handles them. All the time the resolver is solving these problems, new ones are being delivered and the state of those queries already outstanding is also being changed by the arrival of new resources or information.

The resolver claims a query from the list of outstanding ones. This act of 'claiming' probably means the resolver has to notify the helpdesk ('OK I've got that one, leave it with me') and the user who made the query ('Hello, I'm Fred from technical support and I'm going to be dealing with your problem with X'). Some prediagnosis may have to be done, and an assessment made if any further information is needed from the user. If we do need to talk to the user, we can only really get any further if the user is there to talk to, otherwise we leave a message on the user's desk ('Hi, need to talk to you about your problem X, call me when you get back. Fred') and go and claim another problem.

If the user is there, we get the information we need and assess if we have everything else we need to solve this problem X. Maybe we are short of the right equipment or we need some information from a supplier, in which case we put this problem in abeyance and claim a new problem. But if we have everything we need, then we can carry on. We look to see if we will only have these resources (e.g. borrowed software manual) for a while, because if we have a time limit, we had better make this a high-priority job.

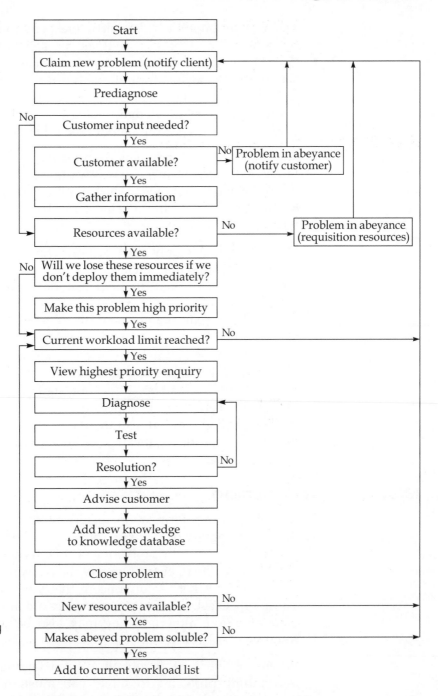

Figure 23.1
Strategy for managing
a personal,
self-replenishing
resolver workload

The next box may differ from support desk to support desk. The
method in this flowchart describes the resolver as going on
claiming problems until she has claimed as many as she can do
that day, so she has a list of work to do. Then she takes her
highest priority problem first.

255

The resolver builds a real or virtual test environment, diagnoses the problem, and tests to see if she has solved it. If she has not, then she readjusts her test environment and goes round the 'solving' loop again until she solves the problem. When she succeeds, she tells the customer, adds any newly gained knowledge to a knowledge database and closes the problem, perhaps by notifying the helpdesk she has solved it.

She checks to see if any new resource has become available, for instance the screwdriver she was waiting to borrow; if it has, she checks whether that means she can now work on a problem she earlier postponed. If so, she goes back through checking whether she can take on another job.

Figure 23.1 shows only one function which can be flowcharted. Other candidates may include plotting how a query is treated when it first arrives at the helpdesk; or deciding what level of service the user should receive; or deciding what network functions a certain type of new user may be allowed access to, and so on. The flowcharts you create can then become part of your procedures manual. Because well-designed flowcharts are also often much easier to follow than textual descriptions, you may choose to give copies to your staff, so they can see at a glance precisely what is expected of them and what needs to happen; or you may publish them to users and other observers of your service for clarification of how you do things.

23.4 Prioritization

In dealing with prioritization, let us first put in place the concept of the inevitability of a queue. You are only human; you can only deal with one item or problem at a time. While you are dealing with that one item, everything else has to wait. The 'everything else' is every other job or concern that you are even aware of. Those other tasks are in a queue. They are at least queuing for your attention, although they may also be waiting for some resource you have yet to acquire.

Wherever there is a queue of outstanding work to do, outstanding problems to solve, you must therefore be using some way of deciding which item in the queue to tackle next. Some people use a simple 'first in, first out' method. This is wonderfully fair, absolutely democratic and for most business purposes utterly impractical. Others set priorities: the most important job gets done first, with some qualification such as the current availability of resources.

These priorities may be business or personal, with the line between the two types becoming more blurred as the professionalism of the individual increases. At the opposite end of the scale, most of us know at least one technician who gives the highest priority to the problem it will be the most fun to solve; and I suspect we have all at some time completed a task first because it was the easiest and quickest to do. If we follow selfish priorities such as these, we should also ensure that the most enjoyable and quickest jobs are also the commercially most rewarding; otherwise we may be doing our company and our users a disservice or even some damage.

User support priorities should always take into account the commercial impact of the user's problem, in terms of the value lost to the company while the user is out of action. If your company is a profit-making or cost-saving enterprise, priorities based thus will be entirely justifiable; if your organization has other motives, look to the organization's stated mission to see which priorities rate most highly, and therefore which should be satisfied first.

It is at this point where we ought to discuss the difference between *importance* and *urgency*. These are two very distinct attributes, though in user support, they are often confused. The result can be that a query gets dealt with first because it is urgent – i.e. time-critical – and not because of its relative importance. At the extreme, the support team prioritizing on urgency may be doing immediately work that does not need doing at all, and this I have found to be a perennial waste of effort in many support teams. It is not surprising that support teams fall into this trap of prioritizing on urgency only – after all, they are the computer firefighters – somebody has to be there to deal with the urgent collapse of the computer system or the sudden shortfall in a user's ability.

23.5 Not worth doing? Then don't do it!

For all the upcoming tasks in your intray, for all the user demands in your list of outstanding queries, and no matter how assiduously you plough through this work, there are still some jobs that will never, ever get done. There may be the new application you have intended to examine, that distant user you meant to attach to the network, that technical newsletter you will one day get round to producing, that software salesman who keeps pestering you to return his call, that report the boss would like 'sometime' – all these and more, these little items of helpdesk hell, the guilt that hangs above every support manager. Be honest with yourself: you have already decided not to do these jobs in favour of doing the stuff you are doing now. The only time you ever claim to 'mean' to do them is when they come back to bite you and somebody reminds you that you have not done X yet. The fact is that you have already prioritized, and the only question here is not whether you prioritize, it is how you do it. That unwritten technical newsletter is your greatest servant – because it shows you that it really is all right, OK and acceptable to prioritize things so low that they will never get done. Now if you can only translate that to certain user and company demands, your prioritization methodology has got it made.

Case Study 23.1: confused priorities

As a helpdesk consultant, I advise corporations on the way they run their helpdesks. One client of mine had this confusion between importance and urgency woven into the very fabric of the way they prioritized outstanding work. They use one of the more popular commercial helpdesk management packages which assigns fix times to query priorities; the higher the assigned priority, the faster you have to fix it and the sooner the helpdesk software chastises you if you look as though you are going to miss that target. They had three levels of priority: 'urgent', i.e. fix within one hour, 'critical', i.e. fix within three hours and 'non-essential', i.e. fix within three months.

Two problems here. First, either a query was urgent or it was non-essential. No real distinction was made between 'urgent' or 'critical', save that if the user was a manager or a manager's PA, then the query was 'urgent' otherwise it was 'critical'. There was no way of classifying a job as being important yet not urgent. As a result, stress levels in the office were extremely high, as more or less everything was treated as urgent. They knew in their hearts that some of these things were non-urgent, and it was the prioritization classifications which were awry. Nevertheless, they had to suffer the constant, ignominious chastizing of the helpdesk system for their not treating something as urgent which it thought was urgent.

Second, they were trying to use a helpdesk system as a workflow management system and it had forced them to make this bizarre distinction, nothing like real life. This led to a blurring between what went on in the user environment and how it was reacted to by the helpdesk. The helpdesk staff found themselves reinterpreting reality for the sake of their computer system. When the accusations began to fly that the helpdesk had 'lost touch' with the users, nobody was the least surprised.

This is where the separation of importance and urgency really come into their own (see Fig. 23.2). This is because urgency can only really be assessed when the problem crops up. Only then do you have the opportunity to consider whether this problem is time-critical or not. If 15 people cannot use their computers, that is time-critical because every moment the system is down is costing a heap of money in idle salaries and lost productivity. If the managing director has a plane to catch and cannot get access to the documents she needs for her business trip, that is time-critical. Urgency is necessarily assessed reactively.

Importance, on the other hand, can and should be assessed proactively. This is the support manager's opportunity to examine the different groups of users and consider their importance relative to one another and relative to the stated goals of the business. If the business goal is to expand sales into Africa and reduce the sales effort in Europe, then a query from the African salesforce will always take precedence over one from the European office, regardless of the relative

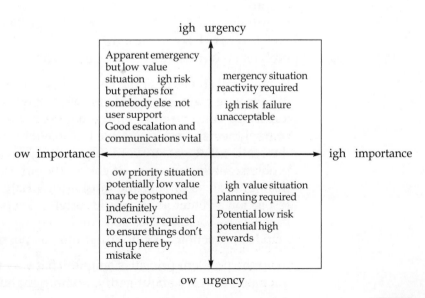

Figure 23.2
Contrasting importance
with urgency

urgency of these queries. Similarly, the warehouse may be more important than personnel, the executive corridor may be more important than accounts, payroll more important than purchasing.

The goal of support query prioritization should be to ensure that what is most commercially important gets dealt with first, especially if it is urgent, but even when it is not. And that may mean that something which is urgent, but not important may not get dealt with until the deadline which made it urgent has passed. Provided that you have set your priorities in keeping with the goals of the enterprise, then they are entirely defensible at any level. All priorities based on business importance should be set in advance and agreed at the highest level where user support performance is measured. Then if these priorities are wrong, then the business is at fault and it may have to put its hand deeper into its pocket so that lower priorities can also be satisfied.

> **Are you overworked?**
> **Or just poorly prioritized?**

23.6 Putting support priorities into effect

First, do not confuse problem priorities with problem categories. The 'priority' of a problem should describe only how soon you should devote resource to solving it relative to other outstanding problems. The 'category' of the problem is an identifier you may use later to look for emerging patterns in the type of problems your users are sending to you.

When a call comes in at the helpdesk, in order that the helpdesk can provide the best possible problem-solving service, it should ideally be concentrating on the nature of the incoming call. To compel the helpdesk operative to consider what priority to give this call, what category to place it in, is to complicate the problem-solving process. Of course the priority is best added at this point, so as to offer the most appropriate speed of problem resolution. Therefore I would advise keeping the helpdesk process as slick as possible and making all administrative helpdesk functions as unburdensome as possible.

Keep the problem priorities simple. That way the helpdesk does not have to worry about getting them right and can concentrate on solving the customer's problem. One way of simplifying prioritization is to use a comparison of importance and urgency as described above. So 'important and urgent' becomes top priority; 'important and not urgent' is next; 'urgent and not important' takes third priority; and 'neither urgent nor important' takes the lowest priority.

Script the sort of questions the helpdesk can ask in order to determine the priority of the query; but remember they only need to go through this process if the query is going to be escalated. One support manager I know sets a default of 60 on all escalated calls. All his helpdesk staff keep beside them a list of the relative importance of each of the user departments. Queries from the sales department get 5 added to that 60; queries from the executive suite stay at 60; queries from internal departments like accounts and personnel get 5 deducted from the 60. There are similar classifications for all the main departments, and any new or unknown users just stay at 60.

After that, where the caller describes his or her computer as being unusable, another 5 is added to the score. A further 5 is added if several users are affected. On the other hand, 5 is deducted if for any reason the user will not be available to help diagnose or solve the problem. The final score becomes the priority of this escalation. Theoretically, queries can enter the system with a priority of anything between 50 and 75 in increments of 5.

After that, the support manager can adjust these priorities by any amount, up or down. That way a list of outstanding queries is produced, sorted under the influence of both importance and urgency (the actual physical sort is performed by the helpdesk package, a custom-written database application). All priority scores are increased, usually by one, for every half-day the query remains unsolved. So older queries are automatically more important than newer ones.

Categories can also be added as the query arrives, and at least one helpdesk book I have read recommends this. I am not so sure, because I believe anything that increases the amount of information that has to be gathered when the call comes in will cause corners to be cut. Most technicians do not like using call-logging systems, and the harder they are to use, the less they will get used, with a detrimental effect on the integrity of the call-log. Call categories are something that can be added later as part of the measuring process, rather than interfering with the helpdesk process.

23.7 Managing multiple support task priorities

Some user support organizations have a wide range of services, committing their resources to various tasks of widely differing priorities. Although we can use something as simple as a comparison of importance and urgency to distinguish the relative priorities of tasks which are more or less all alike, such as user problems, this is not enough to prioritize different types of jobs and compare the relative commitment of resources and the value extracted.

For some functions in more complex support departments, this mixing of priorities does not really matter, because the people who are doing those tasks are dedicated to them. So you may have a professional writer producing the monthly newsletter, a network operator looking after the network design and main-tenance, dedicated problem solvers providing solutions to user problems, and so on. But what if you have just one group of people providing all the services? Then you have to compare different tasks with one another, e.g. an installation project with a product evaluation, a network problem with a management report, and so on, in order to decide where to commit your resources first in the company's best interests.

You cannot compare apples with oranges. They are too different, comparison is meaningless. But if you must make such a comparison, then what you must discover is what apples and oranges have in common and compare these common denomi-nators. So it is with the variety of work in your support department. What do all tasks have in common so that I can compare them and thus decide which is most important?

All support tasks have a certain set of attributes which make them alike. They must, or people with similar skills could not carry out these tasks. Similarity and difference do not mix well. Where you cannot compare the tasks themselves, reduce them to a series of attributes and compare the attributes. I call this method *task attribute scoring* (TAS) and I apologize in advance to anybody who may already have invented it under another name.

All tasks have a resource commitment; they each need a certain number of people for a certain amount of time, and it is quite legitimate to render a lower priority to a task that requires resources you do not yet have than the priority granted to a task that requires resources you have readily available. All tasks will have a client; and as we have already seen the relative importance or influence of clients can be compared. All tasks should have a target completion date; and the targets can be compared with one another for their validity. For instance, a target date set because it reflects a real business need ('the job has to be completed by Thursday or we'll miss a business opportunity') takes precedence over a target set merely arbitrarily ('the job has to be completed by Thursday because it would be nice to have it by then'). You may be able to find further attributes to compare, such as financial justifiability: this project will render a profit to the company, this project will break even, this project will cost more than it saves. Or perhaps general benefits: this project will make all others a lot easier, this project will just add to the support burden, this project will make our lives a misery in future.

The next stage is to weight these attributes against one another; you may consider financial justifiability to be more important than the power of the client, or the availability of resources to be more important than all other attributes. Then the whole thing can be reduced to numbers.

In the table in Fig. 23.3, we can see how different tasks could be compared. For example, a project requiring resources we have available ($1 \times 3 = 3$) genuinely requiring urgent completion ($1 \times 1 = 1$) which will break even ($1 \times 2 = 2$) and has been requested by an important client ($2 \times 4 = 8$, total $3 + 1 + 2 + 8 = 14$) would take precedence over a project requiring new resources ($0 \times 3 = 0$) committed to an arbitrary target date ($0 \times 1 = 0$) only expecting to break even ($1 \times 2 = 2$) and requested by a middle manager ($1 \times 4 = 4$, total $0 + 0 + 2 + 4 = 6$).

Attribute	Options	Score	Weighting
Resource availability	*Resources currently unavailable*		
	Resources available		
Target completion date	*Business-critical target*		
	Arbitrary target		
inancial ustification	*Project will make a profit*		
	Project will break even		
	Project will make a loss		
Client	*Powerful/business critical client*		
	Significant client		
	Powerless/commercially insignificant		

Figure 23.3
A task attribute
scoring (TAS) table

23.8 Controlling demand

As we considered in Chapter 20, the most important bottleneck in any work system is the first one. The narrower this bottleneck, the less work in the system. As the overkeen nightclub doorman found out to his cost, sometimes the entry bottleneck can be so narrow that there is too little work in the system for the system to continue to justify its existence. However, it may be that for your support department, it is worthwhile considering the occasional constriction of demand in order to be able to service the outstanding work at all.

Demand on your services is particularly dangerous at the launch of a new service. There is likely to be an initial surge of demand as the preceding hype has its effect on launch day. That demand can be controlled by keeping advertising of the new service to a minimum, perhaps launching it to a pilot group only. After that first surge, demand could rise or fall. Pushing it up will be increased familiarity, as more people learn how to use the service. Demand will also grow as more people get to hear about the service and at least try it out, perhaps before choosing to use it ('subscribe') regularly. Pushing it down will be any disappointment felt by the users if their expectations were not met, regardless of how they arrived at those expectations.

In the long term, your new service will probably follow the pattern of any new product, finding its own market among the users, enjoying a more or less steady demand and output. Watch for any decline in demand. Indicators include an ever-diminishing group of users using the service, even though you may have launched a replacement service. The workflow in your support department is influenced by the number of directions your resources are pulled in, and old services may have to be discontinued so there are not too many pressures on the workflow and too many opportunities for failure.

23.9 Escalation routes

Your escalation routes are a key consideration in managing the workflow. Ensure that all escalation routes are clear; ideally document these and make reading and understanding the documents a requirement of helpdesk operation. If you have chosen to use query categories for incoming calls at the helpdesk, make sure your documentation shows and that everybody is clear on where calls of which category should be routed. This is especially important for those escalations which are urgent but adjudged to be not important. If they are urgent because of an obvious time-criticality, but they are not important because of your understanding of the business, then you need good escalation routes – both to establish that your understanding of the business is correct and, more pressingly, to escalate this query to a part of the company for whom it is both urgent and important.

Ensure clear ownership of escalated queries once they leave the helpdesk. This ownership is crucial; where it is unclear, it can increase exponentially the work the helpdesk has to do to keep up with the load of outstanding queries. Is the helpdesk's job providing solutions or chasing others to provide those solutions? Chasing is yet another service which has to be managed, and when ownership is clear, chasing should not be necessary.

23.10 Backlog management

Backlogs of outstanding enquiries are dangerous, demotivating and expensive.

The danger comes from the possibility of an important issue being lost in a long list of other work – it may simply be overlooked because there is always so much other work to do. If your staff look at the size of the queue, and feel that the backlog is so impossibly large that it will never be cleared, then in effect it does not matter which problem they select to work on now. This can lead to the practice known as 'cherry picking' – claiming those jobs that are easiest, most pleasant or most distracting. The most difficult work gets left in the backlog, to fester for an indeterminate length of time. Unfortunately, that overlooked or deliberately ignored job might just be the one that would deliver the most benefit to the company, but that benefit may never be realized because the job is so distasteful to the staff. Backlogs discourage ownership and responsibility. In my experience, once a backlog starts to grow, there can be no stopping it unless somebody decides actively to tackle the backlog itself. If that doesn't happen, the culture of irresponsibility it can spawn will seep throughout the department, pulling down service and productivity levels in other areas as well.

This is because backlogs are demotivating. 'Look at the size of that mountain', your staff think. 'We will never get over that – so what's the point in trying?' Morale declines because the efforts of the staff will never bear full fruit – they will just continue to work hard but not actually achieve anything. So the work has no reward, and with a growing backlog, they go home every evening knowing that today the situation got worse, not better. And the manager doesn't seem to care, or lacks the competence to do anything about it, so they lose confidence in you too. So your authority to lead also declines, because under your leadership, things are getting worse, so why should they believe in you or do anything you say?

The cost of a backlog is often overlooked. Every outstanding enquiry suggests that somewhere, a user is not operating to the full potential of his productivity. So the company is wasting money, paying somebody to do less than they actually could if their computer were working properly. Not only that, because user productivity is impeded, the company as a whole is producing less than it could, so less money appears on the bottom line of the annual profit and loss statement than might have done. And the problem of lost productivity is not just a risk to commercial organizations – low user productivity in public service means tax revenues are going to waste, financing inefficient government departments who must therefore spend a higher proportion of their government grant on themselves and consequently less on the services they are supposed to be delivering to the country's population. And what about the more worrying consequences of low user productivity caused by helpdesk inefficiency in charities, the police, hospitals, the armed forces, and so on? In those places, low productivity can literally be a matter of life or death. How would you like to be the helpdesk manager whose unmanageable backlog decreased the efficiency of an intensive care ward, an anti-terrorist defence unit or a third-world food programme?

First, do you have a backlog? Two ways to answer 'No'.

One is that all outstanding enquiries are legitimately waiting for input or activity from some non-IT party, either the user or a vendor. If this is the case, the service level clock should be stopped – do not denigrate your own measure of efficiency when in fact the fault is elsewhere.

The other is a rule of thumb I have, namely that if a 10 per cent increase in support staff productivity would eradicate the backlog, then what you have is not a backlog, it is a mild case of operational inefficiency.

If your insurmountable heap of outstanding work does not satisfy either of those above criteria then your job for today is to read to the end of this chapter, put this book down and get on with the job of eradicating the backlog.

First, check what is in the backlog. This means you have to read every single enquiry in it.

Some helpdesks put all helpdesk work in the same list, and this can distort the view of what is actually outstanding. Helpdesk trouble tickets and change requests should ideally be identified and reported separately. With change requests in particular, separate the jobs in hand from those that are just candidates for a 'wish-list' – some requests are not requests at all, but statements of 'wouldn't it be nice if. . .'. These should not be logged as helpdesk work because they have no specific service level associated with them.

Another type of work that gets mixed in with the trouble tickets consists of the small-scale projects conducted by many help-desks. These too should really be managed and monitored separately. Leave them in the helpdesk system by all means, but in a distinct category that does not impact the trouble-ticket service level statistics. The category itself can be a problem – when your backlog eradication programme starts, you may find that some of the more difficult trouble tickets suddenly magically transmute into 'projects' or 'change requests'. But these too need managing, at least by checking regularly with their owners on progress towards completion.

Next, if it's dead, kill it off. If you have a large backlog, you may well find requests or tickets in there that have been outstanding for months. Nobody in the support team dares to call the user back, for fear of the embarrassment of beginning the call with 'Hi, Mr User. Helpdesk here. Remember that enquiry you logged with us a year ago last October?' The user may have even left the company by now, or moved to a different department. If the job looks as though it will not be missed, get rid of it. Alternatively, you could (and probably should) take the courteous step of sending the user an e-mail, with a copy of the ancient enquiry attached, proposing to close the enquiry by the end of the week unless there is a valid reason for leaving it open. Of course this itself may be a bit embarrassing, but you'll only have to do it once – let's face it, after an humiliating experience like that, you're not going to let your backlog grow again in a hurry.

Of course there may be the occasional user who requests that the call remain open because the problem occurred once, but has not occurred since, but he wants you to hang on to the trouble ticket 'just in case it happens again.' No. Sorry. If we didn't know enough about the problem to deal with it when it happened the first time, that log will be of no use to us when and if it happens again. Our rule is that we only retain in the list of outstanding work those jobs for which there is a promised service level. If we're not going to fix it, we close it.

Next, look for examples of requests coming in that should never have come in anyway because they do not match the helpdesk's published portfolio of services. OK, maybe the facilities department doesn't have a published service level for changing the dud light bulb in the fourth floor men's room, but that doesn't mean the request should have come to the IT helpdesk. In future, make sure your staff know how not to accept such requests.

And now it's time for 'morning prayers'. Or at least that is the name given to a particular backlog management technique used by the service manager at a certain electronics manufacturer just south of London (a man of particular dynamism, charisma and a strong sense of humour). He started with a backlog of 600 enquiries. So every day for a fortnight, he held a 09:30 meeting of 20 minutes' duration for all managers of all the helpdesk and IT resolving agencies. The purpose of the meeting was to examine the contribution to backlog eradication made by each department. They had to promise in front of their peers which outstanding enquiries they would clear by the end of the day, or explain in public the following day why they had failed. The purpose of the meeting was to establish ownership, which means that a known individual would personally see that the problem was completed and closed. It worked magnificently. Within two weeks, the backlog had shrunk to a third of its original size. 'Morning prayers' began to take place not daily, but weekly. After a month, the only outstanding work was known to be because the helpdesk was waiting for activity by or response from the user.

Part Five

Resources management

24 Justifying user support expenditure

If you as the support manager are suddenly being challenged to justify your support services, then you may already have failed. If the powerful people are not already aware of how useful and justifiable you are, then there is a strong possibility that they are coming to you with suspicion in their hearts. Accept that they may need some considerable convincing that you really are worth as much to them as you think you are. After all, they pay the bills – maybe your information about the justification of user support will count, but your opinion almost certainly will not.

Justification probably has three aspects to it, these being your perceived value from the users' point of view, the continued relevance of your services and the real biggy, your financial justification. We looked at your perceived value in detail back in Part Two, so all I have to do here is remind you how important the marketing you do is. Let us look at relevance in a bit more detail.

24.1 Continued relevance

If the design and structure of your support services has not changed for the last three years, you should be worried. Three years ago, the desktop computing scene looked very different; technologies which were unaffordable then are now commonplace, they are on several desks in your company and on the desks of your company's competitors. Competition in your marketplace has probably increased; sources of information have changed, your staff have learned more and they could be offering new services. Some users have moved on, others have joined the company and the skills portfolio of the users in general is different now than it was three years ago. If you have not changed your services to meet those challenges in that time, there is a risk that you are losing touch with the people who bring in the bread and butter. At the detailed level, support managers must keep in touch with the changing patterns of needs, abilities and aspirations among their customers so that they can continue to be relevant to those patterns. If you are not relevant, your customers will try something new that may not include you.

So much for detail. But to be entirely in touch, one should also be looking at wider trends. The company changes because of what happens in the world at large. But the company and the people in it are also part of that world. The company is subject to the tides of fashion in the business world because it is a business; but because it employs people, it is also subject to all those fads of a more personal or cultural nature. This is especially important for a user support manager, because that job is essentially helping people, not just businesses. Keeping in touch with macrocultural trends is part of being ready for the future, if not being part of the trends themselves.

Let us take a specific and relevant example of this broader, cultural pressure. Philosophers and researchers have documented a tidal shift away from the corporatism and conformity which characterized the cultures of many of the developed nations since the end of the Second World War to around the middle of the 1980s. Corporatism and conformity delivered us enormous benefits; it gave us standards for products, which increased competition, bringing down prices, increasing availability, reliability and confidence in the safety of our purchases.

On the back of this corporatism came the success of the 'standardizing' companies, like the computer industry's IBM, AT&T and Microsoft; or in retail, the domination of the British, American and German town centres by the same small groups of chains; or in publishing, the predominance of two-centimetre-thick, pulp sex-and-shopping novels with gold, curly writing on the cover; or in television, the reduction of prime-time to the same group of faces, where for several years, the same soap or the same talk-show host would occupy three or more slots a week; or in travel, where all airports, all hotels and all pizza restaurants look exactly the same as each other, regardless of host nation; or in business attire, where everybody wore a dark suit, white shirt and sober tie and any office floor in the UK looked like a mobilized display of Marks & Spencer. Life was getting boring. Pleasant and cheap but bland and boring. Convenience of production had become a more important feature of many products than customer appeal. We even had slogans, some not invented by advertisers, to honour our own corporate conformity, such as 'you know where you are with a Ford' and the particularly anachronistic 'nobody ever got fired for buying IBM'.

The backlash started in a small way in the early 1980s, with the rising popularity of designer names. This was the dawn of individualism. It is getting vulgar now, where the name is more important than the garment (the designer label is worn outside or the name emblazoned across the front, or worse, across the back). But this merely indicates that another tide of individualism is on the way, to be different from whatever fashion has gone before. Faith Popcorn in *The Popcorn Report*, Charles Handy in *The Age of Unreason* and his quite brilliant *The Empty Raincoat*, and John Naisbitt in *Global Paradox* have all observed this monumental shift away from corporatism and towards individuality. The trick is to spot the pattern – this break from conformity is not just happening in commerce, it is happening in politics (the splintering of eastern Europe and Canada), in publishing (can magazines get any more specialist?), in popular music (how long does a new band last?), even in fast food (Burger King ads offer the product 'your way').

Business is conservative by nature and it has taken a few years for this cultural shift to percolate down into the way firms conduct their affairs. It is happening now in a big way as large corporations switch to their core businesses and break up into smaller, slicker business units. I and others predict this trend will continue and individualism will become even more important. For a while, anyway.

So that is 500 words of commentary on trends that look a million miles from what the helpdesk does; but to remain truly relevant, you have to be watching the outside world to know what is coming next. That will give you the indicators you need to design the most appropriate future services. For example, what will happen to your standard corporate applications interface when individualism hits it? How will the nature of user queries to the helpdesk change when they all begin to ignore the corporate standards and do things their own way? You will not be able to fight it – if you try, these individuals will just see you as irrelevant to them. What about when it swings back to corporatism (as it will)? Your individualistic services will have to be replaced with easy-to-grasp packaged services.

24.2 How to stay relevant

The paradox of all this is that you cannot hope to keep your helpdesk services relevant by concentrating your attention on the helpdesk. That will merely serve to narrow your vision and may even cause you to make the same mistakes repeatedly. As an ambitious young manager once said to me, 'That's old Williams. The arrogant old buffer thinks he knows it all because of his so-called 20 years' experience – what he's actually got is one year's experience 20 times over.' Williams had a reputation for spending years never going outside what little experience he had gained inside his own company.

To stay relevant, to give yourself the vision you need to invent better helpdesk and user support services, broaden your outlook. By all means plagiarize ideas you see working for other support teams. By all means hobnob with the Helpdesk Institute in the US, or the Helpdesk User Group and the PC User Group in the UK. But once in a while, get out of the Support office, broaden your view to look at services in general, and see how other companies and industries go about providing support services, not just computer support services. Then turn your mind to seeing how you could translate those experiences and ideas to your own clientele and range of services.

Earlier in this book, I have quoted some examples of customer service gleaned from experiences with my local retailers. I also get ideas by observing my local municipal swimming pool (how to teach fairly simple concepts like moving your feet to people who are too frightened even to try, how to make a customer feel at ease when she thinks that her life may be in danger, and in one notably hilarious incident, how not to handle a complaint) and from my local freesheet newspaper (how to convey technical and political concepts in an attractively readable fashion) among others.

24.3 Financial justification

It is worth stressing the following idea. Your business uses computers because it has to. The users' technical problems, which keep the user support department in business, exist because they have to. Without computers and all the hassle they cause, the business could not achieve the targets it has set itself. There is a strong business case for the continued existence of the helpdesk. The trouble is, not enough people know precisely how strong a case.

Like every other department in the company, user support exists because its existence is financially expedient. As is the case for every other corporate function, it is cheaper for the helpdesk to exist than for it not to. If it were not cheaper, it probably would not exist. Few organizations are running a charity for helpdesk technicians. Business is business, most commercial enterprises are in it for the profit, and those who are not profit motivated are usually concerned with keeping costs down. No doubt about it, it is cheaper to employ you than not to employ you. The trouble is, not enough people know how much cheaper.

The cost of user support is rarely more worrying than at times of recession, such as we suffered in the early 1990s (things will never be the same again after that one). That recession in the North Atlantic was different because it coincided with the growing maturity of international competition from less-recessed and generally lower-cost economies. This meant that the big, yet recessed economies were under even greater pressure to protect profit margins even though competition was keeping prices down. In many industries, the only option left open was to cut costs to widen the gap between income and expenditure. Some support managers learned for the first time the relevance of world market movements on their peaceful little helpdesks.

When costs have to be cut as radically as the recession necessitated, the helpdesk is an obvious target. It is labour intensive, so it is full of the most draining sort of cost: people. The only comparison some financial managers think they need to make is the money they spend financing the helpdesk against the money they would save by not financing it.

Of course that is a simplistic view, but it is an obvious one. The alternative would be that the helpdesk would be seen as not simply costing, but actually saving money. In most helpdesks that is unlikely. I have yet to find the helpdesk or user support organization which actively pursues a policy of justifying its existence in terms which can be clearly understood by the people who called it into existence in the first place. Businesses think of everything in terms of money: money saved, money spent, money made, money lost. Helpdesks usually think of everything in terms of computers: systems installed, problems solved, upgrades made, downtime experienced. The two factions see the world in entirely different ways. But money created the helpdesk, money keeps it going and money does not give a damn about computers unless it is told why it should, and told in its own terms.

Nobody can expect the financial managers to be any more of an expert in the business benefits of user support than they are in any other specialist area of the business. Only the specialists can explain their world to the generalists, and the support managers therefore have a duty to justify their departments' expenditure to the money men. That expenditure has to be explained, not in terms of money spent, but in terms of money saved and benefits delivered as a result.

The fact is that most support departments save their host companies a great deal of money. This can be brought to the attention of the financiers with a few fairly simple calculations, and some examples are given below. You may find there are other examples for your own organization. A word of warning, however; just as the world of user support is an alien one to accountants, do not underestimate the complexity of accountancy assumptions which may make it less than straightforward to argue these calculations in your company. In your favour, however, is the endless need most companies have for true measures of costs and cost benefits. With these and similar calculations you are offering ways of measuring things they may not have been able to measure before. Take these and other calculations and use them as a basis of negotiation with your accountants as to the true cost benefits of the user support function.

The problem most financiers have with deciding on how much money to invest in the helpdesk is that they don't have all the information they need to make that decision. They know what the helpdesk *costs*, but they don't know what it's *worth*. So when they come to that decision, the one they make is whether to spend money on the helpdesk or not spend money on the helpdesk. Of course, they take the easy answer.

But if they had a cost–benefit analysis of the helpdesk, the decision would be whether to spend money on the helpdesk, or lose money elsewhere because that investment had not been made; and then which is greater, the investment or the potential loss. That is what the calculations below attempt to provide.

24.4 Support cost justification example 1: return on support investment

How much would it cost the user population if you were not there to solve their problems? What would the user have to do to solve a given problem? First, they would have to acquire the technical background knowledge to that problem. At one extreme, that means reading the manual, which they usually prefer not to do because it is so easy to telephone you; at the other extreme, they might need your years of technical insight and experience gleaned from fixing similar problems with this and other products. Either way, it would take them longer than it takes you, and all the time they were spending doing that they would be diverted from doing what they were originally paid to do. This cost would be multiplied by the duplication this would cause; without a central support department, users all over the company would end up solving a problem they were not aware had already been solved by another user in another department.

Let us assume that a support technician can solve a technical problem three times as quickly as a user could. This is a simple calculation: solving problems without the support department would cost three times as much, less the cost of the support department; total, twice the cost of the support department. If the financiers need any corroboration, ask the users; whenever they get a solution from the helpdesk, the helpdesk technician asks the simple question, 'How long would it have taken you to solve that problem yourself?'

But that is not all; to that figure we have to add *lost user productivity*.

24.5 Support cost justification example 2: lost user productivity

Lost user productivity is a fairly complex algorithm about which to make an accounting assumption as to the financial value of the helpdesk. It assumes that the total revenue the company makes is the product of the aggregate work done by all the company's employees. The consequential assumption is that if the employee is not working (e.g. because his computer is malfunctioning) then the company is not making the revenue it would have made if the employee were at full productivity.

So how much revenue does an employee make? Start with last year's financial statement. Somewhere in there will be a 'revenue' or 'turnover' figure, namely the total amount of money the company made last year.

Next, you will need the total number of FTEs (full time equivalent staff headcount) the company employs.

Now because we are going to compare user productivity with helpdesk calls, we need to bring the headcount figure down to something that looks more like a helpdesk call. So we are going to find out the total number of hours of work the company does. So multiply the total FTE by 220, which is the average number of days an FTE is at his desk. Then multiply that by 7.5, which is the typical length in productive hours of an employee's working day.

So now we know how many hours the company works in a year. And from the financial statement we know how much money the company turns over in a year. So if we divide the dollar figure by the hour figure, we know how much money an employee produces every hour they work.

So if the employee, and by that I mean computer user, is not working, that is the amount of money the company could have made for productivity lost per user, per hour. This is the base 'lost user productivity' (LUP) figure.

Still with me? Good. Because now it gets complicated. The fact is that if the user's computer was down, he would be doing something else, like making phone calls, going to a meeting or doing a bit of filing. And not all helpdesk enquiries are about a downed system anyway. So to allow for that, we have to calculate just how dependent the company is on its computer systems. We do this by negotiation with various managers in the organization, to arrive at a percentage figure. This percentage is the 'computer dependency factor' (CDF). It's usually around 50 per cent for manufacturing companies or retail chains with a large blue-collar staff, in the mid-seventies for most companies, in the upper eighties for finance houses and 100 per cent for trading floors.

Now we work out how much productivity is lost given the number of calls the users make to the helpdesk, and the best way to do that is with an example.

A services company has 1000 employees and makes £150 million per year. The staff are 85 per cent dependent on their computers. The helpdesk takes 25,000 calls a year. It fixes half of those enquiries in five minutes and the rest of them average out to around eight hours. So in that case, the potential lost productivity is 25,000 times four hours, or 100,000 hours.

Given the headcount and corporate revenue figures, we know that each employee produces £100,000 per annum, so £90.91 per hour.

So how much productivity is the company losing? 100,000 hours times £90.91 times the CDF of 85 per cent; or £7,727,350. Scary, isn't it?

So, helpdesk manager, how many staff would you need to bring that average service level down from its current four hours to two? Because if you could improve your service level by that much, you would in theory enable the company, with its current resources, to increase its productivity by 50,000 hours and make an extra revenue of £3,863,675.

In a company that size, there would probably be about 11 FTEs in the support department. Its salary budget would be about £250,000. Let's say we double it. So an investment in the helpdesk of a quarter of a million pounds could enable the company to make nearly four million pounds in extra revenue. Not a bad return on investment, I would say.

Impressive though it is, the LUP calculation has its flaws. There is no guarantee that the helpdesk's efforts to free up more user productivity would actually be turned into additional revenue. Given the obvious short-termist knee-jerking of some companies, a likely result would be that the 50,000 hours saved would be turned into 30 headcount layoffs instead. But it would be the helpdesk manager's job to point out the possibilities he had offered by improving his service levels.

24.6 Support cost justification example 3: risk assessment

By being there, support averts disasters, and saves money as a result. To find out how much, calculate the cost of the disaster and divide it by the risk of that disaster happening. There is the example of a small college with an annual turnover of £10,000,000. All of that money is collected in two weeks in the late summer when enrolment takes place. If the computer system goes down in that time, some of that money will not be collected; they will not be able to enrol students, some of whom will go to another college rather than risk not getting a college place. The assumption they make is that 10 per cent of the students will go astray, along with £1,000,000 of enrolment fees. What is the possibility of that happening? Well, the network has been down for one week in the last year (unlikely, I know, but it makes the calculations easier), meaning there is a risk of 1 week in 52, or more or less 2 per cent. So at risk is 2 per cent of a million, or £20,000. That one risk alone is worth £20,000. Now all we have to agree is the amount we will invest in computer support as a percentage of the risk. Get the accountants to agree to pay out 10 per cent of the risk and they are spending £2,000 (on overtime for support technicians, renting a backup server, whatever) to save a cool million.

24.7 Support cost justification example 4: 'repeat business' element

This 'repeat business element' technique is for external help-desks only. It is a way of calculating the financial value of the contribution the external helpdesk makes to the sales effort by playing its part in retaining customers. If the external helpdesk charges for its services, then it is an income stream in its own right – thus calculating its value is the same as making any calculation of the cost of production against the revenue produced. But if the helpdesk makes no such charge, an accounting assumption is needed, through which we can negotiate with the finance director a reasonable level of financial investment in the helpdesk.

The external helpdesk supplies a support service to the company's customers. As such it is part of the selling proposition – the customer is presumed to be buying not just the product, but the 'free' support that comes with it. Therefore, the helpdesk is one of the many reasons why customers keep coming back and spending more money with the company. The value of this money spent by existing customers is known as 'repeat business' (as opposed to 'new business') and for most companies, it is the greater proportion of its overall revenue.

To calculate the helpdesk's contribution to that repeat business, we have to know two things; how much money is made from repeat business, and what value the returning customers place on the helpdesk as one of the reasons why they keep coming back. The money side is easy – just ask the sales director. The value side is more involved, and it requires a customer survey.

Identify a broad range of repeat customers. Help them to make a list of all of the reasons why they keep buying from your company. Once you have that list, assume that in total, it is 100 per cent of why the customers keep returning. Next, ask the customer to put all those reasons in order, attaching to each of them a proportion of 100 per cent so that each reason has a percentage figure next to it.

Next, take the average of all the percentages the customers gave for 'helpdesk' or 'post sales support'. Now you have a percentage figure.

Next, multiply that percentage by the money figure of repeat business, which you got earlier from the sales director.

What you are left with is a dollar figure. And that is the amount the customers think the helpdesk is worth. Prepare to be shocked. It's usually a very big number, far in excess of your helpdesk budget. So if that is what the helpdesk is worth – perhaps the company can now justify spending a little more money on it.

25

Knowledge

How many products does your technical team support? Including the operating system, applications environment, systems hardware, a couple of types of printer, say four or five business applications packages, several add-on bits and pieces hard and soft – the figure typically comes out to around the 30 mark. For each of those supported items, any one of your technicians will be able to claim a level of knowledge anywhere between total ignorance and absolute guru status and a few points in between; let us say five possible levels of knowledge. If your helpdesk has six people in it, then you have $30 \times 5 \times 6$ or 900 permutations of product by knowledge level by knowledge holder. With 900 points to go at, how could you ever be sure that you have deployed the right level of expert at the right time in the right place?

As one would deal with any management problem such as this, the first action should be to take some measurements. Who knows how much about what, is it enough and are those the right things to know about? Start by making a list of all the products you support or suspect the users think you support. At this stage it does not really matter whether you actually (i.e. officially) support all the products or not – as we are going to ask the users to help us compose this list, their opinions count. When we then ask the technicians, we may find that we can support the product anyway.

Having composed the list, we need to find out which of these products are worth supporting. Ask several users and several technicians how important they think the product is to the business of the company. As we are trying to produce a numerical measure, the answers must be in a restricted range of options. The question I ask, for each computer product on my list, is 'To the business of this company, is this product essential, significant, routine or irrelevant?' A response of 'essential' gets a score of 3, 'significant' is a 2, 'routine' is a 1 and 'irrelevant' is a 0. In gathering the responses, I compile a spreadsheet and I calculate averages. This becomes my *product relevance matrix* as illustrated in Fig. 25.1.

Figure 25.1
A product relevance matrix

RELEVANCE	Respondent 1	Respondent 2	Respondent 3	Respondent 4	Averages
Product 1	2	2	1	1	1.5
Product 2	2	1	1	1	1.25
Product 3	0	0	0	1	0.25
Product 4	3	3	3	3	3.0
Product 5	3	2	2	3	2.5
Averages	2.0	1.6	1.4	1.8	1.7

The product relevance matrix tells me how important the company's users consider the products I am supporting. The more people I ask, the more accurate reading I will get, of course; and in any case the more people I ask the more I will be putting myself about; always good for the marketing, but do not overdo it or you may annoy them.

Next, using the same list of products, I ask the user support staff this time how knowledgeable they think they are on each of the products. This time, I miss nobody out; it is vital that everybody who supports users is asked about their ability on every product. This will give you a measure of the technicians' knowledge individually as well as collectively; so if you find any gaps, you will know how to plug them.

I ask the technicians to rate their own knowledge on a level of 4 to 0, where 4 is the highest level and 0 is absolute ignorance. The knowledge levels are described in detail in Fig. 25.2; please note that levels 4 and 0 are there more to put the other levels in perspective than for any identification of genuine genius or gormlessness. An example of the *product knowledge matrix* which results is given in Fig. 25.3.

Now we can compare the results of the two matrices together, and we can see that this particular helpdesk has a number of serious

eve 4	o t s roduct so e cou d ave des g ed t.
eve 3	o t s roduct e e oug to s o ot ers o to su ort t.
eve 2	ca a s er ost uest o s o t s roduct se .
eve 1	ca ot a s er tec ca uest o s o t s roduct ut o at t e roduct s a d o ere to esca ate uer es to.
eve 0	o ot g a out t s roduct.

Figure 25.2
Knowledge levels

problems. First, the overall average of the department's ability at 1.95 is lower than 2, so collectively they can only just support the products. The problem appears to lie with a tendency to rely on specialists; technicians 1 and 3 are clearly the experts and we ought to consider whether the other technicians are being wasted. I would also tend to take technician 1's replies with a pinch of salt; does he perhaps overrate himself slightly?

N LE E	e n an 1	e n an 2	e n an 3	e n an 4	Averages
Product 1	4	2	3	2	2.75
Product 2	3	2	3	2	2.5
Product 3	3	1	2	0	1.5
Product 4	2	0	3	1	1.5
Product 5	1	1	3	1	1.5
Averages	2.6	1.2	2.8	1.2	1. 5

Figure 25.3
Product knowledge matrix

Our next problem is that in product 5 we have an item which most people consider to be essential to the business, yet we seem almost completely unable to support it. Unless this product benefits from contracted-out support, this is a gap we need to plug urgently.

We are perhaps fortunate that technicians 1 and 3 each have fairly balanced knowledge. There perhaps is little scope for doing anything to improve their knowledge as things stand, and perhaps we should look for new areas to involve them in. The other two technicians should each be assigned a product to learn in the very near future.

This comparison of product relevance and product knowledge is an exercise that should be conducted fairly regularly, perhaps once a quarter; and in any case a few weeks after a major product rollout or upgrade, to assess how well the support team has adapted to supporting the product. As a balance to the exercise, check the results with the call-log database to see if the technicians really are as knowledgeable as they say they are. One statistic to use is the spot rate; find out how many queries technician 1 is escalating on product 1; if his spot rate here is less than 100 per cent, perhaps he is not the omniscient wonder he claims to be.

25.1 Acquiring knowledge

One of the most obvious ways to acquire technical knowledge is to go on a training course. This is all very well for new knowledge, but it is seldom the only way or even the best way for increasing the knowledge of technicians in areas they are already aware of. Take the example of the computer technician who knows the spreadsheet package Lotus 123 very well and now needs to be able to support a rival spreadsheet, Microsoft Excel. It would be inappropriate to send this technician on a 'Microsoft Excel for Beginners' course, as some of the course content would probably be on the principles of spreadsheeting, an area the technician already understands well. Boredom would result, possibly along with unconstructive comparisons of the products.

For technicians, training courses are rarely the best way to learn about new products; they would learn more from playing with the products themselves. Technicians benefit from training courses where what is being taught is a new technology rather than a new product.

'Playing with the product' is a euphemism for a more rigorous process the learning technician should go through with a new product. 'Play' is non-directional – the technician needs something more directed, so the process should have an objective. Examples of learning objectives are 'to expose the technician to the product from the user's point of view' or 'to increase the technician's spot rate (or fix rate) on this product by 10 per cent within one month', or 'to report on areas of the product where user difficulty is anticipated'. This way the technician learns the product, but with the direct and measurable result of an improvement in service.

25.2 Where should the knowledge be?

If you operate some kind of helpdesk service, where the users telephone their problems in, the issue of where the knowledge should be in user support is a key one. The fact that the users have chosen to use and presumably you have chosen to offer such an immediate communications method as the telephone suggests they want the answer now. Even if the actual problem may not be urgent, wanting an immediate answer is quite natural – after all, it is cheaper and easier from the user's point of view to request the knowledge exactly when she needs it, rather than have to wait for the knowledge to arrive, or learn it in advance and wait for an opportunity to use it. The use of a helpdesk to get knowledge precisely and only when you need it is just another form of 'just-in-time' deliveries.

When the users call the helpdesk, they want the information now. Because it will disappoint the users to have to escalate the query, because it will depress your spot rate, and because it costs more to escalate, the helpdesk will endeavour to have the requisite knowledge available at the helpdesk.

Some companies see the knowledgeable helpdesk as the high-quality service option; some see it as an opportunity to improve user productivity; others see it as a way of saving money, as the more knowledge the helpdesk has, the fewer resolvers are needed.

Many products exist to help the helpdesk become more knowledgeable, and most of them come in a form of knowledge tools. Often these tools are built into commercial helpdesk packages, and some even go so far as to feature an ability to store scanned pictures and graphical illustrations of potentially useful items of knowledge.

Some companies see these knowledge tools as an opportunity to put in place a helpdesk which is to all intents and purposes technically ignorant; the databases are expected to provide the knowledge the caller or user requires and all the helpdesk does is pass the information on. I find there is only a limited range of helpdesks where such a proposition would be entirely practical; many if not most requests to IT helpdesks are either too simple ('my terminal's locked, would you recycle it please?') or too complex ('how would you recommend I go about X?') to be solved just by a database, no matter how comprehensive, and the patience of the caller would be severely tried by such a process.

There are probably two main types of these tools – the first is the knowledge database, which stores text and graphics in discrete documents of varying size and complexity. By querying this database, a document can be found to give an answer to a given technical problem. The query is normally entered as a series of keywords ANDed, ORed or NORed together.

The beauty of a database such as this is that you can put virtually anything in it; in fact one is encouraged to put everything in it, as this will increase the likelihood of a match to an enquiry. Often, database entries are produced as a result of a user asking a question and the technician researching and documenting the answer. The database can become the repository of all the technical knowledge about old products, when you would rather the technicians cleared their heads of old knowledge to make way for knowledge about new products.

But in the strength of such databases also lies their weakness. The scope and flexibility of them can lead them to reach unwieldy proportions. A query can produce too many answers, so the mere list of 'possibly relevant' document titles can be unusably large. Or the query may produce no answers at all because the database is unaware of that product. Either way the credibility of the database is undermined. As an experiment, I once linked an 18,000-document database direct to the call-logging system of a particularly busy helpdesk. Every time the database was used, a flag was set that I could later count. I found that the database was consulted for around 2 per cent of the queries and useful for even fewer; so the database was virtually useless, despite the fact that I had deliberately invested in its content by having staff and systems dedicated to filling it with relevant documents.

The second major type of knowledge tool is the decision-tree type. This is a structured device which asks questions to try to arrive at an answer by a process of elimination. Even more sophisticated types of such trees are appearing, imbued by artificial intelligence with a rudimentary diagnostic ability. The application for tools such as these is in the ignorant helpdesk. The range of questions may be so wide that it is neither justifiable nor practical to train the helpdesk staff to be able to answer the questions – so either they or the enquirer consult the decision tree.

These too have their problems; for example, the helpdesk staff may learn faster than the machine does and eventually cease to use it for certain types of problems, raising the risk of reduced accuracy of answers; the correct level of simplicity of decisions may be difficult to arrive at, so the enquirer must exasperatingly go through the same questions every time before arriving at something new; a wrong response to the machine's question is given at some point, leading the enquirer up a blind alley.

For both these knowledge devices, some problems will always remain. One is that the system has to be administrated. There has to be somebody there to fill it up with the right information, ensure it is up to date and in a usable form. Often, helpdesks turning to a tool such as this underestimate the secondary investment needed to manage the system and eventually it falls into costly disuse simply because they never allowed for the resource needed to feed the machine.

Another problem is in the use of the tool. When a user calls the helpdesk, he or she is unlikely to want to wait while the helpdesk operative scrolls through a list of possible solutions or navigates round a decision tree, especially if the payoff does not appear to come quickly.

Knowledge is fashionable – the types of questions posed to the helpdesk will change rapidly as the user population acquires its own knowledge by experience and ceases to ask certain questions; at the same time, new products come and go all the time, changing the type of knowledge we need. Any knowledge tool must take account of this simple truth before it can be truly effective. As things stand, I rarely find examples of where knowledge tools could really be as much of a benefit to a helpdesk and its customers as could a proper culture of personal knowledge acquisition.

25.3 The future of technical knowledge

Computers are getting more and more complicated. The massive improvements in processing power, speed and logical size of computers have largely contributed to an alleged increase in the 'ease of use' of computers. So, in theory at least, more people can use them with a lower starting level of computer knowledge. At the same time, computer technology prices have fallen steeply, so more people can afford them. These two pressures have boosted the need for technical knowledge to assist this new user population. Where once there were only a few kilobytes between the user and hardware, now there are several megabytes of interacting layers of device drivers, and so on, any of which is at risk of being at least encountered and possibly damaged by an increasingly technically alienated user. The real high priests of the computer's internal workings have never been in greater demand. Oh, goody, goody, more jobs for us user supporters, I used to think.

Now I am not so sure. Technical knowledge is becoming 'commoditized'; I mean that it is turning into a commonly available commodity, often to be bought on price alone. Lots of companies have technical expertise available as a saleable item. We do not need more low-level analysts, we need more user supporters. True, the machines are getting more complicated, but one machine looks like another – once the manufacturer has solved the particularly knotty problem, a new release is launched and the problem has gone away. It only crops up once, then it is fixed. Whereas the number of users keeps on increasing, and it is the ability to communicate with the user which is more important than the technical knowledge. Now the skill is not knowing the inside of the computer by heart, it is knowing where to go to get the requisite knowledge about such-and-such an innard. Apart from that, the equipment is more reliable, both above and below the operating system. So the people who support the users need to know less, in relative terms, than they did ten years ago. Now it is the use and manipulation of the application the users need support on, not a bug in the operating system. And that kind of knowledge is often operational, commercial even, rather than technical.

At present, much store is being laid by a certain computer network manufacturer's training standards, by which network specialists are created and accredited for their knowledge. This accreditation has become something of a currency, with which accredited technicians can buy themselves better-paid and more responsible jobs. In my opinion, this focus on technical ability overshadows the real need for the ability to support users. Technical knowledge will continue to be needed, but in my opinion by an ever-decreasing élite of people dedicated to the inner workings of the machines. And that type of knowledge will be bought and sold just like the ability to fit a new exhaust pipe to a car. The users do not need that depth of knowledge any more, and with that reduced need will come a decline in the number of companies who consider it worthwhile to retain that specialization on the payroll, when it can be bought from any computer value-added reseller as and when needed.

The future for knowledge gurus does not look bright unless they want to make the final move into the computer industry proper. However, what we are going to need more of is the user supporter – the part trainer, part agony aunt, whose commu-nications skills are more important than how many manuals they have read and whose contacts, insight and experience are valued far more highly than their image as a technical guru.

Equipment

The helpdesk or user support department is just like any other department in the company; it needs its own resources and tools which it exploits to produce results. We have considered people, money and knowledge elsewhere; in this chapter I want to look at the hard resources like computers, telephones, working space, the library, hardware inventory and asset management.

26.1 Who manages these resources?

Who ensures that the technicians' own desktop computers are kept upgraded and in good working order? Who repairs those machines when they fail? Usually it is the technicians themselves, and there is some justification for this; after all, a helpdesk technician's machine is there to be used as a workbench, an adjustable tool for recreating troublesome environments to help diagnose a user's problem. This very process provides an opportunity for the technician to increase his or her knowledge (in some helpdesks it is the only opportunity).

Who looks after the library and ensures that the latest versions of the software and manuals are available for problem-solving use? Who categorizes all the reference items, the manuals, CD-ROMs, bulletin boards, product brochures? Who ensures there is a ready supply of formatted, virus-free floppy disks? Again, in many helpdesks there is no formal library so that issue does not arise; again, it is left to the technicians to retain their own reference material, their own supply of media. As we shall see later, this form of *laissez-faire* creates problems in itself, not forgetting the waste of technical resource.

When deciding on the management of support resources, one principle should be kept in mind – that the resources are there to provide the service, so the service must be more important than the resources. To use personnel who could be providing the end service for administrative or maintenance tasks is to detract from the purpose of the support department. In all probability, it will also be more expensive to have technicians or managers spend time performing functions which could be performed by an office administrator or clerk.

As with all perceived problems, if you think there is a difficulty with the control of resources in the helpdesk, the first step is to measure the problem. Make a list of those non-user support functions which need to be performed but are potential drains on your technical resources. A two-part list might be needed: one for constant or regular activities, one for infrequent ones. Individually, the infrequent tasks may not be a drain, but collectively they may be numerous enough to add weight to your judgement of whether you need a full-time administrator or not.

Typical regular functions might include the following:

- Maintaining library, up to date and correct; ordering replacement manuals and software.
- Monitoring hardware warranties and switching expired ones to maintenance agreements.
- Ensuring summoned maintenance engineers turn up on time and effect the repair.
- Replenishing the stationery cupboard.
- Collecting technician's timesheets.
- General filing.
- Administrating short-term computer rentals.
- Filling in on the helpdesk at peak times.
- Policing the 'clear desk' policy.
- Procuring user computer equipment.

Infrequent functions include:

- Ad hoc reports and counts.
- Reorganizing the library.
- Checking the office complies with safety standards.
- Induction of new recruits.
- Archiving unused software, tidying on-line storage.
- Reassessing user service level agreements.
- Renegotiating hardware maintenance agreements.
- Conducting client satisfaction surveys.

Some of these will require a more senior person than others: it would be unreasonable to expect a librarian to negotiate service level agreements between senior users and the IT department – that is a manager's job. However, it would also be unreasonable to expect the technicians to make sure there are enough pencils, but the department needs pencils to function.

26.2 Inventory and assets

Most commercial helpdesk management software packages now feature some ability to keep records of what equipment is deployed where and to which user. Various packages now use this information to a greater or lesser extent; a typical application is relating a user query to the machine the user has on his or her desk; another is providing IT management with reports of where their budget is being spent. The way this is implemented is to give a code to a user's machine – this code can be made to explode into a full description of that machine, giving serial numbers of all main components (computer unit, monitor, keyboard, printer).

From a support management point of view, there are probably three key issues associated with inventory management. The first is that an inventory bias focuses the technicians on supporting the product rather than the user. This will probably provide an inaccurate description of the support loading because machines do not ask questions, users do. There is no effective correlation between the number of computers and the number of users – a user may have a desktop machine, a laptop for travel, a personal digital assistant and WAP-enabled mobile phone, any of which may be connected to an array of network servers that is constantly growing. To consider the machines as the source of the questions is dangerously close to assuming that you only get contacted when the machine goes wrong, which in most cases is likely to be an utterly erroneous understanding of the service the helpdesk provides; more often than not, support is there to provide help, not simply to effect a repair. Inventory by all means, but be aware of the cultural risk – an inventory bias can cause you to lose sight of what the users (as opposed to the machines) need. Indeed if your helpdesk is a computer industry one – you make or resell a computer product – then inventory is likely to be almost irrelevant to your helpdesk, as you are probably going to be almost exclusively user-focused.

The next issue is the work overhead that inventory brings. Managing the products that closely will mean that you will have to keep accurate records of the logical and/or physical location of each device – and if you go to the level of parts explosion, which peripheral is connected to which device. You may also have to inventory the user himself – which applications, printers and firewalls his logon profile connects him to. If you do not have an inventory to start with, you will have to perform a complete audit, visiting each machine and logging its location against its content. (*Tip*: if you are going to do this, arm your technicians with rolls of coloured stickers, a different colour for each technician. When they audit the machine, they put a sticker on it so you know which machines have been audited and who did it.) You will need formal procedures for logging the movements of all machines to keep the inventory database up to date, and you will have to re-audit at least once a year to keep up with the unauthorized equipment swaps the users make.

The third issue comes right to the crux of whether the inventory is needed at all. With some Helpdesk software, you simply must have some kind of inventory loaded to get anything worthwhile out of the software. But for whom are you managing this inventory? If you have a user rather than a machine bias, do you really need to know as a helpdesk what the serial number of the user's machine is? Maybe – if your department is responsible for ensuring that machine is covered by a warranty or maintenance agreement. Or are you doing this work in order to assist in the accounting procedures? At some point, inventory management crosses the thin line into asset management, where the focus on the installed office hardware is part of controlling the corporate balance sheet. At this point, you are keeping a record of this hardware and software so that it can be measured and depreciated in the business accounts, rather than so that computer user productivity is kept at its maximum. The inventory workload will weigh heavily on what is usually a severely stretched resource – if this is the case in your company, ensure that inventory work gets the appropriate priority.

Case Study 26.1: an administrative revolution

The company had been building ships for ages – the standing joke was that they had even been consulted by Noah. They knew there were some old-fashioned practices still around in their vast ranks, but so long as they continued to make a profit, it was easier to ignore a few little inefficiencies for the sake of stability and peace.

There were ships coming out of this yard before computers were even thought of, but the company was not worried. This was an engineering company – these new electrical boxes would pose them no problem. So when the computer users started to increase in numbers, the company's response was simple, elegant and true to tradition; they set an IT engineer the task of going out and recruiting other IT engineers to form the company's first computer helpdesk.

Then the computers started to change rapidly, every six months, and the company had to keep up or the competition might steal yet another edge. They recruited more and more computer people with a proven technical ability. But the effects of these changes were too profound – more variety in the installed base, more challenge on the technicians to keep up with the technology, more reactivity.

Being engineers, the computer people had to solve user's problems as well as stay up to date. Private libraries sprang up all over IT; half-assembled computer parts lay on desks, on the floor; it seemed that every day users would ring in with a query on a software version they had never come across. Clive, the manager, tried his best but he was spending most of his time placating users.

The turning point came when two things happened at once. One of the senior engineers, John, left to work for one of the newer companies in the town, attracted by the more modern and pristine working environment; and the apprenticeship scheme delivered Vince. Engineering apprenticeships were a tradition for this company, and it seemed obvious to offer them in IT too. But Vince was different; it was not long before Clive noticed that Vince was not really cut out for solving problems; but he was an extraordinary organizer.

Vince started in a small way, tidying an area that had been left untouched for months – categorizing the manuals he found there, asking the technicians who owned which piece of semi-discarded hardware, associating this apparent junk with outstanding user queries. Soon it became logical to make it Vince's job, and he threw himself into it with a will.

Slowly, the department was transformed – the atmosphere changed, became less frenetic. Even John, on one of his 'lunchtime-with-old-mates' visits, commented on how 'modern' the place was beginning to look. Vince's role in this revolution was clear to everybody. Clive's next problem was Vince's apprenticeship: could he now be persuaded to follow an administrative path rather than a technical one? It wasn't hard – Vince was bright enough to know his strengths and he knew he would never make the technical grade and be as happy as he had been as an organizer. So he would never earn the money of a technician – but at least he'd have the contentment of a job well done.

This may sound like a fairy story, but it really happened. And as far as I know, they all lived happily ever after.

26.3 Space – the final frontier

I have to say, all too often I see helpdesks whose skimped space allocation screams the company's negative attitude toward them – miscomprehension of the nature of helpdesk work, low grade accommodation for low grade, lowly paid people whose job function is an overhead and whose salaries are a begrudged draw on corporate resources.

It should never be that way. The typical user support department has the supremely important function of keeping the entire corporation working. In that, it is probably the second most important department in the company after sales, but to look at some helpdesk offices, you wouldn't know it.

The helpdesk needs space, and lots of it. Just like any other corporate function, they will need desks to work at and filing cabinet room. They will also need a central library as well as the unavoidable private libraries that technicians insist on keeping.

Just like many of the company's staff, the technicians will need computers on their desks – helpdesk people are users too. But you cannot assume that will be the only computer ever to occupy that space, because they may often be fixing some user's problem laptop.

Some helpdesks also find that it is necessary to have two (or more) computers per technician – perhaps a laptop and a desktop to represent the different environments the user has to contend with, or perhaps two desktops to mimic the situation where the company is running two operating systems because it has not yet got round to standardizing on one. At least one of these computers will have the formal role as a terminal to the user support technical and helpdesk management databases. Thank heavens for LCD flat screens and CPUs under the desk – because two computers on a standard desk leaves little room for the usual paraphernalia of working, an intray and somewhere for a three-button mouse to scuttle about.

If the support department is also responsible for installing machines, there may need to be a separate transit area where machines are set up, configured and tested prior to delivery to the end user. There may also be a need for a workshop for machines in separate states of repair. (*Tip*: log all jobs, queries, installations, whatever in the helpdesk management system. If a machine needs to be disassembled, stipulate that it must have with it at all times a printout of the job ticket from the system, showing which user the work is being done for, which technician is responsible and most importantly, when the job is due to be finished. It probably will not get rid of all those half-built bits of hardware, but it will start to control them.)

You may also wish to leave space for meetings between technicians or with visitors to the department, away from the hubbub of the helpdesk. Often the manager's office is not enough or already in use. Consider that there are also safety aspects to space, and in some countries that means legal requirements in terms of space per person, overcrowding of offices, access room, and so on.

26.4 The support library

The busy support department is cacophonous enough, without adding to it occasional shouts of 'Who's got the XYZ manuals?' Even the most experienced and knowledgeable technicians will occasionally if not constantly need reference to official material and for the sake of good service, that material had better be available.

26.4.1 Private libraries

The chaotic workspace is part of the technician's response to this need. The technician needs the manual often enough to justify (at least to herself) keeping her own copy. Some technicians need the security of having their key knowledge gathered round them; some are more practical and professional about it than just succumbing to an emotion of personal and intellectual security, but from an administrative point of view, the effect is the same.

Around the support office is a series of unquantifiable and possibly inaccurate private libraries.

Private libraries are an area of difficulty for the support manager. The support manager's dilemma is that the private library makes information available almost instantly, improving the service to the users and keeping the spot rate up, with all the implications therein for providing a good service for the minimum headcount. However, it is no use getting the information out quickly if it is so out of date as to be useless; that will just increase the costs as the false information will eventually backfire and cause another user query, increasing the work and annoying the user. Of course the technician will keep the most-used information up to date automatically. But a private and unmanaged library has a habit of growing, and as it grows, so too does the average age of the documents in it, along with the likelihood that more and more of those documents will be obsolete.

Private libraries feature dubious speed of access to information of dubious reliability. Technicians see them as indispensable – and that simple fact makes them unavoidable. An attempt by management to oppose these libraries would probably be only partly effective and would just set manager against staff. It is not the existence of the libraries which is the problem, it is their lack of reliability. The way to deal with private libraries is to ensure they work rather than try to shut them down. Find out what information is needed in the libraries. If it turns out that that information would be better placed in a central library, probably because it is expensive, accessed infrequently and needed by everybody, then get the agreement of the team as a whole that this would be the way to retain the information.

Look at the private library from the technician's point of view: they need immediate access to commonly needed, low-value information that because of its fluidity or complexity is not worth memorizing. Examples of these are memory upgrade charts, switch settings, option descriptions, service level statements, contact telephone numbers, escalation routes. Produce them in an easy-to-use form. How about designing the private library for them? Try a loose-leaf folder to a format agreed by the whole team and have the responsibility for the folder's integrity taken by support management.

Make the analysis of private libraries a project task for the helpdesk staff. How can they be standardized, centralized, automated, kept up to date? If private libraries exist, recognize, organize and formalize them.

26.4.2 Central libraries

There are two types of central library, the electronic and the physical – here I am dealing with the physical.

The support department's central library also has its problems. It is more vulnerable to losing items than the private library, and it is likely to lose those items outside the support department altogether. Some companies have a policy of not distributing product manuals to their users, in order to control the amount of information the user has access to, and therefore hope to protect the computers from tampering by the users. As well as being a denial of individuality, this is an open challenge, a red rag if you like to some users: in effect, the company pays the user to deliver, then even tries to place restrictions on how the users go about delivering – small wonder that manuals held in a central library can become fair game.

Where the library tries to minimize loss, it must increase security. At a minimum level this may mean keeping a record of who borrows what; at the other end of the scale the borrowing period is limited and policed. The more security is increased, the less accessible the library will be, and the more strictly the security is adhered to, the greater will be the management overhead in running the library.

In a central library, speed of access to the information is less of an issue. The library is a place of reference and, looked at item by item, of occasional use. The central library will have a wider range of information than any private library could, and the essence of the information here is that it is for short-term use – either on loan or for use in research or reference while remaining within the library. Private libraries should almost always feature documents that are for long-term or permanent use.

The centralized IT support library brings a lot of benefits, but it also brings with it the apparent overhead of administration, which may imply having to hire staff who, at least at some point in their working day, are not going to be producing the support department's intended end product: solutions to users' problems. There are overheads in selection, cataloguing, updating, discarding, security, measurement, and so on. You may need to justify a head to do it all; but see the case for what it is. You are not hiring a person to do work which is not done, you are hiring somebody to do efficiently something which is done inefficiently where there is no central library. The ideal solution is to make this one of several administrative and reporting functions.

The alternative to a specialist librarian or administrator is the amount of time your (probably more expensive) technicians will spend running their own less well-organized libraries; there is the additional cost of solving a problem because you did not have the right and most current manual in the first place; there is the shrinkage from your department because nobody is charged with the security of the manuals and software. Of course there is the risk that the librarian will 'make-work': over-complicated cataloguing systems and excessively bureaucratic lending mechanisms are two examples I have seen – but the avoidance of 'make-work' is a staff management issue, which leads us nicely into Part Six.

26.5 The telephone system

With the rise of the call centre came the proliferation of telephone technologies, several of which have been taken up by the helpdesk because of the need for an increasing number of telephone calls to be taken. At Fig. 26.1, I offer an outline of how those technologies may be used in the support environment. I have deliberately left out some technologies, such as pre-emptive dialling, as they are really only pertinent to a call centre environment rather than a problem-solving helpdesk.

The various devices I have described may be connected in a different order, or amalgamated into one another. I've laid them out this way to illustrate the various functions and, frankly, to describe what can go wrong with sophisticated uses of technology such as this.

Caller Line Identification (CLI) picks up from the telephone system which number the customer is calling from. This can then be looked up in a table of known customers and that information used elsewhere. You have CLI on your cellphone – it tells you who's calling you, so long as you have that person's number stored in the phone – but your cellphone knows the incoming number and stores it anyway, so you can call your caller back. In the case of our diagram, the CLI passes the number to a database, wherein are all the customer's details. These details can then go to the helpdesk software, which readies itself for the call eventually getting to the helpdesk operative by gathering information on the enquiry history of that customer.

Once the CLI has captured the user's details and looked up his location, we can start to use that information. If there is a known

Figure 26.1
The user support
telephone system

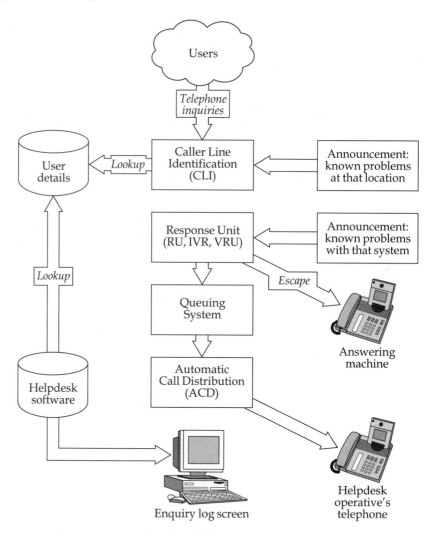

system problem at that location, we can play a recorded announcement to that effect. 'Welcome to the helpdesk. We are aware of the network failure in building six. Service is expected to be restored by noon. If you are enquiring about a different issue, please stay on the line.' This can help in avoiding a sudden rush of calls when there is a failure likely to affect several users.

We can now offer the possibility of a faster service by routing the call to the most appropriate helpdesk operative. The *Response Unit* presents the caller with a range of options he can select from his telephone, so he can go into the appropriate telephone queue. The main issue with these option lists is to keep them short – I know of one company that has eight selectable options at this stage, and it can take a painfully long time for the caller to listen to them all, remember which one he wanted while he waits to see if there is a more apt option, then either select one or forget which number it was and have to start again.

However, now the caller has told the response unit more or less what he is enquiring about, our system can play him an announcement regarding all the known problems with the system in question – for the same reason as we did it at the CLI stage, to avoid an unnecessary deluge of calls on that topic.

The caller now enters the *Queuing System* where he is treated to some delightful Vivaldi and perhaps a regular update on where he is in the queue, along with an expectation of how long he will have to wait.

In some telephone systems, the caller can opt out to an answering machine at any stage.

The next step is transparent to the caller, but the *Automatic Call Distribution* (ACD) system looks after the telephonic availability of the helpdesk operatives, putting the call through to the next available call-taker.

At the same time, the dialogue between the CLI lookup and the helpdesk software has made available the user's details and presented the technician with an already-opened and partially populated enquiry log.

So the potential benefits of this scale of automation can be considerable, especially if the helpdesk is a large one expecting a lot of calls. But it can also go terribly pear-shaped – and that can happen when the wonder of these tools takes precedence over process.

An organization I worked with recently has such a system, and they made that very mistake. They had centralized their helpdesk for several thousand users and found, not surprisingly, that the less efficient regional helpdesks it replaced had rather underestimated their call quantity. As a result, the new desk often presented the caller with the busy signal – so they implemented a system similar the one in the Fig. 26.1, with the promise to the users that as a consequence, they would never miss a call again.

It was sold to the user community (for they ultimately had to pay for all this equipment) on the basis of an improved service and guaranteed access to the helpdesk – but after implementation, that was not how the users saw it. With the announcements coming from the CLI and response unit, the system came to be seen as an attempt to keep callers out rather than bring them in. The length of the announcements meant two things to the users – first, that the computer systems obviously had a lot more problems than the one they were calling about – and second, that if the caller dutifully listened to all the announcements, it could take 13 minutes to get through to a helpdesk operative, even if there was no queue. Not only that, but this system had replaced their own region helpdesk, which had known the users' particular systems and circumstances so well, with a general, central helpdesk populated with staff who had no specialist knowledge because they were dealing with enquiries from all over the company.

There was also a problem with the helpdesk software, which was immensely capable. It had to be – it was dealing with a very wide range of possible enquiries. The project team that had designed it was so impressed by the huge range of data the system could gather, that they had enabled it by default to gather every piece of management information they could think of. So the enquiry log form was roughly three times the size of a computer screen, and to log a call, the helpdesk operative had to scroll his screen around the form. This meant that it took an improbable length of time to log the enquiry – so the form wasn't used. Instead, the helpdesk operatives would write the enquiry down on a scrap of paper – then when the call was complete, the operative would issue a command from his telephone to make himself unavailable to the ACD so that he could complete the computerized enquiry log form. This meant that the wrap-up time, the period after the call was finished to complete the enquiry was considerably longer than the call itself. By the end of the wrap-up time, the call had taken nearly 15 minutes to log, and because the operative was off-line anyway, he would nip out for a coffee or a smoke or a rest break.

The inefficiency of the system directly caused the inefficiency of the helpdesk. The average number of calls per operative per day was only 28 – with an average call length of less than three minutes – so the company was getting less than an hour and a half of real helpdesk productivity per man-day. We calculated that if the operatives had been able to take just over 40 calls per day, which is perfectly feasible for most helpdesks, then given the call quantity they would never even have presented the 'busy' signal in the first place and all that technology would not have been needed.

They had put tool before process. The problem was not that the users got the 'busy' signal (or 'engaged' tone) – it was that the helpdesk was inherently under-productive. Fundamentally, it was a management issue, not a technological one.

26.6 The answering machine

If your helpdesk is typical, there will be clear peaks and troughs of incoming calls throughout the day. Call volume will rise from the start of the day and peak at around 10:30. It will fall off over lunchtime, then climb again to another peak around 15:00, which will be about two-thirds the size of the morning peak. Then it will tail off rapidly.

The answering machine is often used as a way of dealing with these peaks, especially the morning one. On the face of it, the device is a fifty-dollar alternative to hiring another member of staff. But in my view it is a myth and an expensive misconception.

If the user rings in the morning, he may well be experiencing a problem that could impede him for the rest of the day – his machine won't boot, the network won't let him in, he's forgotten his password, the overnight backup failed.

But although the calls come in peaks and troughs, the staffing of the helpdesk is uniform throughout the day. So it has too few people taking calls in the morning and too many in the afternoon, when ideally the staff-to-call ratio should be the other way round.

So in the morning peak, some callers get the answering machine, as a kind of surrogate helpdesk operative. The trouble with this machine is that regardless of the simplicity of the enquiry, it has a first-time-fix rate of zero. Somebody has to go to the answering machine, listen to all the enquiries, then call each user back in turn, because the message they left was devoid of details – 'My computer isn't working properly, call me back. Click.' Then the enquiry has to be logged in the system.

The answering machine inserts delays into the speed at which the helpdesk service can be delivered, and not only increases work in the helpdesk, but causes users to lose more productivity than they would have done had they been able to speak to a technician instead of a voice recorder.

In my view, answering machines do not save headcount – in fact they make extra work for the staff whose headcount is already depressed. What is really needed is a flexible helpdesk work-force, with people who are happy to go on the phone when they are needed there and go on the rounds when they are not. The answering machine is only a viable device for taking calls out of normal service hours, and even then only when the cost of the user's lost productivity is less than the cost of hiring somebody to man the phones outside the normal working day.

Part Six

Staff management

27

The ideal support person

Look through the job advertisements of any computer journal read by IT support people for an indicator of what most corporations seem to regard as the key attribute of helpdesk and support staff. The need, desire, hunt for technical knowledge screams at you from the pages. The ads read like a list of computer software products, and the closest match of the candidate to that list is the first step towards being interviewed.

The software and hardware manufacturers also appear to lay great store by this. Novell, for example, has a range of qualifications which can be pursued by computer technicians. These qualifications have become a marketable commodity: a technician whose technical competence is acknowledged by a Novell-endorsed certificate commands a higher salary and is in greater demand than one whose ability is not so endorsed. A whole market has sprung up to provide Novell-recognized training courses, with a range of quality, pace and price to suit every pocket.

Cynics like me would be very suspicious about training programmes such as these. Of course they create some kind of measure of a technician's knowledge, and that is a useful aid for the company seeking to employ a proven network technician. But a certificate is rarely a true indicator of real knowledge, it is more an indicator of the technician's ability to get through a training programme. The knowledge itself is transient; in six months, Novell will probably have another version of their operating system, in two years it may well look very different than it does now; but the certification will still be valid, even though what it once measured is no longer current.

With these certification programmes, software companies have nothing to lose and so very much to gain; they can sell training courses, appoint recognized trainers, perhaps for a fee. They can ride on the back of the hype the qualification brings in its wake. They can reduce their support burden by encouraging their customers to pay to be able to do their own support. For all the benefits this training brings to the world in general, you can bet your boots it brings a whole lot more to the company that endorses it.

However, I think this relentless pursuit of technical acclaim distracts so much from the attributes we really want in our technicians; and the attributes we seem to mention in our job advertisements all too rarely.

If our technicians only ever dealt with machines, then technical ability is all we could ever reasonably ask of them. But they do not – they deal with people. The true helpdesk and user supporter has to deal with people for the function to have any meaning. Let us go back to the point: the computers were put here to increase the productivity of the white-collar functions of the company. If that increase in productivity cannot be assured, then the investment in computer technology is wasted – worse, it does more damage than good to the corporation's finances.

The only IT function which is solely dedicated to maintaining continued, hour-by-hour productivity through IT usage is computer user support. Therefore, what we need in that department are people and methods that increase or maintain user productivity; and user productivity is not just an 'I've got a bug in my software' issue, it is a 'Help me to know how I go about producing the sort of output I need' issue. The first query requires technical ability alone; the second query is in my experience if not more common then more demanding, and requires technical knowledge coupled with an ability to convey that knowledge in terms the user can understand and believe in.

Without the ability to communicate technical knowledge in stressful and challenging situations, then all that expensively acquired technical knowledge is worth a great deal less than you paid for it. I will go further; it may mean that you have wasted your investment because the knowledge can only ever be used on machines, never on people, so it can never be exploited to increase user (and therefore corporate) productivity. Put simply, technical knowledge without communicative ability costs a lot, but realizes comparatively little benefit. In my opinion, the common tendency to seek computer technicians for their technical ability alone is at best extravagant, at worst futile.

So why do we seldom ask for communicative ability in our job advertisements? One reason may be that it is too subjective and thus difficult to measure; communication is largely a question of rapport, and a good rapport between interview candidate and interviewer does not guarantee a continued good rapport with the users if that candidate is hired. Another reason may be that companies looking for technicians feel that the technical knowledge is the basis for considering a candidate and that the personality can be assessed during the interview.

I too have made the mistake of hiring a technician because I desperately needed his technical knowledge. He cost me a disproportionate salary and was with the company less than a year. During his brief stay with us, although he gained the respect of other computer engineers, he never did gain the respect of the users he was hired to serve. My mistake, and one I hear echoes of from other helpdesk managers. The lesson I learned was that if I need technical knowledge in a hurry, then call in a short-term contractor and milk their knowledge by having them train your own staff; and after they have gone, kick yourself for not having seen the need for that knowledge coming, so next time, plan better.

In my training courses, I ask helpdesk managers the question 'What are the attributes and skills of the ideal support person?', and write the suggestions on a flipchart as they are called out from the floor. Typical responses are as follows:

- *Patience* – to be able to listen to a user describe a situation you have encountered many times before yet still be able to patiently explain the solution; and to painstakingly go through the diagnostic process in search of the cause of a problem.
- *Assertiveness* – to give the user confidence in your ability to solve the problem; to be able to deal with a user whose expectations are unrealistic; to be able to treat the helpdesk manager as an equal so as to recruit him or her as a resource.
- *Thoroughness* – to make sure the job is complete, that the problem is truly solved, the user satisfied and the paperwork filled out.

- *Enthusiasm* – to enjoy the job and stay motivated; to remain positive in a challenging situation; sometimes, to convey cheerfulness to a user who might otherwise think that a situation is irredeemable.
- *Responsibility* – to be able to take on the burden of a task, set oneself an objective and maturely follow it through to a successful conclusion without unnecessarily involving others.
- *Technical knowledge* – to have acquired, and continue to acquire naturally, the sort of technical knowledge the job requires.
- *Empathy* – to be able to put oneself in the user's position so as to understand the real nature of the difficulties the computer presents them with, and therefore to treat the problem with the appropriate priority.
- *Communicative ability* – to be able to use language well enough to convey confidence, to ask the right sort of questions to solicit information about the nature of the user's problem, to use the right register and phraseology so that the user can understand the solution as described without being alienated by technical jargon. This skill is as important over the telephone as it is face to face, although the challenges of the two situations differ considerably.
- *Works well under pressure* – this can range all the way from staying amusing and positive when the office gets noisy to being able to handle quite dangerous levels of stress.

When the ideas are exhausted, I then go round the room and ask at what age people typically begin to acquire their technical computer knowledge; the responses range from mid-teens to late twenties. I follow this up with a question about what age people acquire their ability to communicate, their patience, empathy and enthusiasm; these are much earlier, with most respondents acknowledging that these are personal skills and largely acquired in childhood, maturing in later years.

The fact is that technical knowledge is learned by experimentation and education, and relatively late in our personal development. We can continue to acquire technical skills throughout our lives, and from a corporation's point of view that means that where they are missing, they can be taught. It is also possible to change and improve personal skills, where they are lacking – but this is much more difficult.

What this all comes down to is that the ideal user support technician needs to have the appropriate personal skills to deal with the users – for the users come first. What our ideal helpdesk needs is genuinely personable people who, by the way, are also accomplished computer technicians. Indeed why should the corporation ever take on the burden of changing dysfunctional or inappropriate personalities? It is much easier to hire personable people and teach them to be better technicians than it is to hire clever technicians and teach them to be better people.

27.1 Inherited staff

However, this ideal of hiring good people and developing them technically is in practice one that can only really be pursued during recruitment. When staff are inherited rather than chosen from an open field, then it is more a case of making the best possible use of what skills and attitudes are available, while improving in areas of weakness.

It is difficult, but not impossible, to change and improve the non-technical skills of our staff. The first hurdle we have to get over is the attitude held by some organizations that personal and social skills are a prerequisite for employment, and thus the corporation should take no responsibility for helping people who fall short in that area. This attitude is justifiable to some extent – but it can also be self-defeating. If the corporation gives no clear indication that good human interaction is desirable, while simultaneously indicating (as many do) that technical skills are vital, then technical employees can hardly be blamed for following that emphasis by conducting themselves and their services as though computers were more important than users. The most effective way to get technical staff to engineer good user relationships is for the corporation's managers to publicly lay as much store by, say, good communications skills as by the ability to configure a network server. In practical terms, that means using the same management techniques for personal skills as we do for technical skills. That means advertising for good personal skills, not just for recruitment purposes but also because your own staff will see those ads and so will see what it is you are looking for. It means sending people on personal development training courses as well as teaching them to be better computer engineers. And it means identifying and measuring the growth of social as well as technical prowess.

27.2 Hijack the knowledge matrix

In Chapter 25 we looked at a method for measuring the department's technical knowledge (see Figs 25.2 and 25.3). The knowledge matrix can be expanded to accommodate the controlled growth of almost any skill, simply by adapting the five 'skill levels' to give a score more appropriate to measuring personal skills rather than just technical knowledge.

The intangibles of personal relationships – good communications, empathy, popularity, ability to inspire confidence – can all be improved simply by controlling how we appeal to the subjectivity of others. By keeping in mind how others view us when we are deploying these skills, we will be communicative from their point of view, empathize with their problems, take account of their weaknesses, and so on. This is where technical and social ability part company: to be good at technical stuff, what you have to keep in mind is what you are doing; but to be good at social stuff, what you have to keep in mind is not what you are doing, but who you are doing it to and how they are perceiving it.

Of course all this is subjective – but the success or failure of personal relationships is undeniably a product of subjectivity anyway. All this method tries to do is put some kind of measure on what is unavoidably subjective, and in that respect alone it is an improvement on having no measure at all. An example of these subjective measures is given in Fig. 27.1; in this case, 'telephone manner' is being measured.

Figure 27.1
Measuring telephone manner

Level 4	Sufficiently skilled telephone technique to motivate and train user over telephone.
Level 3	Solves most problems over telephone to user satisfaction.
Level 2	Can use telephone to gather sufficient useful information for subsequent solving problem.
Level 1	Fails to get all required information during call, necessitating other calls.
Level 0	Telephone manner tends to annoy or irritate users.

The measure does not have to be purely subjective, however; Fig. 27.1 shows how a mix of subjective and objective measures can be used. Attainment of level 3 can be measured partly by monitoring the technician's spot rate (see Chapter 22 for a full description of the spot rate and its uses).

27.3 How much professionalism?

Naturally you want professionalism from your user support staff. Let us look at professionalism more closely. Professionalism is apparently the art of doing your job well, afflicted with the minimum of emotion. To be professional is to consider the approach you take to your job and the way you do it, rather than just what you do. The true professional should convey an image of cool competence to customers and colleagues alike.

But not too much.

To be without emotion is unnatural and mechanical; and it is the opinion of this author that one of the weaknesses of Northern Hemisphere societies is that the whiter the worker's collar, the less room there tends to be for emotion in the way they carry out their work. Humans are emotional creatures, so work and service must have their fair share of emotion just like any other human activity. Any person or department which strives or is considered to be utterly professional is living to work rather than working to live. Enjoyment, for example, is an emotion. So are enthusiasm, passion, positivism, creativity, self-confidence, humour and all the other things that make the job worth doing. It is only when emotion is applied to the job that people do it extraordinarily well (or exasperatingly badly). And do not forget that taking the job too seriously is one of the quick ways to too much stress.

Professionalism is doing the job to the best of your ability, with enjoyment and enthusiasm and without taking it too seriously, while considering the needs of the peers and clients around you. The 80/20 rule strikes again: be reliable and controlled 80 per cent of the time, but once in a while, let go. If you believe in yourself and your job, you will still be safe, and that will probably be the time when you are at your most creative.

> **Show me a company that shuns emotion for the sake of professionalism and I'll show you an invariable, boring machine.**
>
> **Show me a company that still has room for emotion, innovation and a passion to change the world and I'll show you a professional, productive, likeable environment.**

28

Motivation and productivity

Start with good people, lay out the rules, communicate with your employees, motivate them and reward them. If you do all those things effectively, you can't miss.

Lee Iacocca

Low morale. Poor motivation. Under-productivity. Call it what you will, many user support groups suffer from the problem. The helpdesk team is not as happy as it could be, so they are not as productive as they could be. The fact is that staff motivation is massively important, and it is not just a matter of a happy atmosphere: motivated IT technical specialists have been shown to be not just a little, but many times more productive, in terms of output and reduced numbers of mistakes.

A lack of motivation can show up in many ways, such as absenteeism, lethargy, work-shyness and short-temperedness. But these are the obvious ways we can spot low morale. There are many ways that low motivation can affect work which cannot be seen by the naked eye. If a technician turns up for work every day and always seems to be busy, he will appear to be motivated; but the outward signs can be misleading if the manager has no way of measuring what the technician is busy doing. However, measurement in and of itself is not enough – it has to be measurement of factors which the manager and technician have agreed are pertinent, and these measures must not simply be seen as a means of control.

To explore this more fully, we must understand the different types of motivation. The burst of enthusiasm one shows at the beginning of a job is one type of motivation, but this is hardly likely to maintain a buoyant personal morale for the length of a project or the long haul of a career. There has to be a different, more profound kind of motivation, an innate attitude rather than a solicited rebel-yell. Good oratory can get the rebels yelling, but no manager can truly be the architect of the attitudes of a member of his or her staff, and this is especially the case among computer support technicians, from whom we expect so much independence of thought and action.

As manager, your scope for motivating your people is severely limited. You can motivate all you want, but if the technicians choose not to be motivated, your efforts will be wasted.

28.1 Inspire and aim

The manager trying to achieve better staff motivation has got her or his work cut out. First, there is the mistake so many managers make: they assume that it is up to them to motivate their staff. Fact is, there are some people reporting to us who are content to be miserable – it gets them attention, pity, help, whatever. There are others who may appear unmotivated but are in fact extremely motivated – but only when they are doing something other than what you pay them to do. Trying to 'motivate' people like these is a waste of time – worse, your direct efforts, no matter how deft, may have precisely the opposite effect. The whole thing is confused by some of your staff who do actually appear to be motivated by your efforts to make them so.

The truth is you cannot motivate anybody. They can only motivate themselves. Some people choose to be motivated, others do not. The best you can hope to do is inspire and aim them, and if they then choose to be motivated, great. But let us get the cause and effect relationship clear. Motivation is not the cause, it is the effect. Do not try to 'motivate' them – inspire them and aim them.

In practical terms, this may mean that you will have to give examples of motivation passively, rather than actively trying to motivate. If the circumstances of your department cause low morale but those circumstances are unavoidable, then you must indicate that you too have to live under those circumstances yet still remain personally motivated.

Leadership is an immensely powerful motivator. As a manager, you must ask yourself if you espouse it. Are you like your technicians, coming into the office in the morning, doing a job of work and then going home – and doing that day after day after day after day with no prospect of change or improvement? That is the opposite of what your team needs. The reason people follow a leader is because he knows where he is going, and it is bound to be better than here. Separate yourself from your staff. Visualize a better future for them and yourself. Know what that future will look like and have a strategy for getting there. Tell your staff where the department is going and give them roles in creating that future. Keep on telling them, and keep on exhibiting behaviours that demonstrate that you are still following the dream they have chosen to take part in.

Believe in them and your department. Make sure they know that this department is the best in the company. It is better than the customer service desk at taking calls, better than the facilities department at fixing problems, better than the accounts department at analysing figures. There are very few people in this company, and probably none in the IT department who even come close to being good enough to work in this helpdesk. We are the best.

Establish an identity for your helpdesk. Have a badge of excellence to which all your people can belong. Get a mission statement that clarifies your purpose. Have goals that your people can strive towards. Give them objectives to achieve, so they fill their personal histories with a catalogue of personal and professional success.

Incentivize their work. Have them compete with one another, because nobody wants to let the team down. Let them expect excellence from each other.

28.2 Money does not motivate

This begs a big question straight away, that of *money* – because since when did money do any inspiring or aiming? I subscribe to the school of thought that in the non-incentivized professions like user support and customer service, money is not a motivator. It may work in the greed-based professions, but even there it depends on what you are trying to achieve. Let us test the money theory – when was the last time you bounded from your bed screaming 'Look out world, here I come' just because you had remembered you were going to be paid three weeks on Thursday? Rather than waiting for and being driven by the same old salary you will be getting whatever happens, is it not more rewarding to have your work recognized and appreciated by those you do it for?

Do not use money as a motivator in user support. It does not inspire user support people in the long term. If your technicians do not think they get enough money, the topic may even demotivate them. And giving them the rise they think they want only works for a short while, until their expectations start to grow again. Then the whole sore topic comes back to haunt you. I am not saying you should not give your staff a merit rise, but do not treat it as an incentive when it is not one.

Where money does work is in an incentive towards productivity. A support manager at a supplier of computer components in northern England has a complicated and flexible cash incentive scheme which he brings to bear on certain areas of productivity throughout his large user support department. For him, it works; his concern is more with the numerical production of solutions to problems rather than maintaining an inherent atmosphere of positivism. However, it would be unjust to say that his financial incentives have not produced motivation. By inducing an atmosphere of activity and productivity, his staff can feed off that to boost their own motivation. But let us not forget that the attitude comes first, the motivator comes after.

28.3 Staff attitude

Even after you have done all your inspiring and aiming, there is still the problem to contend with of the attitude of the staff to your best efforts. Sometimes, even with the clearest of goals, with the most involving of departmental communications, the most charismatic of helpdesk managers, the most consistent of managerial behaviour patterns, attempts at motivation still fall flat. Why?

The key to this is the attitude of the staff – not just to your efforts to motivate, but to anything the company, the job, the weather, or the users may throw at them. Do they shrug off the pressures, even enjoy them, or do they let the pressures add to one another? And what do you do as a manager to help them to survive those pressures? For only if your support staff can automatically and subconsciously survive the pressures of the user support job can they hope to retain a positive attitude to both the good and bad of the job they do and who they do it for.

Again, this leads us to the logical conclusion that we must develop our staff's personal skills as well as their technical knowledge (see Chapter 27 for more on this theme). Only when they have the abilities to survive and deal competently with life itself, can we hope that they will also be as productive as they can be on the corporation's behalf.

28.4 How to motivate technicians

In my seminars, I routinely run the exercise of asking for suggestions of what motivates technicians. The usual suspects invariably come up – good working environment, powerful computer, good canteen and coffee, doughnuts in the afternoon, recognition of a job well done. Yes, these are admirable, but they are not motivators, they are morale boosters. There's a big difference.

Motivation is the prospect of getting somebody from this state to a different one. The state may be emotional, professional, career, level of productivity, and so on. But in all cases, a transfer of state requires the individual to change in some way. And when people are satisfied, there may be no real reason for the change. So there has to be some form of incentive. Morale boosters are not incentives, because they are after the fact – so they are rewards, not incentives. The state of motivation is achieved not by the reward itself, but by the *prospect* of the reward – which is when the reward becomes an incentive.

Think of the professional soccer player. Which is more likely to motivate him – the reward of somebody patting him on the shoulder after he has scored the goal, or 20,000 people screaming encouragement at him while he is running with bursting lungs and a well-controlled ball towards the goal? It is not the praise itself that motivates him, but it may be the promise of the praise – but even that is not as powerful as the vocal encouragement from his peers and supporters. From them he gets the incentive, in the form of their encouragement.

So the manager keen to inject more motivation into the support team should have four points of focus: inspiration, aim, encouragement and staff attitude. First, inspire your staff. Find something to lead them towards, rather than just having them drearily turn out the same old work day after day. Why do they do what they do – because you pay them to or because there is a greater purpose? Remember money does not motivate, but everybody likes to be part of a success story. Find the success stories in the support department and publish them, inside and outside, so both your staff and the users they serve can see your people for the successes they are.

Second, aim your staff. Give them objectives to achieve rather than mere tasks to do. Watch them – and tell them when they are doing it right, at least twice as often as you tell them they are doing it wrong. Look for opportunities to tell them when they are doing it right: it will show them you care, force you to keep up to date with them, demonstrate that you know what they are doing (and what they may be up to), and encourage them to reproduce the sort of productive and positive behaviours you want from them. Report back to them how they are performing, individually and collectively.

Make them realize they are part of a whole; individually, they are a function in a bigger device, whose goal needs their efforts to be achievable. Anticipate what they will need and want to know about the bigger picture and keep them apprised – few things can have a more profound and lasting corrosive effect on group morale than poor communications, rumour and speculation.

Third, and probably most importantly, expose your staff to the right attitude. Support can be a disheartening profession at times – give them the tools to win against the discouragements and stay positive. Where they do not have those personal and social tools, find them on their behalf by example and direct training.

Above all, do not forget how the world looked when you were a technician or a lower employee like them. What suspicions did you have of your management? Where and why did you feel under-informed? Did you feel your boss trusted you? All these and more you can think of will be going round the heads of your staff, and they all erode their ability to stay motivated in the high-pressure (and these days, insecure) atmosphere of the modern helpdesk. Anticipate these thoughts and fears in your people's heads and quash them.

28.5 Avoiding burnout

Your user support technician comes into the office, reacts to several user questions and problems, solves most of them, and goes home after a job well done. The next day, she comes in, solves more or less the same problems but perhaps for a different set of users. The next day looks the same, and the one after that. All the time, the technician is subjected to an environment of things going wrong, people being frustrated, and is probably overworked. How long can we expect them to do that for without burning out?

Burnout is a recognized problem in helpdesks and user support departments. It manifests itself in boredom, absenteeism and a drop in motivation despite success and adequate money. It makes technicians look for another job, for slightly more money, yet where they may suffer the same burnout in another year or two.

The key to avoiding burnout is to combine work variety with an appeal to the computer technician's most primeval drive – the quest for increased technical knowledge. Most computer support people around today are self-taught or have picked up their technical knowledge by default and circumstance rather than design. The best ones are the ones who have been most motivated and skilful at this process. By their own motivation, they acquire their computer knowledge, then they realize they can both continue this process and earn some money by going to work for a helpdesk; and from the day they get there they have to give that knowledge out over and over again. This is completely at odds with their original motivation, which was to acquire knowledge, not vomit it forth repeatedly.

We must introduce a variety of activities, one of which will be the structured acquisition of knowledge. Without giving them some respite from the pressures of the helpdesk, their motivation may suffer. In Chapter 29 I offer a structure for a support department to formalize this process.

28.6 Individual productivity

One of the jobs I had as a support technician consisted of long periods of virtually fruitless activity interspersed with brief but intense periods of high-value, highly stressful activity. My graph of motivation looked like the Alps in profile. I realized that the difference between the peaks and the troughs was the difference between having an objective to strive for and being without direction. My boss simply made this worse; when I asked him what I should be doing, his infuriating, stock reply was 'You carry on as you are – I'll tell you when you're doing wrong.' Such a negative attitude could produce precisely the wrong effects for a manager such as this; without guidance, I might shoot off in a completely false direction, or worse, I might fear to start anything in case I got it wrong and got into his bad books. Where in a more positive, directed environment I could have started things, achieved some goals, won my spurs, or furthered my career, under this management it was safer to keep my head down, only move when I had an objective and when I was sure someone was watching, never achieve my full productivity potential. My employer was wasting money and skills and I thought less of him for it; I felt I could have been giving the users a better service, but because of my lack of experience I did not know for sure what or how, and my manager should have been the one to tell me.

In his book *The Human Side of Enterprise* (McGraw-Hill, 1960), Douglas McGregor described his Theory X and Theory Y schools of management. McGregor holds that Theory X managers believe people will naturally shirk and so have to be coerced and persuaded to be productive. I am a Theory Y manager, believing as I do that most people, probably out of self-respect and the avoidance of boredom, want to be productive and that it is my managerial duty to agree with them what productivity means to me, to them, to my department, to my users and to my company.

We must not confuse activity with productivity, however. If all you can see is activity, you cannot be sure that there is any point to it, so it cannot be said to be productive. That is why managers can be fooled by the 'quick, look busy, here comes the boss' office environment. This is especially the case in user support – you may not even be able to see the activity, for it is going on outside the office, at the user's desk, in the computer room, in that forgotten basement where they store all the old monochrome screens, in your technicians' heads. The activity may even be 'make-work' – the creation of activities which serve no purpose other than their own existence or which exist merely for the self-justification of the person carrying out the activity. Some cases of 'make-work' are products of working practices described by Professor C. Northcote Parkinson:

> *The man who is denied the opportunity of taking decisions of importance begins to regard as important the decisions he is allowed to take. He becomes fussy about filing, keen on seeing pencils are sharpened, eager to ensure that the windows are opened (or shut) and apt to use two or three different coloured pencils.*
> (Quoted in Helen Exley's *The Best Business Quotations*, Exley Publications, 1993.)

If we were to extrapolate this observation into computer support, perhaps it would read 'he becomes fussy about tidying his hard disk, eager to ensure uniformity in Microsoft Windows and apt to use several different fonts in his reports'.

To ensure that all activity has a point and to avoid 'make-work', never look at the activity – focus on the result.

Key result areas for 'J. Smith'	Relative importance	Available performance levels	Achieved performance level
1. Answering queries	20%	1. 80% spot rate	
		2. 85% spot rate	
		3. 90% spot rate	20% x **2** = 40%
2. Learning software	5%	1. Can take queries	
		2. Can solve problems	
		3. Can teach product	5% x **3** = 15%
3. Writing reports	10%	1. Legible	
		2. Informative	
		3. Innovative	10% x **3** = 30%
4. Teaching colleagues	20%	1. 1 person taught	
		2. 2 persons taught	
		3. 3 persons taught	20% x **2** = 40%
5. Motivating team	25%	1. <3 people	
		2. Half team	
		3. All team	25% x **3** = 75%
6. Admin. duty I	5%	1. 1 day late	
		2. On time	
		3. Early	5% x **1** = 5%
7. Admin. duty II	5%	1. You satisfied	
		2. Me satisfied	
		3. All satisfied	5% x **2** = 10%
8. Managing budget	10%	1. On budget	
		2. 5% under budget	
		3. 10% under budget	10% x **2** = 20%
TOTALS	**100%**		**235% / 300%**

Figure 28.1
Measuring individual productivity

Figure 28.1 shows how personal productivity can be measured, technician by technician, activity by activity. Some organizations draw up charts like these at appraisal time, maybe once or twice a year. There is a strong argument for doing this once a month, as projects and objectives come and go. This chart also recognizes that there are several activities any one technician may take part in, which increases the importance of work variety.

The chart shows the work objectives of a given individual 'J. Smith' in the Support Department. He has eight areas where he is expected to produce a result; some of these are more important than others, and this 'relative importance' is expressed as a proportional percentage, where all these percentages add up to 100. In each of the eight areas, J. Smith has been given scope to achieve at one of three levels. This means that the maximum possible score that could be achieved is 300 per cent, by achieving level 3 in each 'key result area'.

When we last assessed J. Smith on his performance, we wrote down in the 'actual performance' column what level he had actually achieved in each key result area and multiplied that by the weighting factor in the 'relative importance' column. In key result area 1, 'answering queries', we discovered that J. Smith had actually achieved a spot rate of 85 per cent, which means he hit level 2. So we multiply the relative importance for this area – 20 per cent – by the level achieved – 2 – and we get 40 per cent. Finally we total up these achieved portions of the maximum possible 300 per cent to give a final score.

J. Smith is clearly astute: he has ensured he has scored well in the areas where it matters and deliberately let slip the less valuable areas like the administration duties – but that is not a problem, because the manager set these relative importances just to cause J. Smith to concentrate on the most valuable work areas.

If it so happened that J. Smith had achieved level 1 or lower in each of his key result areas, then we might be looking for an urgent explanation or perhaps J. Smith's departure. In fact we can apply an interpretation to the whole spectrum of results, where a score of 0–100 per cent gets J. Smith a severe reprimand, 100–200 per cent means he gets a bonus, 200–300 per cent means he gets the support supervisor promotion (or as I once heard it put, 300 per cent gets him a bottle of champagne, 200 per cent gets him a glass of champagne, 100 per cent or less means he gets to wash the champagne glasses).

A chart like this is quick to draw up and can rapidly be customized to suit the different jobs of individuals as well as the coming and going of various projects and priorities. It does not have to simply focus on statistical information, but allows the manager and technician to agree a healthy mix of both statistical and emotional input.

28.7 Dealing with prima donnas

The knowledge matrix described in Chapter 25 encourages the twin benefits of a general level of knowledge held by all technicians complemented by high expertise in some areas. Having experts is one matter – but those experts can in some circumstances be allowed to develop a disproportionate view of their own value. It is at this point that we find ourselves with the dilemma of the *technical prima donna*. On the one hand, we have a person whose technical knowledge and skills are second to none in the department and vital to user support operations; on the other hand, we have this individual's arrogance which threatens to erode any team spirit and severely test the user support manager.

In Chapter 19, I said that in departments suffering from extreme reactivity, often the manager has, perhaps subconsciously, shied away from challenges such as this. One reason might be the eventual action, unpalatable to many managers, of having to let somebody go. Another might be the difficulty of measuring the true value of the prima donna. By design, the manager's technical knowledge is no longer strong enough to engage in complex discussion of the technical nature of a problem, so it is possible for the so-motivated technician to allow his or her boss to retain an inflated picture of the technician's worth – in effect, pulling the wool over the boss's eyes.

The dangers of doing nothing about the technical prima donna are many, and will often considerably outweigh the benefits of having a technical guru on the staff. The daily pressure to provide the fastest possible solution to a user's problem will cause technical problems to gravitate naturally towards the person most able to solve them. This 'technical favouritism' can cause the department to miss opportunities to expose other technicians to those problems and learn how to solve them in future. Some experts may even engineer this flow of work to their own desks and away from other technicians; after all, knowledge is power, and while one technician holds all the knowledge and controls access to it, that power makes that individual so much more valuable.

However, the benefits of retaining one highly capable and experienced team member may well be outweighed by the damage such advanced individualism can do to the department's 'team spirit'.

Where the other members of the team feel collectively aggrieved by this individual and the situation in general, staff confidence in the support manager can suffer; and this in itself can jeopardize many more of the department's functions. Eventually the manager may have to take direct and even drastic action simply because the interests of the team are much more important than those of any one of its members.

Case Study 28.1: the Fictional Finance Company Inc.

Moving from minicomputers to PC networks was a major decision for the company, and most people in the computer support group agreed that if they had not had Mike in the team, they would never have been able to keep up with the speed of change the company needed. Mike had been the first to get to grips with the network and he knew the system inside out. Whenever there was a problem on the network, whenever a change needed to be made, Mike was the first one everybody went to.

It was a while before the general view of Mike began to change, but when it did, it took hold fast. Mike was good at installing networks; in fact, the other team members began to see that it was all he was any good at. Once upon a time they had been grateful for that, but now, all Mike wanted to do was go on installing networks, but as the project was over, there were no more networks to install; Mike seemed to spend most of his time tinkering with and reinstalling the existing system. It seemed to the team that this was at the expense of the time Mike could have been spending helping out with users' problems.

Julia, Mike's boss, knew this insufferable situation was partly her fault. Time had been tight during the installation project, so she had paid over the odds to recruit Mike; then she lumped all the difficult networking work onto him. The result now was that we had a bored network installer who effectively had nothing to do and was being paid too much to make it worth his while to look for another job. Mike's continued presence was a source of frustration both to him and the rest of the team – where once he had assisted them, now they were carrying him. The other technicians were looking to Julia to do something about it.

Julia had considered and tried several options; these included setting Mike new objectives and measuring him more closely, but that did not work because the new objectives were nothing like the job he had originally come to do, and Mike never bothered with the measurements because he seemed to think they did not really apply to him – he saw himself as too technically valuable for paperwork. It was that attitude that eventually gave Julia her solution.

Measurement was now important; good records had to be kept. There were no records of the installations Mike had done on the network and he kept no records of the work he was doing at present. After Mike failed for the third time to document the network so that others could support it, Julia called in an expensive external consultant to draw that documentation up – and immediately asked Mike to leave.

29   Staffing and structure

29.1 How many people?

How many staff does your user support department need? Different sources give different numbers. It depends on several factors, including the range of services you will be providing and such performance indicators as spot rate, fixes per resolver, and so on (see Chapter 22 for a fuller explanation). The range of services will depend on what 'computer user support' means in your organization. Before computers were downsized to the extent they are now, 'user support' was typically just one of a number of groups in the IT department, and things like user training, computer operations and software development sat outside. Now in many companies, the developers have been replaced (either by off-the-shelf software or contractors brought in on a project-by-project basis), computer operations has been subsumed into the computer support department, and user training is commissioned from outside by the user's own line manager. Of course this is not the case everywhere, but the various permutations of computer support structures complicate still further the process of deciding how many people you actually need.

In 1997, and then again in 2000, the author conducted a survey of the global helpdesk industry, it yielded the following figures:

- Average number of queries posed per user per year: 26.
- Average number of problems taken per first-line technician per day: 32.

- Average spot rate of a helpdesk: 59 per cent.
- Average number of fixes per dedicated resolver per day: 8.
- Ratio of support managers to staff: 1:9.25.

These are a long way from excellent helpdesks. I am mindful of a helpdesk at a healthcare manufacturing company near London, whose figures are 42, 76, 76 per cent and 16 respectively – as a result they need many fewer staff than the industry average, and the service is faster, so the users perceive a higher quality service. Yes, in user support, cheaper can also mean better.

Going with the industry averages, however, a benchmark staffing level can be calculated. Let us assume a company with 1000 users. At 26 calls per user per year, that's 26,000 enquiries. Over the 250 (normal) working days of the year, that's 104 enquiries a day. Divide that by 32 enquiries per first-line technician per day, is a little over three first-line heads. They will fix 59 per cent of those 104 enquiries over the phone, so they will escalate 43 of them. These will be dealt with by the second line, at eight resolutions per resolver per day, and 43 divided by eight is work for almost five and a half full-time equivalent second-line staff. Add the three first-line heads to the five and a half second line and divide the total by nine to see how many managers. So the total is nine-and-one-half people in the user support group.

All these averages are subject to fairly wide variation due to the number of factors influencing them. The users never pose an 'average' number of queries. What tends to happen is there are some users who use the service constantly and others who almost never do; in larger organizations there are even competing helpdesks, where users have set up their own, local service and thus seldom need to call the central helpdesk, or use it just as an escalation route. Organizations of up to 500 users may make nearly 50 enquiries per user per year – this tends to be because in smaller firms, many users may be working alone or in small groups, so they do not have as large a peer group to share knowledge – so they tend to call the helpdesk more often.

29.2 How expert can they be?

If everybody in the team knew everything there was to know about all the products, we would have more flexibility in the support team and that might mean we would need fewer people. But there is a limit to how many products a support technician can keep up to date with. If we knew that limit, we could build it into our planning.

I tend to take a pragmatic approach to this one. Take a look at the skillsets of your most experienced, capable or long-standing staff. In how many products can they claim to be truly expert, the people everybody else in the helpdesk turns to when an enquiry with that product arrives? The average number of high-expertise areas they hold is a benchmark. In theory, that's the level everybody could attain, with the right training and exposure to the product's typical problems. So that is what's possible – that's the ideal.

Take into account how many enquiries you have on those products and how many calls or resolutions your team can produce in a day. From that, you will be able to work out how many experts you need to make available to take those enquiries. And if the number you need is less than the number you have, then start aiming your staff development at that ideal.

29.3 The 'Resource Allocation Spreadsheet'

If you have followed my ideas throughout this book, you will by now have a portfolio of services produced by your helpdesk. What you really need to know is how much resource each of those services consumes – not just answering the telephone but all the projects, installations, configurations, resolutions, reports and all the other myriad things the helpdesk does. Also allow for other time and manpower consuming activities, such as training courses, sick leave, meetings, and so on. Turn all those consumptions of resource into the horizontal axis of a spreadsheet.

On the vertical axis, list all the members of staff.

Then ask your staff to log the time they spend over a given period in each activity, and write those time amounts in the cells of the spreadsheet.

What you now have is what I like to call a 'Resource Allocation Spreadsheet'. Adding the vertical columns gives you the precise amount of manpower resource it took over that period to produce any service or conduct any activity.

It's particularly useful when somebody complains at you that 'You have ten staff down there – how come it's so hard to get through on the phone?' The spreadsheet may tell you that in fact, you only have 2.75 *logical* helpdesk staff, although you may indeed have ten FTEs.

And if the manager comes to you and demands that you take more helpdesk calls, you can show him the spreadsheet, and in your sweetest and most reverent voice, say 'Certainly, we can take more calls. Here is my resource allocation. In order to put more staff on the telephone, which service would you like me to shut down?'

29.4 User support group structures

Structure is a natural and essential element of any group of workers. Structure makes production lines possible, and without it, we would risk organizational chaos. As a concept, 'organizational structure' has been dealt several blows of late, usually through (deliberate?) misinterpretation of the works of visionary management writers like Rosabeth Moss Kanter and Tom Peters; and I wonder if the critics of structure have forgotten the benefits of structure and the risks of trying to function without one. If your team decides to function without a structure, the risk is that the members of the group, lacking a clear view of their position in the group, will then begin to expend effort trying to build themselves a position, and a structure will evolve whether the host organization ordains it or not. However, this effort they spend is at the expense of effort they could be expending improving user support services.

Structure creates hierarchies, which give those on the lower rungs an example of what they can aspire to through success and seniority; structures show that there is a future. Structures create and enable identities and subfunctions, give people a sense of belonging and purpose. Structures show people where the default communication channels and responsibilities lie.

It is in this placing of responsibilities that group structure really comes into its own. Ideally, the structure should reflect the group's objectives, in that clearly identifiable parts of the structure are clearly responsible for stated objectives. If one of your main services is network management, then consider having a network management section, even if it means there is only one person in it. One support team I have worked with has a structure describing sections to which no staff are devoted full time, but to which all the other sections contribute staff because of job rotation. The purpose of this is to ensure the objectives of that section, in this case product evaluations, are fully met, with the technicians in that section suffering the minimum of interruptions from the sections they normally belong to. The section becomes a psychological barrier: it is much more final to say 'I'm sorry, she's unavailable – she's working in a different section today' than it is to say 'she's doing a product evaluation'.

Figure 29.1 shows a user support department structure which implements these ideas of placing responsibilities, ensuring communications channels and demonstrating routes of future progress for the more ambitious members of the team. The

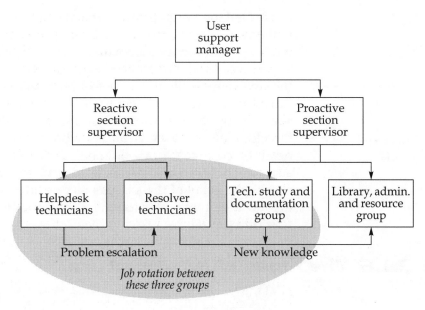

Figure 29.1
Proactivity built into a
user support structure

reactive (i.e. helpdesk) and proactive (i.e. increasing and publishing knowledge) functions have been structurally split apart; this is to ensure the proactive work gets done, as it is so easy to let the reactive work come to dominate and preclude all else. The technical functions are all interlinked by job rotation, so the technicians can move between these functions and get regular exposure to each of the three main technical functions, namely answering technical questions (probably over the telephone), solving problems (possibly at the user's desk) and increasing technical knowledge (and writing about it). The library function stands alone, probably not staffed by technicians at all, but by professional administrators and librarians.

29.5 Organizational flattening

In recent years, 'organizational flattening' has been a popular bandwagon in management theory. I believe that in a user support function, more harm than good might be done if some of these theories were taken up. Much damage has been done to concepts of organizational structure by the recent fashion for the 'flattening' of organizations. The flattened organization has fewer tiers of management, so that staff report to a higher manager than perhaps they would have in a more pyramidal hierarchy. The theory gained enormous popularity in the late 1980s and the recession fuelled it, being an opportunity to shed layers of middle management, thus reducing headcount costs.

In the flattened organization, the manager is closer to the staff, without having a supervisor in between. More people report to a manager than might have done earlier. The manager is closer to the 'coal-face'. However, this does not necessarily mean that the manager will be in a better position to manage her department. The more senior the manager, the more removed she will be from the detail of the job, necessarily taking a broader view. That view can be so broad as to be useless to the detail of 'coal-face' work. So the flattened organization ends up stripping out the supervisors, leaving nobody except the staff to ensure the detail of the job gets its due attention. Flattening the organization may save money, but potentially at too great a cost to service levels.

29.6 The 'boss plus' structure

Some support departments arrive at a flattened structure by default rather than design, particularly if the department has grown up organically in response to perceived user demand. The resulting structure is a simple one; there is 'the boss' (often the longest-serving technician) and below him or her, everybody else. Such a department will often have a limited number of functions, perhaps dedicated user support and problem-solving, possibly equipment installations also. In the short term, this is a very effective structure and keeps the manager close to the end product. In the long term, such a structure can be disastrous. It has no career path within the support function, tends to preclude the manager from developing managerial as opposed to technical skills, and is ineffective for man-management purposes if the department gets beyond, say, four or five strong. Such a structure is also likely to be purely reactive, which is a recipe for losing control of the present, let alone the future.

29.7 Teamwork and individualism

Throughout this book I have tried to be careful about the use of the word 'team' to describe user support, and the reason is that it may not always be appropriate that the department operate as a team, or that the staff are necessarily recognized for their 'team-player' qualities.

There are two types of team. One is the beautiful mix of mutually complementary skills and responsibilities, where a problem moves smoothly between individuals who each add their unique value to it, the whole producing a greater result than could the individuals alone. You can see it in any well-structured organization with different skills and responsibilities and good lines of communication between them. The job flows smoothly through the group to an inevitable and beneficial end. A Mancunian by birth, I see that beauty in some of the playing style of our own Manchester United football team. There is another type of 'teamwork' which can be seen in less sophisti-cated and less mature workgroups. Although the members of the less well-orchestrated team may ostensibly pursue the same goal, often the skills are not unique and complementary, they are all very much the same. Consequently, to return to the soccer metaphor, when the ball swings wildly to the left wing, they all lurch lemming-like after it, as it bounds chaotically to the right, they all huddle uncontrollably to the right also.

Teamwork, done properly, takes a problem which no one skillset could solve, and by orchestrating different skillsets, produces an otherwise impossible solution. Teamwork, done badly, takes a problem which one skillset could eventually solve alone, but because it is a lovely juicy problem, allows lots of other skillsets to have a go, causing more heat than light and more distraction than production. Which type of team looks most like yours?

One person, working alone on a problem, will be free of distractions and people offering advice. That person will have an opportunity to take full responsibility for the problem and its resolution, and responsibility is the seed of *ownership*. Without ownership, nothing would ever get done; with ownership, your staff have another, probably better reason for coming to work than just their salary. One person will have the opportunity to make mistakes in private, not in full view of his or her colleagues, and will therefore be less fearful of trying more options, and stretching their skills further. And it is only through trying and seeing results that you acquire experience, which is so much more valuable than mere knowledge. One person working alone will be able to build up a rapport with the user, who will welcome being dealt with by a person rather than a faceless 'department'. One person will be able to bask in the glory of success, where that glory is irredeemably diluted by being claimed by a 'team'.

At one support team I worked with, I saw this failing in action. They were stumped by a particularly knotty problem. The helpdesk technician would listen attentively to the description of the problem – then go and interrupt his colleague for more advice. Ownership of the problem was unclear. The helpdesk technician was out of his depth – the person he kept distracting was already occupied. This was a bad example of teamwork. Only one member of the 'team' could add value to the problem – the other merely frustrated the user, the problem and the rest of the team.

Most problem-solving support departments have four basic functions: user support (the helpdesk), the problem resolvers (those who answer what the helpdesk cannot), resources management (the library and administration) and functions co-ordination (the boss). Of these, the most glamorous and probably the most problematical are the problem resolvers. These sometimes work as a team, but often they are individually embroiled in a problem which only one of them can solve; and if that is the case, 'teamwork' or the ability to work as a 'team player' may be an ancillary skill at best, a hindrance at worst. More often than not what is required of a problem resolver is an ability to work alone, to take responsibility and to produce a result from their own efforts. However, they also need to appreciate that the other three functions exist to enable them to solve user problems; were those functions not there, the job might be impossible.

Teamwork, though desirable, may distort the picture of the individualism that is needed in many user support departments, particularly among the users. Teamwork, and the departmental structure that embodies it, should never be allowed to stifle individuality, or with it you will stifle creativity and the natural learning process.

29.8 User representatives

When designing the structure of the support department, it is wise to take into account not just the staff who work under you as the support manager, but to cast one's view rather wider to look at the whole provision of user support across the corporation. Certain user departments may have their own user support functions, whose job it is to provide an internal helpdesk but also to represent the interests and computing needs of the users back to the IT department or central helpdesk.

These people should be seen as an extra arm of the user support function. They are there to deliver a service, and through them you may be able to deliver services which would be impossible were you to be restricted to operating solely through your own limited headcount. For example, they could operate as a conduit for launching services, a publicity medium, an additional helpdesk to take the load off you, an extra on-site resolver. They can be brought into your structure, perhaps not as direct reportees, but as additional resources. As resolvers in any case, they will have to have access to the communications and knowledge channels your own resolvers enjoy, for this is the way you can ensure the standard of support they provide. Remember too that they are your link with the users; where your view may be from the computer outward, theirs is from the user inward, and a marriage of these views can ensure a better and more relevant service for the users in future.

User support management considerations

The object of this final chapter is twofold: first, it tries to consider some of the less academically definable areas of interest to existing or would-be user support managers. In this, it is unashamedly gut-feel; it is what I have found in my work with support departments to be common areas of failure, those parts of our job where most of us could do better.

Second, this chapter acts as a kind of epilogue, a way of winding the book up just in case you have done me the great honour of reading it from cover to cover.

30.1 Why support managers fail

Support management is simple – but that is not the same as easy; the job is downright difficult. There are many reasons why the support manager may fail. Some of these are a matter of technique, like slack communications or poor staff motivation. Other reasons are circumstantial, like a lack of senior management commitment (no matter how hard you try to convince them), underfinancing or poor resources. But there are other reasons why support managers, like any other leaders, may fail. Some of these reasons are psychological. We should not shy away from them because like all other problems, they can (with a little personal courage and honesty) be measured and dealt with. Some of these reasons are examined below.

- *Support management creativity.* A common tendency of recent times has been to reduce costs, and a common victim of this policy has been headcount. As support is essentially a labour-intensive function, it comes under constant pressure to do more with less. This is a problem in itself; but it can be compounded by a lack of creativity or vision on the part of the support manager, who may fail to spot new avenues and ways of meeting the twin pressures of increasing demand and diminishing resources.

- *Conservatism.* Closely aligned with a lack of creativity, the tendency of some technical managers to hang on to what they have got can result in their being labelled 'inflexible' by peer managers. Sometimes stemming from fear, this can result in support managers deliberately limiting themselves to what they are confident they can do, rather than taking risks or suffering change. The fear is to some extent justified; the recession of the early 1990s saw whole ranks of middle managers discarded, and for some this was not a good time to get noticed and assessed. Conservatism can work the opposite way, however; an American management recruitment consultant claimed in the IT press that inflexibility was one of the main reasons for firing IT managers. For our purposes thus far, however, it remains a possible factor in defining the type of support service to be found in a given company.

- *Technical predominance.* Despite the pressures on so many support organizations to move more towards a customer service and away from a machine service bias, there are many who remain fundamentally technical, often out of the personal preferences or skillsets of the support management and staff. This is typical of the older support departments with a low staff turnover. It is understandable; as industry stands at the moment, there are few formal routes into support, so technical staff tend to be largely self-taught, often hobbyists who began by conducting their pastime in a work environment, perhaps in addition to at home or school. They have chosen to work in support, rather than been vocationally guided into it. Support staff are often technicians by choice and choose to remain so. The manager attempting to design services around an existing staff conforming to this norm will find his or her options limited.

- *Senior management understanding.* Support is a peculiar activity, not prolifically documented, not always formalized, and often misunderstood at senior management level. No surprise in that: for various reasons, there are not many ex-IT support professionals on the boards of the world's major corporations, especially when compared with the numbers of representatives of the better understood commercial activities like finance, accounting, sales, general management, personnel and production. This lack of understanding can give rise to unrealistic expectations of what can be achieved per unit of support resource. It is exacerbated by continued computer illiteracy among so many senior managers, alienating them from the problems of maintaining high technology. In all, the support service which exists will often reflect this mis-comprehension, by steering clear of subtleties which may be strategically desirable in favour of more tactical, high-profile service delivery.

- *Negativism.* Faced with headcount restrictions, living within the confines of a cost centre, struggling with a limited budget perhaps controlled by another manager; all these impedi-ments can clip the wings of an ambitious support professional if they are taken to heart. It is not unusual to see the demise of the 'can do' attitude in circumstances such as these. It results in deliberate or subconscious self-limitation and a narrowing of the horizons. What could be achieved begins to appear less possible, and the support service structure which emerges from one so affected must reflect these reduced expectations. And negativism such as this can be self-perpetuating, as low expectations are just barely met and managers convince themselves that they were right to expect so little and aim no higher. At this point, only encouragement from outside can break the downward spiral, to encourage the manager to focus on what can actually be achieved within the company or possibly elsewhere.

- *The installed base.* There is an irreverent joke which asserts that the reason that God only needed seven days to invent the world was that He did not have to worry about being compatible with the installed base. To the support manager, this means having to take into account not only the technolo-gies currently in use in the building but the existing expectations of the users and support staff he or she will have to work with. For example, a client of mine asked me to recommend a management and reporting structure for her support department; but it had to have two management positions and a word processing function, not necessarily because that was what the users needed, but because she already had two management grades and a word processing specialist on her staff: restructuring those jobs was not an option. Stunned though I was, in the then climate of industrial retrenchment, I had to accept that this was a feature of her installed base as she understood it to be. The result at that company is that word processing support is far better than it needs to be, necessary growth in support for other applications is restricted and two managers pass responsibilities between them, not always to the benefit of the users. The structure of the support department is a result of the existing staff profile, not the other way round, which may have been more logical.

30.2 The support manager as leader

In business in general, much is spoken about leadership. From the textbooks I have read and the management speakers I have heard, 'leadership' might be seen as the prerogative of the most highly placed of executives. This is an emphatically false view of leadership. Good leadership is needed whenever a group of individuals is striving towards a common goal, regardless of how big or how small the group may be.

Accusations of a failure to lead are levelled at politicians and captains of industry. It is certainly true that when any team or workgroup fails, it is the manager who must shoulder the responsibility. After all, it is the manager's job to co-ordinate the often unrelated efforts of his or her charges to produce what is expected of the group as a whole. So the success or failure of the whole body is in fact produced by the manager. There is also the numerical fact that there are more staff members than there are managers. If the department fails, it is unjustifiable to blame the employees; that they should all individually be failures and the manager a success is statistically improbable.

Leadership is an appropriate group response to change – if we as a group need to change, let us have a leader to make the decisions, set the direction, delegate the responsibilities, keep us on course. On the other hand, a lack of leadership will invariably not produce change, but status quo or stagnation. To meet a challenge, appoint a leader with the courage of conviction, an eye for the future and an ability to instil confidence. To produce a period of calm after a period of upheaval, elect or appoint a weak but inoffensive leader. In a time of conservatism, the leader changes role to become a coach, to keep skill levels up; in a user support context, this would work admirably because technicians usually have enough skills, resources, and motivation to continue doing what they do without leadership, but perhaps needing a little steering now and again to keep them productive and not making-work.

As an industry sector, IT user support is desperately short of leaders. It is safe to say that most technicians are naturally conservative, and as these are the seedbed for our future IT support managers, the future is a little worrying. Information technology is currently changing faster than most business sectors, and strong leadership is needed to meet change. Leaders come into their own in an atmosphere of change; after all, the reason people follow leaders is because they believe that where the leader is going must be better than here.

30.3 Manager or supervisor?

They may call you the helpdesk manager, but you may really be its supervisor. On the other hand, your title may be 'supervisor' or 'team leader' but in fact you are a manager (but perhaps they dare not call you a manager because then they would have to regrade your job and pay you more – then again, that's just my cynicism).

In the 20-odd years I've been in user support, I've seen the position and role of helpdesk manager change dramatically. In some cases, it is the helpdesk leadership itself that has caused this, by keeping its head down too much, failing to lead and behaving like a member of the team rather than a manager. In others, it is because the company has finally accepted how important the helpdesk is, and made it part of a larger department (commonly 'IT services') with an intermediary manager between the helpdesk and the IT director or VP IT.

There is a functional difference between the roles of a manager and a supervisor or team leader. The manager is an orchestrator, a strategist, one who marshals resources and publishes services. His view is outward looking and focuses on the overall picture and how that should be delivered to a customer base he identifies.

The supervisor is a ticks-in-boxes person, making sure that people turn up, things get done, objectives get met, productivity targets are adhered to. The helpdesk needs both – the team leader to monitor the production line, the manager to design it in the first place.

All too often in the helpdesk, the supervisor is doing a management job but perhaps does not realize it. When this happens there is often some hint of an inferiority complex, or an artificially high level of respect for corporate hierarchy, leading the misguided supervisor to the erroneous belief that those higher in the company therefore also have more authority and know all the answers. Take it from me – that ain't necessarily so.

If your company is typical, there will be few if any people higher than you in the hierarchy who have ever worked on the helpdesk, and as such, they know even less about how to run it than you do. If you want it, the power of helpdesk management is there for the taking. Don't wait for authority to be conferred upon you because you'll wait forever. If you are hanging back waiting to be promoted to a position of higher authority, consider this – if you were a senior manager, who would you promote? The one who waited for management authority, or the one who took a few risks and made innovations in order to create that authority for himself?

If you want to be the helpdesk manager, don't dream it – be it.

30.4 Some closing comments

Do you need to follow all the advice in this book? Of course you don't. Taken literally, this book describes an ideal, and there is no such thing. Besides, if you had an ideal today, by tomorrow the circumstances which created it would have changed. Not only that, but the book makes few allowances for the individual difficulties you will have in implementing its lessons in your corporation, because I have never met the people through whom you are going to try to do that implementing. I do not know who or what is going to get in your way, who or what is going to support you, or who or what is going to be utterly indifferent to your efforts. In the end, it is all a matter of payoff: whether it makes commercial or ideological sense to you to manage such-and-such a function of user support in the way I recommend.

For example, take the lessons on queue management; for you, improved queue management may be the boon your service has been desperate for; but I have a client who does not care about queues, and has the money and justification to throw limitless resources at any queue, because it is that vital that all users get an immediate service on everything; yet I have worked with another organization which deliberately engineered an ever-lengthening queue for certain types of user support simply to make the demand go away. Everybody has different reasons for doing (or not doing) anything.

This book has offered guidance towards an ideal. If you can implement any of it I shall be flattered. If in the true spirit of the Pareto principle you can implement 80 per cent of it, you will be doing almost superhumanly well. And if you implement it all, you will be at least a far better support manager than I ever was, because although I have used all the winning techniques I have described in this book, I have never been able to implement them all in the same place at the same time.

What I do not want this book to have left you with is the feeling that to win at user support you have simply got to do everything this or any other book suggests. You do not, nor should you lose any sleep trying. If you are going to achieve truly effective computer user support, then at least as important as the methods is your motivation. If you do not have the motivation, enthusiasm and a real desire to do the job and be good at it, all the winning techniques in the world will not make the slightest bit of difference. Support management (for me) is fun. Winning is fun. Being good at your job is fun. Providing effective computer user support should be, above all else, fun. Get out there and enjoy yourself. If anything in this book makes that enjoyment a little easier to come by, then I have done my job.

Further reading

With this list, I am not saying that you should read them all, but I think that each of these books and others have contributed to making me a better user support manager. Some of them I have quoted in this book. Others are just a very good read and present new ways of seeing the world. As things stand, there is a frustrating shortage of good literature for aspiring helpdesk and support managers, and I scoured bookshops in the US and the UK to find research material. So please see this list as something for you to be creative with. These books may give you ideas, but as most of them do not specialize in the support field, you will need to do some creative thinking to implement the ideas they give you. Good luck.

Armstrong, Michael, *How To Be an Even Better Manager*, Kogan Page, London, 1988.

Bittle, Lester and Newstrom, John, *What Every Supervisor Should Know*, McGraw-Hill, Singapore, 1990.

Bliss, Edwin, *Doing It Now*, Futura, London, 1984.

Bryce, Lee, *The Influential Manager*, BCA, London, 1991.

Czegel, Barbara, *Running an Effective Help Desk*, John Wiley & Sons, Inc, 1998.

Clutterbuck, David, *The Power of Empowerment*, BCA, London 1994.

Denikas, Marie and Lapcewich, Dennis, www.ksasystems.com/prolink

De Marco, Tom and Lister, Tim, *Peopleware*, Dorset House, New York, 1987.

Douglas, Merrill and Douglas, Donna, *Time Management for Teams*, Amacom, New York, 1992.

Goldratt, Eliyahu and Cox, Jeff, *The Goal*, Gower, Aldershot, 1989.

Handy, Charles, *The Empty Raincoat*, Hutchinson, London, 1993.

Handy, Charles, *The Hungry Spirit*, Arrow Books, London, 1998.

The IT Infrastructure Library, HMSO, Norwich, 1990.

Martin, Chris (ed.), *Supporting End Users*, Xephon PLC, Newbury UK, 2000.

Middleton, Iain, *Key Factors in Helpdesk Success*, http://www.rgu.ac.uk/~sim/research/helpdesk/keyfact.htm

Peters, Tom and Waterman, Robert, *In Search of Excellence*, Harper & Row, London, 1990.

Townsend, Robert, *Further Up the Organisation*, Coronet, London, 1970.

Verghis, Philip, www.philverghis.com/helpdesk.html

Wilson, Ralph, *Help! The Art of Computer Technical Support*, Peachpit Press, Berkeley, Calif., 1991.

Index